A Guide to Third Generation Coaching

Reinhard Stelter

A Guide to Third Generation Coaching

Narrative-Collaborative Theory and Practice

 Springer

Reinhard Stelter
University of Copenhagen
Copenhagen
Denmark

ISBN 978-94-007-7185-7   ISBN 978-94-007-7186-4 (eBook)
DOI 10.1007/978-94-007-7186-4
Springer Dordrecht Heidelberg New York London

Library of Congress Control Number: 2013944559

Tredje generations coaching – En guide til narrativ-samskabende teori og praksis

Printed on acid-free paper

Springer is part of Springer Science+Business Media (www.springer.com)

In true dialogue, both sides are willing to change.

Thich Nhat Hanh
Buddhist monk and peace activist

Preface

Since the Danish Psychological Publishers published my first coaching book *Coaching – læring og udvikling* (Coaching – learning and development) in March 2002,[1] the field of coaching has undergone tremendous development, both in Denmark and around the world. With some 25,000 copies sold in Denmark and Sweden, this book has influenced and promoted the field in Scandinavia. For me as an author, it has been very gratifying to see the book in use in a large number of educational programmes and courses with a focus on learning, leadership, team development and communication with coaching as pivotal point.

In 2009, Birgitte Lie Suhr-Jessen and Mette Popp-Madsen, then both editors with the Danish Psychological Publishers, approached me with a request and a proposal of revising the aging bestseller and preparing a new edition of the book. I declined, as I felt it would be too daunting a task to incorporate all the new developments into the existing framework and to decide what was 'worth' preserving, and what needed to be rewritten from scratch. The book would not become the coherent whole that it has become in its present form. Therefore, I suggested to the editors that I write an entirely new book on coaching, a book that would reflect my own learning and developmental process during my past 10 years' journey in coaching and coaching psychology.

In the 10 years following the publication of the first book, I have developed numerous international contacts, including my involvement with the Global Convention on Coaching in Dublin in 2007, where I served as a working group chairman and was involved in shedding light on many key issues in coaching. Over the years, I have developed close relations with many key figures within the field, including strong professional ties with coaching psychology units at the University of Sydney, London City University, the University of East London, Oxford Brooks, the University of Middlesex, the University of Johannesburg and, in Denmark,

---

[1] I still remember the amazing collegial cooperation with my fellow authors who contributed to the success of the book: Stig Eiberg Hansen, Peter Hansen-Skovmoes, Allan Holmgren, Lotte Møller Elleberg and Gert Rosenkvist.

with my colleagues at Aalborg University, Copenhagen Business School and the University of Copenhagen. As a member of the International Coaching Research Forum; as a Founding Fellow of The Institute of Coaching at Harvard Medical School, where I continue to be a member of the institute's Scientific Advisory Council; and through my membership of the Scientific Committees of five major international coaching psychology conferences, I have had rich opportunity to expand my international collegial relations and gain insight into the most recent research and practice development within the field – an amazing opportunity for professional development. Since early 2008, I have organized the lecture series *Coaching – research and practice* in my department at the University of Copenhagen, which I hope has been a significant driver of professional development in the Danish coaching environment. For more than 5 years, the lecture series has attracted many with an interest in coaching and thus developed into a professional development forum for coaching in Copenhagen and environs; it has also resulted in many personal and professional contacts.

Without the many travel companions and new professional contacts after the publication of my first book, the present book would not have become what I now present, with a certain amount of pride. My own activities as a researcher, teacher and practitioner in the fields of coaching and coaching psychology have had a significant impact on my development and professional learning. I have learned so much from my many teaching sessions in various places of education – especially in my own workplace, the Section of Psychology and Educational Studies, Department of Nutrition, Exercise and Sports at the University of Copenhagen; at the Copenhagen Coaching Center (CCC); and at the Master of Public Governance programme that is run jointly by the Copenhagen Business School (CBS) and the University of Copenhagen, where I am responsible for teaching the compulsory module *Personal leadership and dialogical coaching*. I have also highly appreciated my new professional challenge at the Copenhagen Summer University, where I have been course director for the week-long course *Coaching, Kierkegaard and leadership* since 2011. My interactions with students and course participants, their willingness to reflect and their many questions have provided food for thought, forced me to seek new paths and facilitated my own development as a coaching practitioner and theorist. Through theory development and through developmental and research projects, I have sought to offer my contribution to documenting the role of coaching as a practice field.

Coaching should be understood as a dialogue form that focuses especially on the coachee as a fellow human being. In the present book, I shall be using the term *coachee* rather than *focus person*, the term I used in my first coaching book. I view my conversation partner less as a focus person and more as a partner in a shared process of learning and development. With the term *coachee*, I aim to highlight this equality of roles and my effort to reduce the asymmetry. This forum of shared learning and development becomes even clearer when I work with group coaching. I would describe coaching as interaction and dialogue – not as intervention. My conversations with a coachee constitute a search and a quest for third-generation coaching, where shared meaning-making and reflections on essential life values carry special importance in the conversation. I seek to underpin this new understanding of coaching with relevant theory and research, and in addition I will point to links with current societal (post-modern) challenges that we all have to be ready to deal with. It is precisely the analysis of these social conditions and challenges that inspired me to continue developing third-generation coaching as a new dialogical practice.

The book is not merely a handbook aiming to cover anything and everything within the field. As the author of the book, I have a special ambition: I hope to provide a direction for coaching where I view the development of new forms of dialogue, in a broad sense, as a key and possibly novel basis for developing our society on many different levels – in conversations with each other, in small learning situations, in specific work contexts, in developmental and team contexts, in organizations and many other settings. Coaching and coaching-inspired dialogues should help build new social realities that revolve around the development of our abilities, a desire to engage in reflection and a striving for a better understanding of each other. My hope is that the differences between people will not be an obstacle to genuine meetings but instead can facilitate development for both parties. Obviously, I sometimes fail to live up to this vision myself. Sometimes it is necessary to give yourself a push to speak to the other person in a new way, but it also requires willingness and readiness from the other person. Hopefully, the book can give readers the courage and the urge to spark new conversation processes.

Acknowledgements

I would like to take this opportunity to thank my most essential travel companions[1]: First, I would like to mention my wife, Shereen Horami, a psychologist and a trained coach, who discusses my ideas with me and who is always there for me as my personal 'supervisor'. I thank the wonderful and close professional partners in my research section – Helle Winther, Anne-Marie Elbe and Charlotte Svendler Nielsen – and my current Ph.D. scholars in coaching psychology – Morten Bertelsen and Ebbe Lavendt. A very important source of inspiration in my professional development as a coach over the past 10 years has been my collaboration with Ole Fogh Kirkeby, a professor of management philosophy at the Copenhagen Business School, who introduced and developed protreptics as a special form of third-generation coaching, and with whom I enjoy a good collegial friendship, in part through our shared teaching in the Master of Public Governance programme. Further, I would like to mention my good professional relations with people from the Copenhagen Coaching Center – Mette Mejlhede, Andreas Bering, Jeannette Nyrup Hansen, Kim Gørtz, Jens Larsen and Thomas Mosfeldt – and with Britta Ankerstjerne from Peak Balance. I thank the director of the Søren Kierkegaard Research Centre and my good co-director of the course *Coaching, Kierkegaard and leadership*, Pia Søltoft, for bringing me closer to an understanding of the role of existentialism for coaching. Other colleagues from the Danish coaching environment also deserve thanks for good collegial collaboration: Tobias Dam Hede and Morten Ziethen, both coaching researchers and consultants with Attractor, and my colleagues from Aalborg University, including Ole Spaten, Thorkil Molly-Søholm, Søren Willert and Helle Alrø. Among my international colleagues, I would especially like to thank Tony Grant, Michael Cavanagh, Suzy Green and Gordon Spence from the Coaching Psychology Unit at Sydney University, where I visited as a guest professor in spring 2011; Ann Whyte of the Melbourne Business School and Whyte & Co.; Carol Kauffman, Susan David and Lew Stern of the Institute of Coaching at Harvard; Ho Law of the University of East London and David Drake,

---

[1] I regret that I was unable to mention everyone who deserves mention here.

with whom I enjoy good cooperation on narrative coaching; Stephen Palmer of the London City University, whom I admire for his efforts to develop international coaching psychology; Jonathan Passmore for good collegial conversations; David Lane for his effort in transferring his considerable psychological knowledge to coaching; and Aletta Odendaal of the University of Johannesburg, for her ability to combine personal charm with admirable professional integrity.

I would also like to thank all my students, course participants, workshop participants and coaching conversation partners with whom I have been in contact over the years. You have all helped me move forward and contributed to this book.

Finally, I would like to thank Rikke Schou Jeppesen and Marianne Brandt-Hansen, the department's competent and ever helpful research employees, for the initial proofreading and assistance with the development of the book; Inger Lomholdt Vange from the Danish Psychological Publishers and Stefan Einarson from Springer, for good cooperation on editing and producing the present book; and the anonymous reviewer for feedback and comments. And last but not least, I would like to thank Dorte M. Silver for her professional translation of the Danish original.

Copenhagen, January 2013   Reinhard Stelter

Contents

About the Author

 Reinhard Stelter is a Ph.D. in psychology and a professor of sport and coaching psychology, the director of the Coaching Psychology Unit and head of the Section of Psychology and Educational Studies in the Department of Nutrition, Exercise and Sports, University of Copenhagen. He is a coordinator in the Master of Public Governance programme at the Copenhagen Business School and the University of Copenhagen with responsibility for the compulsory course module 'Personal leadership and dialogical coaching', course director at Copenhagen Summer University for the course 'Coaching, Kierkegaard and leadership', and a member of the Danish Psychological Association and an accredited member of the International Society for Coaching Psychology.

His current research interests are aimed at the development and research-based testing of a narrative co-creative approach in coaching psychology. He has also studied the topics of identity and learning processes, mindfulness and embodiment as well as motivation and developmental processes. Reinhard Stelter is also a trained psychotherapist and has additional training in sport psychology and coaching psychology. He is the author of several books, including one of Scandinavia's bestselling books on coaching: *Coaching – læring og udvikling* (Coaching – learning and development).

In addition, Reinhard Stelter is a member of the editorial boards of *International Coaching Psychology Review*; *Coaching – Theory, Research and Practice*; *International Journal of Mentoring and Coaching*; former associate editor of *Psychology of Sport and Exercise* and the author and/or editor of ten books and more than 150 articles and chapters in journals and books. He is a member of the Scientific Advisory Council, Institute of Coaching, Harvard Medical School (2009–); a former board member of the European Mentoring & Coaching Council (EMCC) in Denmark (2007–2009); honorary vice president of the International Society for Coaching Psychology (2008–); an associate of the TAOS Institute; and a lecturer and workshop leader in high demand, both in Denmark and abroad. Reinhard Stelter is a member of the Advisory Board of the Copenhagen Coaching Center, where he also works as a senior coach and teaches in the centre's 2-year coaching programme.

Reinhard has an independent business as a coaching psychologist and lecturer. Reinhard is German citizen with permanent residence in Denmark since 1984. www.sp-coaching.dk & www.nexs.ku.dk/coaching.

Chapter 1
Introduction

Coaching has changed considerably over the past 15–20 years. Coaching has become a well-developed practice field with a variety of different approaches. At the same time, coaching and coaching psychology form a young and budding research field.[1] Previously, coaching was often associated with the world of sport. A few years ago, Diane Brennan, Global President of The International Coach Federation (ICF) in 2008, told me, "Whenever I told people in my peripheral social circle that I work as a coach, they did a double take and then asked me which sport I was coaching." In recent years this question has become less common. Now, in the world of sport, sports coaches apply principles and ideas from coaching psychology that were developed in other organizational contexts, and which help change management principles in sport from a highly autocratic to a dialogical style of cooperation and leadership (see e.g. Hansen & Henriksen, 2009; Hardman, 2011; Stelter, 2010a).

In this book I use the terms *coach* and *coaching psychologist*, respectively *coaching* and *coaching psychology*, as more or less parallel concepts. As my historical review will show, coaching has roots both within and outside psychology – sport is often considered real origins. But within the past ten years or so, psychologists and their organizations have begun to discover the use of coaching as a psychological discipline, as reflected for example in the formation of societies or interest groups under the national psychology associations. Thus, coaching psychologists can claim their field as an actual profession. Coaching is not quite in the same position,

---

[1] In Denmark, a number of Industrial Ph.D. scholars are currently working on their research projects. Some of these scholars have a background in philosophy, while some come from the field of psychology, and others again come from business colleges. Further, there are modest-sized research environments in coaching (psychology) at Aalborg University, the University of Copenhagen and the Copenhagen Business School. Internationally, a group of researchers has formed the International Coaching Research Forum. The European Mentoring & Coaching Council holds an annual coaching and mentoring research conference. Furthermore, The Institute of Coaching at Harvard Medical School (www.instituteofcoaching.org) has a research fund that funds coaching researchers all over the world.

R. Stelter, *A Guide to Third Generation Coaching: Narrative-Collaborative Theory and Practice*, DOI 10.1007/978-94-007-7186-4_1,
© Springer Science+Business Media Dordrecht 2014

and it will always serve as a supplement to other professions (cf. Lane, Stelter, & Stout-Royston, 2010). According to the Danish legislation on psychology,[2] the title of coaching psychologist is a protected professional title.

Let us begin with a brief historical review: The history of coaching and coaching psychology can be traced back to two key roots: Sport psychology and the Human Potential Movement. In the 1970s in the United States and in Europe about a decade later, concepts from sport psychology (Singer, Hausenblas, & Janelle, 2001; Stelter, 1999) and the world of sport in general such as 'competitive mindset', 'motivation' or 'peak performance' appealed to managers and business executives. Intervention strategies and tools from sport psychology were transferred to business-related areas as tools for staff development or management. In fact, many sport psychologists (even previously successful elite athletes) have changed over from sport to business. The world of sport offers metaphors but also theories and a practice that are appealing in relation to management and organizations. Originally, sport psychologists had a mainly task-oriented focus, were motivation and performance maximization were the key to initiating processes of change – a typical approach from traditional elite sport psychology.

Human Potential Movement (HPM) is mentioned as the second source of coaching and coaching psychology, as highlighted especially by the well-known Australian coaching researcher Anthony Grant (2007) in his discussion of the strong emphasis on humanist and existentialist psychology in the 1960s and 1970s, a psychology that was particularly focused on personal liberation and self-realization. With its eclectic orientation and many self-development strategies such as encounter groups,[3] self-development courses and experiments with alternative ways of living as well as a variety of therapeutic methods, HPM stimulated the growing interest in psychology and personal growth in Western societies, which has influenced so many areas of life. According to Grant, HPM provided powerful impulses to the development of coaching and coaching psychology and formed the basis of today's more sophisticated practice forms in coaching.

In terms of its application, however, coaching is not merely a tool for personal development and self-realization. Today, coaching is applied in a wide range of contexts (including education, healthcare and social services, career, management and staff development and personal challenges). At the same time, coaching unfolds in a wide range of practices, not all of which can be considered equally effective,

---

[2]*Psykologloven* (The Danish act regulating psychology practice) of 1 January 1994 states that "The right to call oneself a psychologist is reserved for individuals who have passed a master's exam in psychology at a university or other institution of higher education or who holds an equivalent degree," (translated for this edition). The regulations also apply to compound titles that include the term *psychologist*, thus also *coaching psychologist*. Violations of the regulations are punishable by a fine, cf. Sec. 23, par. 1

[3]The open online encyclopaedia *Den Store Danske*, Gyldendal, says, "In the 1960s, encounter groups were developed in the United States, consisting of 8–15 individuals, with the objective of creating emotional openness, intimacy, self-insight and personal growth in the members" (translated for this edition).

theoretically founded and evidence-based. That raises a number of important questions: What are the key topics and challenges with regard to the function and role of coaching today? What role does coaching play in the many areas of society today, and how does one explain the proliferation of coaching in just the past ten years? The basis of my argumentation and of the theories that my understanding of coaching relies on, rests on a societal understanding of coaching. Coaching has become as widespread and as important as it has because society has developed the way it has. (The key considerations are presented in Chap. 2, where coaching as a dialogue form is linked with various social change processes).

In viewing coaching as a dialogue form that revolves more around questions than around answers, one phenomenon in particular should be highlighted, a phenomenon that characterizes today's society, and which helps explain the growing use of coaching: a new concept of knowledge – or the lack of an unambiguous orientation, which can be related to the development and prominent role of coaching in our world today.

1.1   The Breakdown of the Knowledge Monopoly

Whether we are looking at politics, leisure time, private life or working life, our social situation is characterized by a growing degree of uncertainty, complexity and disorder. In our current society we have lost the direct access to relevant knowledge – despite our easy access to information via the Internet etc. – or, in other words: We no longer have access to knowledge that offers immediate answers to the challenges we are facing. Because of the high degree of complexity in many areas of our life, applicable knowledge is mainly developed in relation to specific situations and is only relevant in very specific contexts. Values, norms and attitudes, too, are often associated with particular groups, situations and lifestyles. It has become difficult to offer firm directions for actions and decision-making; this is especially true with regard to education and work. On the one hand, it is up to the individual person's creativity and adaptability to develop a useful and situationally appropriate action orientation. On the other hand, the individual's partners and opponents in the social environment help define what is considered right or wrong. The knowledge that is applicable in specific social contexts or at work is created in that context and in specific social practice and work communities. There are no clear-cut answers to the questions we ask. Epistemologically speaking, this assumption is based on *constructivism*, which has philosophical roots that go back to Giambattista Vico (1668–1744) and Immanuel Kant (1724–1804). From a constructionist perspective, we have no direct access to perceiving reality; instead, people actively (co-)create their knowledge about the world and each other. In the framework of this understanding, one will never arrive at any final truth; instead, what we define as truth is culturally determined and depends on the social context that is involved in determining the 'truth' (Gergen, 1994). Both in our private lives and in the public space, we therefore need to learn to *negotiate*: In any given situation, there are many solutions to be explored and developed. Ready-to-use solutions, for example from teachers, parents, colleagues or leaders – do not exist or are extremely rare. Knowledge has become contextual and dynamically variable. And here, coaching can play a crucial role. In a dialogue perspective, the point is to present one's particular position at that point in time while maintaining an open-minded interest in learning from other people's contributions and perspectives. In that way, coaching and coaching-inspired dialogue can help generate new knowledge.

1.2 The Need for a New Coaching Concept

The challenges I have described place demands on coaching. Coaching should be in the service of learning and development, but who defines the terms for coaching processes?

1.2.1 Coaching as Self-Bildung

Demands for reorientation and continued development appear an absolute necessity. These demands are becoming increasingly specific and unrelenting: 'If you are not developing, you are on your way out.' Nikolaj Kure (2010) of the Department of Language and Business Communication, Aarhus School of Business at Aarhus University raises legitimate criticism of this trend:

> [It] is a problem that companies *feign* their demands on personal development: On the one hand, the work place *pretends* that development is a personal and voluntary matter, but on the other hand, it *requires* that the employees make themselves the subject of personal development. ... [P]ersonal development is the new currency in the relationship between companies and employees and is now literally taking over the company with body and soul (p. 3; translated for this edition).

Ole Fogh Kirkeby (2006a), professor of management philosophy at the Copenhagen Business School, phrases his reservations – especially with regard to management coaching – in his usual provocative style:

> Coaching is an intimate technology. Like in the brothels in St. Pauli and Amsterdam, where you can open a couple of small hatches in a wall and check out the breasts of your selected prostitute in order to test the goods, coaching can open a few tiny hatches in the coachee's front. Then the manager can check the amount of commitment meat on the soul. Let's just hope that he can pull his hand out again. Coaching is an intimate technology. It is intimidating because it combines the gazes of the confessor, the interrogator and the executioner. The interrogator goes for confessions. The executioner goes for blood-letting, he is a surgeon of profession. The confessor's currency is remorse. When this mix is balanced properly, one arrives at the condition of 'utterly and completely brain-washed' (p. 11; translated for this edition).

These analyses and perceptions should be taken very seriously, especially when the leader acts as coach. In that context, coaching as a productive dialogue form can be discredited and lose its worth with regard to facilitating ambitions of development and *Bildung*. Coaching can be combined and associated with various forms of self-guided learning and should be understood as an offer to an individual or a group of people to be used within a framework that they are involved in defining. Here I would highlight the role of coaching as a *personal Bildung project* that the coachee can initiate in relation to himself: A given reality has revealed itself to a person (here the coachee), and the person has opened himself up to this reality – by virtue of his experience, insight and understanding (Klafki, 2000). Reality needs to be explored anew, as it takes shape for the coachee as meaningful and with a particular worth that may have gone undiscovered and inexperienced. The person's self is challenged in its view of reality – a need for further exploration arises. Here, coaching becomes part of the person's *self-Bildung*. Self-Bildung can be defined as a process of continuous self-development that involves virtually all life and work situations. Self-Bildung involves personal, social and professional development and is a process that relies on one's *own* (i.e. *existentially meaningful*) development ambitions (see also Hansen, 2002). According to Danish educational philosopher Schmidt (1999), the concept of Bildung no longer has anything to do with coming from a cultured background. In a highly individualized society, where everyone is required to work with their own identity, personal self-presentation and specific learning and development projects, Bildung becomes self-Bildung, where the individual shapes his or her own identity. From a critical perspective, this may be viewed as a new form of disciplining.

It is in this self-formation perspective that I see the core purpose of coaching. The old mentors are losing their authority. In virtually all life situations we miss a basic orientation and a guideline that no one can really offer. At times we feel uprooted, and increasingly – each in our way – we feel compelled to find appropriate 'solutions' to challenges that no one dares to offer any advice on. In this situation, coaching can help us reflect and discover the potential answers that we all have to find for ourselves. Coaching can thus promote agency and facilitate the self-Bildung process. To support the coachee's self-Bildung, the coach must meet certain requirements: The coach must understand and empathize with the person's life situation and help the person (as well as him/herself) grasp a variety of perspectives and understandings of the situation that is addressed in a specific coaching session. Although a life or work situation is experienced by an individual, it is, to a high degree, created by the relations and the context that the individual enters into. Self-Bildung thus relies on the individual's ability to present him/herself in a new way in relation to certain social relations and in selected life and work contexts. A successful coaching process creates the basis for new stories about situations that the person originally perceived as entrenched, challenging or difficult. Furthermore, a coaching conversation can help the person develop new practices and action alternatives in relation to these situations.

1.3   What Is Coaching?

In the following, I will take a brief look at the phenomenon of coaching, outlining it by means of two metaphors: 'coaching as a journey' and 'coaching as a story'. These metaphors help define my perspective on coaching – and I use them being fully aware that other actors in the field of coaching will have different perceptions. In this introduction and the subsequent chapters, I seek to describe my understanding of coaching and anchor it in a discourse that is driven by specific social and societal developments that will also be used to explain the growing use of coaching (Stelter, 2009a).

1.3.1   Coaching as a Journey

There are many views of the nature and purpose of coaching. At first glance, many would agree with the aptness of describing coaching as a *journey*. There are many ways to travel, and coaching displays a similar diversity. Let us take a closer look at this metaphoric description of coaching as a journey, first by examining a common notion of what a journey is all about:

Most people lead busy lives and have limited time available for travelling, so the route, destination and accommodation typically have to be clear and determined ahead of time. Many choose package tours; they are cheap and offer a product where everything seems simple and adapted to the customer's needs. We often attach high hopes and dreams to our journeys. Every journey should be a pleasant break, an opportunity for pleasure and new experiences, but we also want some assurance that we will not be disappointed. Travel companies do their best to present their wares in glossy catalogues to offer the customer a preview of the form and quality of the journey. We want new experiences, but we also want guarantees and predictability.

But is that the kind of journey coaching offers? A straight answer would be NO. This book does not describe a pre-packaged solution. Coaching is a complex process, a journey into the unknown, where neither the coach nor the coachee knows the destination or the route. It is more like a journey of discovery into relatively unknown territory. Both parties – coach and coachee – are travel companions, and none of them knows the road ahead. Their journey is based on the agreement that something may occur. The coachee often comes in with a desire to discover something new, a change of course or new perspectives on his or her life. The coach strives to create a safe atmosphere by being present as a good (i.e. empathic and professionally qualified) travel companion, but the journey might still hit some rough ground. In this sense, coaching is a journey into the unknown, although it proceeds in a context that is essentially safe and often produces a satisfactory and life-affirming outcome.

1.3.2 Coaching as Storytelling

In my view, defining the coaching process as a way to shape new stories about specific events and situations is really an expansion on the journey metaphor discussed above. Coaching as *storytelling*, however, is not based on just a single storyteller; instead, the story is created in an interaction between coach and coachee/coachee group. The coachee indicates a beginning and suggests an idea of an ending, but things will develop differently as the process unfolds. A story revolves around a plot, a storyline and a structure. However, when coaching is viewed as a story, the plot is not pre-determined. It unfolds in the process and is co-created in the dialogue between coach and coachee. That is in fact the underlying idea in coaching: changing the plot and the storyline, creating a new and often more uplifting story about certain events and linking events together. One of the common reasons for a coachee to seek coaching is the desire to find new perspectives on one's life, certain events and oneself. This understanding – in both coach and coachee – shifts during the coaching process; new meanings emerge, precisely because the coach asks questions that help invite new actors, new perspectives and new events to take part in the journey. Both the coachee and the coach can develop new understandings of issues, circumstances and phenomena that are important to many people. This concept of coaching as storytelling suggests a new understanding of the relationship between coach and coachee, which is traditionally described within a framework of asymmetry – a fact that I have also noted earlier (Stelter, 2002b), but which I aim to address in a new way in this book. The new assumption about temporary periods of symmetry in the dialogue is also part of my reason for speaking of *third-generation coaching* (see more in Sect. 3.2.1).

1.3.3 Definition of Coaching: An Attempt

Many definitions of coaching have been put forward, all reflecting the inherent basic orientation and intention that the coach and the coachee pursue in their dialogue. Coaching has an intentionality that becomes evident in the basic definition. That makes it virtually impossible to offer an explicit and adequate definition that all the actors in the field will embrace. As a very broad and relatively non-specific definition I still like John Whitmore's (2002) basic view of coaching, where he highlights that coaching "is helping them to learn rather than teaching them" (p. 8). I also maintain my own broad definition of coaching (Stelter 2002a): "Coaching should be understood as *participation* in the focus person's/focus group's development and learning process" (p. 15; translated for this edition). Anthony Grant and Dianne Stober (2006) offer a similarly general statement: "Coaching is more about asking the right questions than telling people what to do" (p. 3) and describe coaching relations in terms such as 'collaborative and egalitarian' rather than 'authoritarian'.

In *The Complete Handbook of Coaching*, Cox, Bachkirova, and Clutterbuck (2010) largely avoid offering a single specific definition of coaching. They note that coaching cannot be defined by virtue of an ultimate purpose, a particular type of clients or a uniform process. The book presents a broad spectrum of coaching approaches which to some extent are distinguished by their intended application, and which are covered by the following matrix (Table 1.1).

Generally, I propose the following definition of coaching:

> *Coaching is described as a developmental conversation and dialogue, a co-creative process between coach and coachee with the purpose of giving (especially) the coachee a space and an opportunity for immersing him/herself in reflection on and new understandings of 1) his or her own experiences in the specific context and 2) his or her interactions, relations and negotiations with others in specific contexts and situations. This coaching conversation should enable new possible ways of acting in the contexts that are the topic of the conversation.*

This somewhat complex definition reflects my epistemological position. I wish to highlight the individual's *experiential* embeddedness in the situation here and now, which is partly manifested in the individual's implicit (i.e. bodily, non-verbalized) connectedness with the specific practice context. In this understanding I draw mainly on a *phenomenological theoretical tradition* that underscores the individual's (bodily) intentionality (= orientation) in relation to the specific environmental situation.

Experiences and thus learning and development are always situated, and the coach will be wise to anchor the conversation in specific contexts and situations.

Furthermore, the individual is an actor in a social world, a participant in specific social contexts and communities of practice. The individual's reality is shaped and created in relations and interactions with others. Here I incorporate the *social constructionist theoretical tradition*, which highlights interactions among individuals as they unfold in *social negotiations* and collaboration, both physical and verbal. It is through these negotiations that the person and his or her social reality are created, and in coaching, these negotiations become the topic of the coaching dialogue, where verbal interactions from the world outside the coaching dialogue are articulated. Coherence and understanding are achieved by means of specific narratives that link certain events together and thus create meaning in the coachee's life universe. These narratives often unfold a story about times when life was not quite successful, and thus they are not always particularly uplifting. It is the desire to discover a new perception and understanding of these experiences and events that motivates the coachee to seek coaching.

The definition presented here will guide the book with regard to the way I incorporate and address specific theories and recommend and assess coaching practices.

Table 1.1 Coaching matrix (Source: Cox et al., 2010, p. 10)

Section 1: theoretical traditions of coaching	Skills & performance	Section 2: genres and contexts of coaching									
		Developmental coaching	Transformational coaching	Executive & leadership	The manager as coach	Team coaching	Peer coaching	Life coaching	Career coaching	Cross cultural coaching	Mentoring
The psychodynamic approach to coaching	*	*		**		*				*	
Cognitive-behavioural coaching	**	**	**	**	**	**	**	**	**	*	
The solution-focused approach to coaching	**	**		*	*	*	*	**	**		
The person-centred approach to coaching	*	**		*		*	**	**	**		*
The Gestalt approach to coaching	*	*	*		*	**		*	*	*	
Existential coaching	*	*	*	*	*			*	*	*	
Ontological coaching	*	**		*	*				*	*	
Narrative coaching		**			*	*			*	*	
The cognitive-developmental approach to coaching	**	**	**			**			*		
The transpersonal approach to coaching	*	*	*	**		**		*	*	*	
Positive psychology approach to coaching	**	*		*	*	*		*	*	*	
Transactional analysis and coaching				*	*	*		*	*	*	
The NLP approach to coaching	**	*		*	*	*	*	*	*	*	

1.3.4   Coaching: Urging Self-reflection and New Perspectives

In my view, *stimulating the coachee's self-reflection capacity* is the first main goal
of the coaching dialogue. In a globalized world we have to accept that the world
is diverse and rich in perspectives on life's many challenges. Acknowledging and
appreciating diversity or *multiversality* can be considered an advantage and an
opportunity: Developing one's capacity for entertaining different perceptions of the
world and incorporating other people's perspectives on specific challenges may be
viewed as an invitation to expand and enrich one's own perceptions. Coaching is
about focusing on making meaning, both personally and with regard to the relations
and contexts that one is a part of. In that connection, I consider the *narrative co-
creative practice,* which is this book's main orientation, particularly valuable. The
main goal of the coaching dialogue is to achieve coherence (1) with regard to the
coachee's identity, self-concept and agency and (2) with regard to integrating events
from the past and present and put them into the perspective of a future that offers
direction and meaning and appears uplifting.

A coachee or coachee group invites a coach in because they want development
and a reorientation. The main condition for the coaching conversation is the
coachee's desire and readiness to change. In addition to self-reflection I therefore
consider the *adoption of new perspectives* the second main goal of the coaching
dialogue. The coach should ask questions that help initiate a shift in the coachee's
perception and spark impulses to a shift in the narrative plot. The coach's questions
should ideally encourage in-depth reflection as well as change. Further, the co-
creative process between the coach and coachee should help shape a new coherent
whole and new meanings in relation to the challenge that was the topic of the
conversation.

1.4   The Goal and Structure of the Book

With the present book I hope to invite the reader into a coaching approach that
is under development, and which will probably never be completed. The goal
is to qualify a dialogue form where coach and coachee(s) develop together in
a coaching partnership, but where the coach is also aware that he or she has
taken on an obligation, which is to support and participate in another person's
or group's learning and developmental process. Unlike first-generation coaching,
where the goal is to help the focus person achieve a particular objective, and unlike
second-generation coaching, where the coach assumes that the coachee implicitly
knows how to deal with a particular challenge, third-generation coaching has a less
clear and goal-oriented agenda but is hopefully more in-depth and sustainable, as
coach and coachee create something together where meanings are co-created during
the conversation, where both parties partake in a journey, and where new stories

gradually take shape. A story will always contain a deeper meaning and rest on a value-based conviction – and this value base creates a degree of sustainability that goes beyond simply accomplishing the next objective.

Approaching third-generation coaching is a process of searching and testing in a permanent professional development process. Sometimes, on appropriate occasions, one will include elements from first-generation coaching and, more frequently, from second-generation coaching (see more in Chap. 3, Sect. 3.2.1). However, the coach's search is aimed at finding a depth that can help the coachee understand him/herself, his or her basic experiences, special events and the relationships that the coachee enters into and hopes to understand better or develop further.

My other goals for the book can perhaps best be laid out with a brief overview of the structure of the book:

The following chapter, Chap. 2, presents *theoretical perspectives on coaching*, reflections to help provide a basis for understanding *coaching* as a contemporary phenomenon. (1) Within the framework of a societal analysis, coaching is viewed as the answer to post-modern challenges, (2) Coaching is viewed as a space for identity development and self-construction, (3) Coaching is viewed as a special form of learning, and (4) Coaching is viewed in the perspective of organizational and management theory.

In the rather comprehensive Chap. 3, I focus on *intervention theories in coaching and coaching psychology*. Coaching is presented as a special kind of dialogue where the dialogue partners seek to alter their perspectives in order to generate development and new insights. I present the key underlying intentions of the three generations of coaching: from a problem focus over a solution focus to a reflection focus. Following that, I present my basic theories and their possible inclusion in third-generation coaching. I move from a systemic over a social constructionist to a narrative co-creative theoretical universe and present additional theories that I find it useful to integrate: elements of positive psychology and of experiential and emotion-focused approaches.

In Chap. 4, I present *narrative co-creative coaching in theory and practice*. My intention is to connect phenomenology and social constructionism by placing the concept of meaning at the centre of my theoretical reflections and the practical consequences for the conversation process.

In Chap. 5, I present *some case studies from my own practice*. This should offer the reader an impression of my version of third-generation coaching in practice. I also present qualitative and quantitative research findings in a form that will appeal to the reflective practitioner. I present *stories told by participants in group coaching and document the effect* of narrative co-creative group coaching, which I have researched for years.

In Chap. 6, I invite the reader into a developmental process toward a reflective practice, a *professional practice in between research, knowledge and reflection*. I engage in critical reflection on the concept of evidence and suggest a path for developing the reader's knowledge, practice and professional growth.

In Chap. 7, I present case studies where I describe and analyze *how coaching experts reflect on their own practice*.

In the closing chapter, Chap. 8, I round off and seek to offer additional perspectives for third-generation coaching.

It is my hope that the book may contribute to a further development of coaching and coaching psychology in theory and practice. Obviously, not all readers will share my views, but hopefully everybody will feel inspired to continue working on their own understanding of coaching. My ambition with the book is to support the reader's own ambitions of becoming a reflective practitioner.

Chapter 2
The Origins and Development of Coaching

In this chapter I present the origins and development of coaching in order to provide a foundation that offers theoretical evidence for the suggested coaching practice (cf. Stober, Wildflower, & Drake, 2006). The following four perspectives may serve as a framework and a basis for the coaching practitioner and clarify how coaching practice rests on a social science basis. My discussion addresses the following themes:

Societal legitimacy: coaching as the answer to late- and post-modern challenges
With reference to several sociological theories I offer an explanation for the role and proliferation of coaching in today's society. I will argue that coaching can be viewed as an answer to late- and post-modern challenges, which may be part of the reason for the widespread use of coaching in so many areas of society.

Coaching, identity and self-constructions
Coaching as a dialogue form is an offer that lets you reflect on yourself and review certain positions and possible selves. Identity should be understood as a relational process, where coachees are invited to see themselves in a new light. The general understanding that is presented will be based mainly on social constructionist theory, which has as a key tenet that we create our identity in interaction with others.

Coaching and learning – between personal experience and collaboration
Coaching contributes to learning and development. A number of learning theories will be presented in relation to their impact on the shape and format of the coaching dialogue. The main focus will be on theoretical perspectives that take their point of departure either in experiential learning or in learning as a social and collaborative practice.

Coaching in the perspective of organization and leadership theory
Indisputably, coaching has seen its main growth in relation to leadership and organization. This chapter focuses especially on the new challenges that today's leaders are facing, and on the associated consequences for the leader's self-presentation and the action possibilities available in his or her position. In this connection, I discuss the interrelationship between leadership and coaching as a specific challenge; several researchers have criticized the use of coaching as a leadership tool.

R. Stelter, *A Guide to Third Generation Coaching: Narrative-Collaborative Theory and Practice*, DOI 10.1007/978-94-007-7186-4_2,
© Springer Science+Business Media Dordrecht 2014

2.1   Societal Legitimacy: Coaching as an Answer to Late- and Post-Modern Challenges

A strong argument in favour of the considerable role of coaching in many professions is based on an analysis of societal developmental processes. In the past 20–30 years, Western society, indeed the global society, has undergone fundamental changes with profound effects on all members of society, in both their private and professional lives. In the following, I present sociological and social science theories that highlight these change processes in a variety of ways. The social scientists quoted below do not necessarily have the same point of departure but emphasize different perspectives in the developmental process. Therefore, the following review should be understood as a mosaic that aims to shed light on processes of change and suggest the big picture, outlining how individuals are affected as members of a society. My message is the following: Social changes have helped create the widespread need for coaching and other dialogue tools (e.g. mentoring, counselling, process management etc.) today. In coaching and related fields it is therefore important to include the social perspective and consider the special societal challenges in one's concrete work with the clients.

Here I am thinking especially of the challenges related to three main trends: (1) globalization, (2) hyper-complexity and (3) late-modern reflexivity. Their unique conditions and meaning for the life of individuals will be addressed in the following.

2.1.1   The Globalized World

The increasingly global character of our world can be seen as the first aspect influencing the role and development of coaching and coaching psychology today. Globality can be defined as the end-point of the globalization process and may be seen as a condition that frames our mutual interactions. The well-known German sociologist Ulrich Beck (2000) notes, "Globality means that we have been living for a long time in a world society, in that sense that the notion of closed spaces has become illusory. No country or group can shut itself off from others" (p. 10).

The financial crisis that began in 2008 has painted a clear picture of the effect of globality on the life of virtually everyone on this planet – in the form of growing unemployment, falling real estate prices, reductions in aid to developing countries, growing budget deficits etc. Climate changes, migration, global media coverage (e.g. in connection with the Danish Mohammed cartoons in 2005/06 or the Japanese tsunami in 2011) and their related consequences are further examples of how globality invades our lives in the Western world. Beck (2000) highlights the following consequences:

> Globality means that from now on nothing which happens on our planet is only a limited local event; all inventions, victories and catastrophes affect the whole world, and we must reorient and reorganize our lives and actions, our organizations and institutions, along a 'local-global' axis (p. 11).

Local and global phenomena are closely interrelated. Some of our everyday challenges, both in our private lives and in our work lives, can be understood in the light of globality – and that is the case also when these challenges are the topic of a coaching conversation. The world view of globality is affected by change processes that are characterized by growing diversity and multiple perspectives with regard to their interpretation and in relation to the development of possible action strategies. Furthermore, it seems that we have to adapt to a reality where we are less able to control certain factors locally. In fact, the very notion of control has been devalued as a result of the impact of globality on individual lives. Based on these reflections, I point to the following consequences and action strategies for the coach's and the coachee's dialogue in relation to specific challenges:

- It is rarely possible to offer or devise simple solutions during the coaching conversation. The complexity of the world does not invite simple answers.
- Focusing on reflection processes in relation to the challenges is a crucial aspect of the dialogue. The parties use reflection to achieve profound and necessary understanding.
- Examining differences and diversity becomes a quality in the format of the dialogue.
- Striving for a more open and non-judging approach to environmental influences is a new form of 'problem-solving' strategy.

2.1.2 The Hyper-Complex Society

In our late- or post-modern society, individuals confront growing diversity in the social world where the organizations, institutions and cultures all have their own autonomous 'developmental logic'. Various social contexts are characterized by specific cultures and organizations, and the members in the specific contexts develop their unique form of communication that matches the local culture, and which is simultaneously shaped by this culture. As a consequence of this development, society is increasingly losing internal coherence and cohesion. The German sociologist Niklas Luhmann (1998) puts it as follows: "The system tends towards 'hypercomplexity', towards a multitude of opinions and interpretations about its own complexity" (p. 876; own translation). According to this argumentation, it becomes impossible to achieve a uniform and concordant understanding and interpretation of specific societal phenomena or of society at large. Particular observer perspectives determine how the world is perceived. We create our world from the vantage point and the angle from which we view the world. A term that is used about this condition is *contingency*: the notion that everything can always be viewed and interpreted differently. This increased complexity or contingency can lead to stress or to a sense of freedom, implying new possibilities for action. As citizens in society we are therefore increasingly confronted with the question of how to manage differences in perception, and how the various social environments and cultures can communicate, given that each environment and each culture speaks its own language and has its own interpretations of the way things are.

Even within the same context there are different perceptions and different forms of contingency: On the one hand, the individual has to develop his or her competence to adapt and attune with the norms, values and behaviours of the specific culture in order to function as a member of it (e.g. an organization, a workplace). On the other hand, there will also be differences in perception among the parties within the same cultural and social field; for example in the workplace: How does the individual perceive the concrete challenges? Or in a marriage: Do husband and wife have very different perceptions of their involvement in household chores? As long as the parties are not engaged in conflict, the differences are manageable, but as soon as one party attempts to convince the other of the correctness of their particular position, differences and disagreements between the parties will increase.

As a consequence of this growing cultural diversity, the American social psychologist and social constructionist Kenneth Gergen (2009a) says that "the major challenge of the twenty-first century is how we shall manage to *live together* on the globe" (p. 114).

Looking at coaching practice in this light, it becomes essential for the coach to include and examine relevant contexts and positions. The basic position for the coach should be that the concept of 'truth' depends on the context and on social agreements in the local culture. Thus, 'truth' is an issue of power or social negotiations. Therefore, coaches and consultants should strive to heighten cultural sensitivity in the individual clients as well as among their clients with regard to both organizational and personal aspects, which are often interrelated (e.g. work-life balance). Indeed, one may expect the same from one's manager. In order to increase understanding and develop good working relations, the coach – or the manager and other people who are responsible for others – should initiate *transformative dialogues* (Isaacs, 1999; Phillips, 2011; Strauss, 2002; Winslade & Monk, 2001). These dialogues, according to Gergen (2009a), should be considered "a joint creation of meaning, one in which the parties draw from tradition, but in which they can create new realities and ways of relating" (s. 118). The strategy in this process will be to focus on the cases and situations where one has had shared successes rather than normatively indicating how things should be. Further, it is helpful to articulate visions and dreams for a possible shared future for the group.

2.1.3 Reflexivity in Late Modernity

In this section I want to focus on the understanding of the concept of reflexivity that was put forward by the English sociologist Anthony Giddens to describe the special challenges facing individuals in today's world. Giddens wonders how the individual is affected by the vast social change processes that are unfolding in this late-modern age. In that connection he introduces the concept of reflexivity, which he describes as the ongoing revision based on new information that is a characteristic of and a necessity in late-modern societies. Giddens (1991) says,

> Each of us not only has but *lives* a biography reflexively organised in terms of flows of social and psychological information about possible ways of life. Modernity is a post-traditional

order, in which the question, 'How shall I live?' has to be answered in day-to-day decisions about how to behave, what to wear and what to eat – and many other things – as well as interpreted within the temporal unfolding of self-identity (p. 14; italics in original).

Giddens (1991) sees the development of self-identity on the one hand as the individual's permanently ongoing reflexive project. He describes self-reflexivity as "the process whereby self-identity is constituted by the reflexive ordering of self-narratives" (p. 244). On the other hand he speaks of institutional reflexivity: "The reflexivity of modernity, involving the routine incorporation of new knowledge and information into environments of action that are thereby reconstituted or reorganised" (p. 243). Giddens (1991) describes reflexivity as follows:

The reflexivity of modernity extends into the core of the self. Put in another way, in the context of a post-traditional order, the self becomes a *reflexive project*. ... Modernity, it might be said, breaks down the protective framework of the small community and of tradition, replacing these with much larger, impersonal organisations. The individual feels bereft and alone in a world in which she or he lacks the psychological supports and the sense of security provided by more traditional settings (pp. 32–33).

This analysis of society makes it clear that personal development is not merely a requirement from 'official' entities, for example one's employer; it also appears to be a necessary project for the individual today. Strengthening one's capacity for self-reflexivity has become the key factor for the individual's ability to find and understand his or her place in the social (dis)order. One result of this requirement of development, which has accelerated in recent decades, is the central and widely accepted position of psychology and coaching in society.

In extension of the social analysis presented above, the following question becomes urgent in relation to the effort to develop the values, objectives and goals attributed to coaching in society: How can this requirement of personal development and self-reflexivity contribute to the ongoing development of coaching and coaching psychology? Until now, one of the key perspectives in coaching has been to focus on results and solutions and to facilitate the coachee's ability to accomplish his or her goals quickly (see e.g. Jackson & McKergow, 2007; King & Eaton, 1999; Pemberton, 2006). Many coaches – and probably also their customers – labour under the belief that it is possible to achieve change quickly simply by planning out a course: "What are your goals? What results would you like to achieve in the near future? – Once you find out, I'll help you get there." But if we incorporate Giddens' analyses, the matter looks a little more complex and complicated: A coach or a coaching psychologist should not suggest that it is possible to offer a simple path to solutions, a quick fix. Our social world has become so complex that it is more helpful for the coachee if the coach offers a *reflective space*, where both the coach and coachee engage as partners in a dialogue that makes room for self-reflection and in-depth reflection on essential and existentially meaningful topics. With this approach, coaching can provide a forum where there is time to think and room for pause, and which lies outside the *production domain*. In the production domain, the perspective of the conversation remains logical-rational, and the focus is on the objective reality. The linear cause-and-effect mindset prevails, and the goal that frames the process is clarity and a reduction of ambiguity in relation to, for example,

Fig. 2.1 The domains and
their relative weight in the
coaching conversation

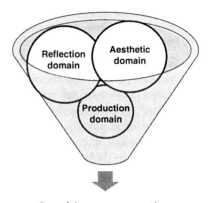

Coaching conversation

rules, norms, goals and demands. Instead, to a much higher degree, the coaching
dialogue should take place in the *reflection domain* and the *aesthetic domain*, which
makes it possible to see new ways of acting in specific and sometimes challenging
situations in a long-term perspective. The *reflection domain* refers to the explorative
angle of the conversation, where the coach and the coachee focus on multiple
possible versions of reality. This domain allows for diversity, stories of equal worth
and multiple perspectives in order to achieve a nuanced understanding of reality.
The *aesthetic domain* allows for the personal and emotional angle, where it is
possible to present desires, values, attitudes, experiences and morals and reflect on
ethical issues. In the aesthetic domain, we attribute meaning to a given action. The
domain theory was originally conceived by Maturana, although he never actually
wrote about it himself. The theory was presented by Lang, Little and Cronen (1990)
and is particularly widespread among systemic and social constructionist coaches
and consultants (Haslebo & Haslebo, 2012; Hornstrup, Loehr-Petersen, Vinther,
Madsen, & Johansen, 2012; Stelter, 2002a; Storch & Søholm, 2005). The role of
the domains in the coaching dialogue and their relative weight are illustrated in the
following diagram (Fig. 2.1):

In this section, I have attempted to clarify the impact of social and societal
changes on organizations, personal interactions and individuals. In the following,
I seek to specify the direct impact of these new trends on individual identity
development as well as the potential role of coaching and other forms of dialogue
in this process.

2.2 Coaching, Identity and Self-constructions: The Self Is at Stake in the Coaching Dialogue

In a conversation of any depth – and thus also in coaching – the conversation
partner/the coachee has some desire to challenge his or her own identity and self-
concept. In a conversation that revolves around reflection, this is both desirable

and unavoidable. Identity is first of all defined as the individual's self-reflective process in relation to his or her interactions with the environment; in this process the individual attempts to strike a balance between his or her sense of continuity (being and resembling him/herself) and a degree of conformity (being like others versus standing out from others). Markus and Wurf (1987) propose the following definition of self-concept. To them, self-concept is

> a dynamic interpretive structure that mediates most significant intrapersonal processes (including information processing, affect, and motivation) and a wide variety of interpersonal processes (including social perception, choice of situation, partner, and interaction strategy, and reaction to feedback) (p.300).

In the late- and post-modern age, the person's search for an identity, however, becomes an increasingly complex process. The term patchwork identity has been proposed (Keupp et al., 1999; Stelter, 1996, 1998), reflecting the notion that, depending on our current context, we create and construct ourselves in a variety of ways. In a sense, we may consist of several individuals in one, depending on the situation and setting that currently frame our behaviour. The individual 'patches' in the quilt describe the multiplicity and variety of possible actions and the many ways of developing an identity, depending on the individual's given contexts – but when the person's identity patchwork is viewed as a whole, a coherent impression nevertheless emerges, despite the diversity of the individual patches – or self-presentations. Identity and self-concept have become key themes in our society; as individuals, we strive for a certain self-presentation and a life-long search for who we want to be, and where we want to go. Kenneth Gergen (1991) describes the post-modern being as a "restless nomad" (p. 173). In Gergen's perspective, the post-modern self is overwhelmed by countless possibilities and possible actions and faces a situation of disorientation in terms of the best way to address the situation. The Norwegian psychiatrist and writer Finn Skårderud (2000, 2001), who has extensive experience with treating patients with anorexia nervosa, and who relates experiences from this field to a social analysis, uses the concept of 'unrest' to characterize the psychological challenges that many people are facing today. He discusses how a growing number of people in our society experiment with themselves in a search for purity, control and meaning. A growing proportion of the population find it difficult to achieve stability, control and direction, and in this search, individuals arrive at extreme techniques and ways of life, either in the form of socially acceptable behaviour, like a multiple ironman challenge or other mad or extreme sports quests, or in the guise of various forms of psychological and psychiatric 'dysfunction' – from stress and depression to eating disorders and self-harming behaviour/cutting.

What conclusions can we draw in relation to coaching practice? In a coaching dialogue, the coach may assume that the coachee has a pronounced desire to explore him/herself in interaction with a specific environmental situation, for example the desire to 'come to terms with' his or her relationship with a co-worker or a manager, to focus on career opportunities or to achieve a healthier lifestyle. The coachee's fundamental interest in change and development is the condition for a successful conversation process. The coaching dialogue can also examine the coachee's different ways of behaving in different situations and address how and when the coachee feels best about him/herself. Here, the coach or coaching psychologist may draw on his or her theoretical knowledge about the particular psychological challenges faced by individuals in late-/post-modern society. It will also be helpful to apply a more in-depth psychological understanding of the underlying processes in identity and self-development, which I will present in the following in a version that I have previously developed and tested in a number of research projects (see e.g. Stelter, 1996, 1998).

2.2.1 Identity Theory: Between Phenomenology and Social Constructionism

In my theory development I have aimed for a balance between a *phenomenological* and a *social constructionist* understanding of identity and self-concept. This linking of theories is a consistent feature that characterizes my basic position, which is also evident later in the book when I present my practice and intervention theory for coaching (psychology). What is the significance of these two theoretical perspectives for the development of identity and self-concept? The *phenomenological* perspective focuses on *subjective perceptions and experiences and the individual's open-minded approach* to the situation here and now as a basis for the individual's concept of reality and self. The *social constructionist* perspective, on the other hand, addresses the individual's identity development as a result of the relationships that the individual enters into.

This theoretical coupling of an experiential and a relationist perspective is becoming increasingly widespread and appears in works by Crossley (2003), Sampson (1996), Shotter (1993, 2003), Shotter and Lannamann (2002) and Stam (2001, 2002).[1] Crossley (2003) presents her position as follows,

> I felt there was a need for a different kind of psychology – one which retained the ability of appreciating the linguistic and discursive structuring of 'self' and 'experience', but one which also maintained a sense of the essentially personal, coherent and 'real' nature of individual subjectivity (p. 289).

In the following, my theoretical approach to the development of self and identity[2] will be founded on two basic orientations that the self has in interaction with its environment, and which should be seen as inextricably integrated in the specific action context:

---

[1] In August 2009 I was among the presenters at the summer university on coaching organized by the consultancy firm Attractor. Here I was surprised to find that the systemically anchored consultancy firm had invited several speakers who focused on subjective and experiential perspective as a necessary element for developing the systemic/social constructionist position. In addition to myself, this included Helle Alrø, John Shotter, Morten Ziethen, Finn Thorbjørn Hansen and others. Many participants welcomed this perspective. Perhaps we are approaching a new understanding?

[2] The theory was originally developed in my Ph.D. dissertation (Stelter, 1996) and has undergone continual further development (Stelter, 1998, 2002b, 2006, 2008b).

1. The striving of the self for stability and consistency, where the focus is especially on inner processes. Here I consider *perceptions and experiences* key dimensions of self-development.
2. The striving of the self for an ongoing re-anchoring in varying social contexts and situations, where the individual focuses on the environment and on social relations. Here I consider *self-presentation* as a key aspect of identity development.

In the following, I present these two basic orientations, fully aware that the distinction is an analytical one. The self develops in a dynamic interaction of varying contexts and situations, and both perspectives are in constant interaction.

2.2.1.1 The Striving of the Self for Stability and Consistency

The self is characterized by an inner conservatism that is expressed in its striving for stability and consistency. A person to some degree perceives him/herself as consistent; the same is true of other people's perceptions of the person. (In some identity theories, the characterization of the predominantly stable self is assumed as a central perspective; see e.g. Greenwald, 1980). The theoretical understanding presented here underscores this striving for stability, albeit only as one perspective on the construction of self and identity. (The word 'identity' in fact comes from the Latin word 'idem', which means 'the same'). This perspective should not, however, be perceived as an assumption of a permanently stable personality core, where the individual appears unchanged over time, regardless of social context and situation. I want to address what happens with the individual when he or she 'enters' a particular situation: What is the interaction between the person and the specific situation? And what is the source of this form of stability in the individual's self-concept? To answer these questions, I would point especially to the body as a crucial element in our ability to perceive and sense the environment. The individual's meeting with an environmental situation is always initially corporeal. The body is always a part of the person's action practice. In order to understand individual experience and embodiment, I include phenomenological theory, which views the body as the individual's anchor in the world (Merleau-Ponty, 2012). Via the body, the individual is always *intentionally* oriented in relation to his or her environment, and this orientation conditions the individual's ability to perceive him/herself and the situation as meaningful. By virtue of its function as a perceiving organ, the body attributes the external world with meaning that springs from the individual's perspective on the given situation. In this sensory and experiential process, the individual develops his or her *body self*, which is actualized continually via sensations, perceptions and cognitions that emerge from body sensations in the given environmental situation. The body sensations reach our consciousness via sensory organs, proprioceptors, kinetic sensations and the vestibular system. These sensory perceptions of the self are always related to an actual practice – actions that are performed in a specific situation based on the body's intentional orientation in relation to the environment.

The body self is developed through *habits and routines* in the individual's day-to-day practice, whether it is cooking in the kitchen, the performance of particular skills in the workplace or regular jogging after work. As a result of these habits and routines, the individual develops a form of stability and inner consistency in relation to his or her self-perception, which produces a basic sense of safety and security that is an important condition for the individual's self-development. The individual may also achieve this essential sense of security in his or her self-perception, which is so crucial for stable self and identity development (Stelter, 2008b), through *observational learning based on certain models* or *supportive learning processes with experienced others*, for example in training situations in work or education – also described in the didactic concept of apprenticeship learning (Nielsen, 2006; Nielsen & Kvale, 1997).

The person's self-concept develops via the body self. *Body self* and *self-concept* are inextricably linked. I would define *self-concept* as an affective-cognitive structure that shapes perceptions and experiences via an embodiment of the environment into a subjective environment or individual reality. A person's self-concept reflects his or her understanding of him/herself and the environment that he or she lives in. Through this self-concept, the person presents his or her *subjective reality*.

2.2.1.2 The Striving of the Self for Continual Re-anchoring in Selected Social Contexts

With these individually interlinked constructions, here defined as body self and self-concept, the person steps out 'in front of the public'. (In this presentation of theory we will view the situation as separated in time. In fact, the two aspects of self-construction are temporally integrated, but this quality cannot be captured in words). The subjective reality – which is anchored in the individual's self-concept – encounters other individuals' realities in certain social contexts and situations. This is where the dialogue with the *social* environment begins. Thus, identity is not simply the result of a subjective perception of the environment – it is also to be negotiated in various social environments. Identity is shaped in one way in one environment (for example in the workplace) and in another way in another environment (for example in the family); that is to say, we *negotiate* our identity or present ourselves differently depending on our current social environment. Thus, the self not only has a personal dimension – as described above – it also has a social dimension that is influenced by the social relationships the individual enters into. This concept of the *self as a social construct* is developed in an active dialogue with the social environment. The self as a social construct or the *relational self* (Gergen, 2009a, b) is continually anchored in a variety of social contexts. This understanding clearly shifts the focus away from the individual. The perspective shifts completely, and consciousness, cognition and emotions become anchored in the relationship itself as "the property of ongoing relationships" (Gergen, 2009a, s. 106), not, as assumed in traditional psychological theories, as a strictly personal property.

The theoretical expansion that is presented here, with its emphasis on relational interpersonal dynamics, is an important step in a new direction in relation to the huge impact of societal changes on our self and identity development. To capture the diversification in individual ways of life and the individual's attachment to many different social contexts theoretically, it is helpful to move away from a strictly *egocentric*, individually oriented concept of identity and instead enrich the perspective with an open-minded stance toward theories that are based on *sociocentric* assumptions. The sociocentric, relational and social constructionist orientation seeks to examine the self in a system of multiple social relations and varying social contexts. Already a quarter of a century ago, Sampson (1985) argued that it might even be helpful for the individual to understand the self from a sociocentric point of view, abandoning the traditional personality concept:

> Our personhood ideal does not lead toward either individuality or freedom; it only catches us in a contradiction that produces frustration and slides us inevitably toward a socially self-destructive pattern. The freedom that self-organizing systems represent can never be reached from a self-contained stance about personhood. Only a decentralized, non equilibrium conception of personhood that allows our multiplicity and interconnectedness a time to live can possibly encourage the problem solving that is necessary to achieve the utopian dream we share (p. 1210).

Self-development and identity formation in today's world rely mainly on *social processes such as weighing, adapting, changing and selecting social situations and contexts*. These processes highlight the individual's striving for continually anchoring him/herself in a network of social relationships. The self is thus not an autonomous entity, as assumed in the traditional (egocentric) personality psychology, but can be defined as "a node in a chain of social relationships" (Gergen, 1990; translated for this edition). Identity thus becomes a social construction, a "processual event of ongoing day-to-day identity work"[3] (Keupp et al., 1999, s. 30; translated for this edition).

According to social constructionism, social self-construction processes are relational in character, as the individual's identity develops through others and in relation to specific social contexts. The following definition describes the self in its network of social relationships): "The self as a social construction is formed by active interchange with the social environment and society in general. In a verbal discourse, the subject is forced to defend his or her personal constructions of the world in relation to (significant) others, and the subject has to adapt this personal perspective according to the power structure of the social group or society in general. Furthermore the subject has the possibility of negotiating his or her identity via different impression-management strategies and via the choice of social setting" (Stelter, 1998, p. 18).

---

[3]German original: "*Prozeßgeschehen beständiger 'alltäglicher Identitätsarbeit'*."

2.2.2   Identity Negotiations in the Coaching Dialogue

In the following, I seek to strengthen the reader's focus on the impact of the coaching dialogue on self-development. I consider it crucial to link two key identity-forming perspectives, which are reflected in a focus on the individual's *experiences* and *self-presentation*, in order to promote the integration between the coachee's awareness of his or her subjective life world and social relationships. This integration forms the basis of the coaching dialogue, where the dialogue itself can be viewed as a form of identity negotiation that contributes to establishing a holistic perspective on the coachee's life situation. In this perspective, the coaching dialogue is about (a) *describing, reflecting on and speaking about the coachee's own experiences*, (b) *reflecting on the coachee's own self-presentation* in selected social contexts and thus generating development, change, new perspectives and integration in the two previously mentioned areas (c). This process of identity negotiation takes place in the coaching dialogue itself, which may serve as a venue for self-reflection and for testing new forms of self-narratives and self-presentation. In the following, I will elaborate on these three dimensions:

(a) By *telling the stories of own experiences*, the individual can connect his or her subjective realities to the challenges of the social world. Subjective perceptions, experiences and notions and the resulting personal self-constructs need to be tested, confirmed, defended, replaced or modified in social discourses that are relived in the coaching dialogue. In this conversation, stories take shape (Bruner, 2002; Gergen & Gergen, 2006; Kraus, 2006) in a co-creative process either between the coach and coachee or in a coaching group. Stories are also generated on the basis of interactions between the coachee and certain individuals in the social contexts that the conversation addresses. The coaching conversation pursues a particular perspective, where stories from everyday life, ideally, are developed further to form a progressive, uplifting storyline (see Gergen, 1994). The possible uplifting stories that are generated during the conversation may influence the coachee's self-concept and may also have a positive impact on the social interaction that was the topic of the dialogue. In this way, language and action have a positive mutual effect on one another (Cronen & Lange, 1994) – a perspective that may be considered on the most important hallmarks of the coaching dialogue.

(b) The *self is presented* in social contexts by means of selected forms of self-presentation strategies and through the choice of particular identity-stabilizing environments and situations that help promote the individual's identity projects and social self-constructions.

First of all, identity negotiations depend on the individual's capacity for predicting expectations in selected social contexts (e.g. a difficult conversation with a co-worker). This 'internal analysis' is a precondition for the individual to develop strategies for his or her self-presentation. According to Goffman (1959), personal aspects such as 'appearance' (the person's social standing), 'manner' (social conventions) and 'setting' (the situation's social, organizational and interactive

2.2 Coaching, Identity and Self-constructions: The Self Is at Stake...   25

circumstances) are all involved in framing the person's self-presentation. The individual ascribes particular meaning to the social signs and codes of the given context. Social signs refer to group affiliation, membership and social positions, such as job titles as an indicator of the person's standing in the organization. Social codes refer to an integrated system of signs, for example etiquette as a reflection of certain social interactions and fashion as the reflection of a particular social identity (Manning, 1987). In life in general and also in the coaching conversation, selected social contexts are ascribed specific meaning and importance through what I call 'internal analysis'; this influences the person's/coachee's way of presenting him/herself with the intention of handling the situation in a more satisfying way.

Secondly, the individual manages his or her self-presentation by *selecting certain contexts or settings*. Seeking out certain environmental situations that promote the person's identity and self-concept is crucial for the person's identity development. With reference to several authors, Swann (1987) points out that people often seek out social contexts that are sure to offer *self-confirmatory feedback*, and which thus support certain preferred modes of self-presentation. These social situations, contexts and settings, which the coachee chooses or prefers, contain social relationships that strengthen or at least do not threaten the individual's existing self-concept. By selecting certain social situations and contexts and rejecting others, the coachee can consolidate certain 'personality characteristics'. The choice of context is thus an effective means of stabilizing one's identity, as the context and the social relationships that exist in the given context determine the scope of the person's behaviour and appearance (Gergen, 2009a).

(c) In the coaching dialogue, the coach and coachee work together to achieve development and integration in relation to these two overall dimensions. The intention is to enable the coachee to develop a deeper understanding of his or her subjective experiences in specific situations and to facilitate insight into his or her interactions with various actors in a variety of social contexts. The dialogue generates new meaning, which is often presented in new stories about certain experiences, tasks, situations or events.

Identity development is thus an integrative process balancing between individually specific, experiential aspects on the one hand and relational interaction aspects on the other. The coach may focus on these dimensions of identity development, and the theoretical considerations that have been outlined here may help heighten the coach's attention of the particular dimensions that are in focus in the given conversation situation.

In the following, I will focus on some considerations in relation to learning theory. Coaching and learning are inextricably linked. Broadly seen, coaching always constitutes a learning situation. On a theoretical level, the concept of learning that is presented here lies in extension of the understanding that was presented in the previous section. In the following I continue to strive to integrate experiential and relational/social perspectives.

2.3 Coaching and Learning: Between Personal Experience and Collaboration

I define learning as a life-long, permanent process as part of individuals' or groups' efforts to meet society's demands for active participation in work and civil life. This concept of learning has become a fundamental condition in the life-long education of modern man and the democratic process in society. During the last decades of the 20th century, a situated and context-dependent concept of learning has largely replaced the former concept of learning, which was often associated with the rote acquisition of simple action patterns or cognition processes. This new concept of learning is one of the causes of the growing popularity of coaching in late-modern society: Life-long learning and development have become fundamental requirements for all members of society, and coaching may be seen as a form of dialogue that is capable of supporting individuals and groups in their efforts to learn and develop.

As it becomes increasingly difficult to establish specific development goals, coaching and learning come to focus on the process and on what might unfold in *personal interactions*. Learning and development often take place in creative practice communities, where the individual works, develops and learns together with others.

Learning can be viewed as a *transformative* process (Mezirow & Associates, 2000; Illeris, 2004) based on reinterpreting one's own experience. The way we learn and develop often involves a reinterpretation of the way in which we have created meaning. This reinterpretation may involve reflection processes, where the individual explores certain perceptions and experiences in an effort to achieve a new understanding and a new assessment. But learning is also a communicative process that aims to understand the meaning of what others communicate. This is often the case, as Mezirow and Associates (1990) put it, in regard to "values, ideals, feelings, moral decisions, and such concepts as freedom, justice, love, labour, autonomy, commitment and democracy" (s. 8). Certain events may force a *perspective transformation or a shift in perspective*, but that may also be triggered by conversations with others. Later (in Chap. 3), I mention a *shift in perspective* as a key objective of coaching. Mezirow and Associates describe *perspective transformation* as

> the process of becoming critically aware of how and why our presuppositions have come to constrain the way we perceive, understand, and feel about our world; of reformulating these assumptions to permit a more inclusive, discriminating, permeable, and integrative perspective; and of making decisions or otherwise acting upon these new understandings (p. 14).

In that sense, *reflection* as a basis for a further development of meaning plays a key role in transformative learning, a circumstance that characterizes coaching in the framework of learning theory.

In the following, I address learning with a focus on two key dimensions, which are also crucial for coaching in practice: (1) Learning through experience and (2) learning as a social and collaborative practice.

2.3.1 Coaching and Experiential Learning

According to the American organizational psychologist Kolb (1984), learning can be defined as "the process whereby knowledge is created through the transformation of experience. Knowledge results from the combination of grasping and transforming experience" (p. 41). I thus present learning as an experiential and action-oriented process of cognition and development, where cognition is understood as *enaction*, which Varela, Thompson and Rosch (1993) describe as follows:

> We propose as a name the term *enactive* to emphasize the growing conviction that cognition is not the representation of a pre-given world by a pre-given mind but is rather the enactment of a world and a mind on the basis of a history of the variety of actions that a being in the world performs (p. 9).

This understanding suggests that experience, cognition and action are interwoven into one and the same meaning-making process, which I will call *experiential learning*. In the understanding presented here, cognition does not stem from the person's inner consciousness. Cognition is thus *not* anchored in intrapsychological factors but is the result of a dialogue or an interaction between a person and his or her given environment, where experience and actions are not in a cause-and-effect relationship; instead, they condition each other in a circular process in the sense that experience always contains an action perspective, and action is always based on experiences and perception. The person perceives, discovers and understands his or her environment via action, and action is the precondition for perception and experience. Action can thus be defined as the *realization of certain meaning relations*, and cognition is embedded in the action process itself. In the dialogue between person and situation, the person shapes *his or her own* meaning in relation to the given situation. This dialogical process also forms the theoretical basis of coaching as a process tool; here, one of the objectives is to help the coachee better understand his or her dialogue with specific situations in the environment and to use this understanding to shape cognitions about him/herself and his or her behaviour.

According to Kolb (1984), the course of the learning process is divided into distinct stages (Fig. 2.2), and each stage is associated with different types of knowledge production:

1. Concrete experience
2. Reflective observation
3. Abstract conceptualization
4. Active experimentation (action)

This staged structure should be seen as a purely analytical understanding; in fact the stages transition into each other, seamlessly and continually.

I will present these four stages as a possible orientation framework for the course of a coaching conversation – one possible method that pays particular attention to the sensory and experiential perception of a given challenge:

Stage 1: Learning may spring from the coachee's *concrete experiences* in relation to a specific situation or event; this situation or event may constitute the point of

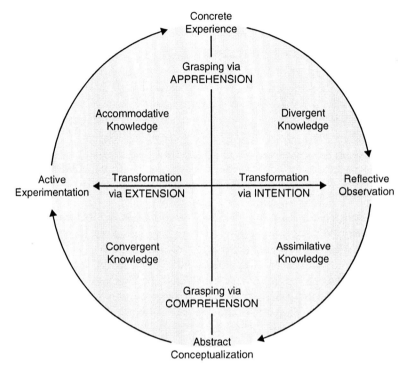

Fig. 2.2 Kolb's experiential learning cycle (Source: Kolb, 1984, p. 42)

departure for the coaching conversation. To develop a sense of the situation, the coach may ask the coachee to focus on the sensory-aesthetic[4] dimension of the events. The coachee adopts a first-person position (Stelter, 2008a). According to Varela and Shear (1999), first-person events are lived experiences that are linked with cognitive and mental events. This first-person perspective can be considered the sensory and experiential foundation of the self, where self-development rests on the interaction between person and environment in the field of concrete action: The coachee is directly involved in events, and the situation is initially perceived on very sensory terms due to the concrete experiences which the coachee relives. The coachee's focus on concrete experiences is framed by basic attitude perspectives that frame the subsequent reflection process (cf. Stelter, 2008a):

- The coachee always adopts an *intentional perspective* on the situation: The coachee's intentional relationship with the specific practice context is an essential cornerstone for his or her sensory-aesthetic involvement in the situation. This sensory involvement is based on the coachee's situation-specific and embodied experience; this experience is often based on habits and routines and is typically not verbalized.

---

[4]The term *aesthetics* stems from the Greek word *aisthetikos*, which means *sense perception* (see also Stelter, 2008a).

- Sensory-aesthetic experiences are enabled by the coachee's orientation to the here-and-now situation. In the form of selected *present moments*, the focus is on the immediate experiences related to the situation. Stern (2004) describes these moments as "a subjective, psychological process unit of which one is aware" (p. 25). He emphasizes a number of characteristics that define the present moment more specifically. As a key characteristic, Stern mentions, "The present moment is not the verbal account of an experience" (p. 32). The present moment can be experienced, for example, in the concrete *practice situation*: I am aware of what I am doing, and events unfold in the flow of the action.
- This attention and alertness to the here and now of the situation are based on *epoché*, a Greek word describing a basic stance where the individual avoids and suspends any judgment of the situation or him/herself. The founder of phenomenology, Edmund Husserl (1931; Zahavi, 2003), describes his understanding of *epoché* as an opportunity to enhance one's self-awareness. The unprejudiced or non-judging attitude that is the central aspect of epoché may constitute a fundamental basic stance in certain stages of the coaching dialogue.

Stage 2: Via *reflective observation*, the coachee can expand on the meaning of the concrete experiences and capture the effect of the situation on him/herself and the environment. The coachee's goal should be to enhance his or her awareness of the situation, of others and of the event and to explore nuances and differences. Through reflective observation the coachee can achieve a deeper understanding of the various facets and vantage points of the situation, and in this reflective process the coachee increasingly perceives his or her interaction with the situation as meaningful. In this stage in particular, knowledge production and learning take a *divergent* and explorative form. The key is to capture and articulate the full diversity of the situation and its many details, which may initially seem surprising. The basic stance in this reflective process of observation can be described with the terms *mindful* and *mindfulness*. Mindfulness is defined as a specific intentional orientation that has to do with paying attention in a certain way, with a specific purpose and without judging, focusing on cultivating a deliberate awareness and alertness from one moment to the next in an open, curious and accepting manner (Germer, 2005; Kabat-Zinn, 1994). The Harvard psychologist Ellen Langer (1997) speaks of *mindful learning* and describes her approach as follows: "A mindful approach to any activity has three characteristics: the continuous creation of new categories; openness to new information; and an implicit awareness of more than one perspective" (p. 4). To her, mindfulness expresses a basic awareness to the details of a given context or situation.

Through this reflective observation the coachee puts differences and details into words and is thus able to appreciate the full richness of the situation, which often goes unnoticed in everyday life. It is no *easy task*, however, to have a conversation about these often implicit, i.e. unarticulated experiences. Verbalizing sensory-aesthetic experiences requires a *transformation* (Stelter, 2000): In a process of symbolization, the *felt sense* (Gendlin, 1997) of concrete persons, situations, tasks or events is reformatted to a verbal expression that becomes meaningful in relation to the often implicit experiences that are embedded in the concrete practice situations. This articulation can best be achieved by means of specific strategies, which are described in detail in Sect. 4.3.1.1.

Stage 3: In the stage of *abstract conceptualization*, the coach directs the coachee's attention toward *grasping* the multitude of reflections on the concrete perceptions and experiences that were prominent in Stage 2. At this stage, the emphasis is on *understanding*. Kolb (1984) describes this as an *assimilative process of learning and cognition*, where reflective observation is, for example, coupled with the coachee's experiences and knowledge from previous situations, and the coachee tries to discern a pattern in his or her way of acting in certain situations. The coachee seeks to find a position that can be compared to the perceived reality that begins to take on prominence. The coachee develops a form of subjective theory[5] with regard to his or her interactions with the concrete situation in order to create a personal explanation of his or her experiences. Through this process, the coachee develops a basic, generalizing and abstract understanding in relation to the situation. For example, a coachee might arrive at the following statement: 'When I wind up in a conflict situation, I tend to get insecure, but I react somewhat aggressively toward my counterpart.' This stage is dominated by rational considerations, logic and generalizing conceptualization. To incorporate a narrative theoretical position here, it is important to *name* or find a term that best captures the person's generalized experiences in relation to the situation or event. The coachee also compares the current situation with previous situations in order to generalize the experiences and observations from the concrete situation. In the course of the conversation, naming can also cause the coach to focus on what this generalization/naming reveals about the coachee's identity and how it is associated with the coachee's values and aspirations.

Stage 4: This is the *action* stage or, in the context of the coaching process, the stage of *active experimentation* in relation to potential actions that the coachee might initiate in extension of the meeting with the coach. The subjective theories and general reflections (via naming) that were developed in Stage 3 may be viewed as an invitation and a precondition for establishing hypotheses about future action patterns in similar situations. They can be used spontaneously in new situations or in planning a specific future event. In order to concretize this understanding in relation to the coachee's conflict situation, the coachee may for example say, 'When I wind up in a conflict situation I will be aware of my own insecurity, describe it to my counterpart and attempt to suggest a constructive way out of the conflict.' This process of outlining possible solutions or developing concrete hypotheses about ways to handle future situations describes a *convergent process of learning and cognition*. The subjective theories and generalized considerations from Stage 3 provide an orientation framework for the new action situation. The person's actions will then form the basis for initiating a new learning cycle.

---

[5]See mere in Groeben and Scheele (2000) and Groeben, Wahl, Schlee, and Scheele (1988).

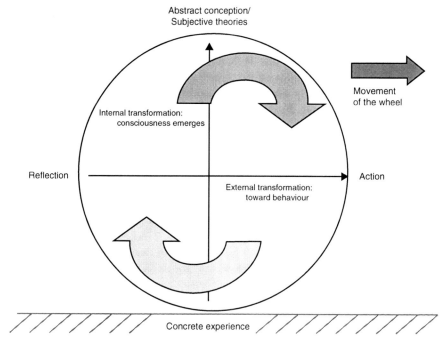

Fig. 2.3 The learning wheel (Source: Law et al., 2007, p. 36; with modifications)

A group of English coaching psychologists (Law, Ireland, & Hussain, 2007) have turned Kolb's learning cycle upside down. Their graphic presentation suggests a stronger dynamic in relation to the coachee's learning progression. Kolb's learning cycle becomes a wheel that rolls forward. Internal and external transformation processes are interwoven (Fig. 2.3).

2.3.2 Coaching and Learning as a Social and Collaborative Practice

With Kolb's learning cycle as my point of departure, I have described how coaching can be viewed as a learning process that revolves around, for example, the coachee's concrete perceptions and experiences. In the following, I will explore the social component of learning. In many contexts, we learn in interaction with others in a classroom, a department, a production team, a sports team or a work or self-help group. The group's learning process can be intensified by means of coaching methods and coaching questions techniques. The group leader may serve as a coach. Here one should be aware of the leader's dual role as both participant and coach. This dual role may pose special challenges, and in work contexts especially, coaching-oriented leaders need to be aware of their power position, which may make it difficult to be an effective coach.[6] A group or team coach may also be an outside person engaged by the group or team, for example with view to developing a strategy, resolving a group conflict or facilitating a development task.

The social perspective can also be included in a one-on-one coaching situation. The coach then actively builds on the others' positions, for example by asking the coachee to consider one or several colleagues' reflections in order to develop and create new perspectives in the conversation. In many cases, it is the involvement of these different perspectives that makes a real difference in the coaching situation (Bateson, 1972). This fundamental idea is also present in the model of *double-versus single-loop learning* (Argyris, 1992). Single-loop learning is based on an assumption of certain more or less stable conditions – such as goals, values and presumptions in relation to a given situation. *Double-loop learning*, on the other hand, means rejecting these pre-existing assumptions. Thus, the coach helps to bring the coachee in a position where he or she includes a new perspective on the situation and the coachee's assumptions about the situation.

With regard to coaching as a socially mediated learning process, the basic point of coaching is to *'learn' in interaction with others*. The group serves as a community of learning and collaborative practice. To avoid complicating matters in this presentation, I will temporarily suspend the discussion of power in relation to the coach's position. In their social learning theory the American social learning researchers Lave and Wenger (1991) speak about learning in communities of practice. The key point in their understanding is that all the actors are 'legitimate peripheral participants', that is, the participants have an *intentional orientation* toward being part of the community of practice, and every participant is accepted by everyone else as a legitimate participant. The peripheral aspect of this form of learning is explained as follows: The point is not to transfer knowledge from one person to the other; instead, knowledge emerges as a product of the joint practice that all the parties contribute to as best they can. According to Lave and Wenger as well as to social constructionists (Gergen, 2009a, b; Paré & Larner, 2004),[7] learning and knowledge production is locally and contextually anchored. Thus, this position corresponds to a learning concept that characterizes late- or post-modern society (Lyotard, 1984), where knowledge production and learning to a high degree rely on their *utility value* for the participants in the process.

The smallest practice community is the dyad, for example that of a coach and a coachee. Ideally, this relationship can be considered an interaction between two

---

[6]In their book *Ledelsebaseret coaching [Leadership-based coaching]*, Søholm et al. (2006) have described the manager's possibilities and limitations in the role as coach. Kirkeby (2009) notes, however, that leadership coaching does not adequately ask itself how much leadership power blocks the dialogical potential for symmetry. Therefore, Kirkeby proposes a protreptic form of coaching that focuses especially on reflection on the fundamental values that guide our actions in certain contexts.

[7]I am aware that Lave and Wenger and social constructionist authors do not normally refer to each other or are normally placed in the same category, but their basic ideas about knowledge production and learning appear fairly compatible. Later in this section I offer an overview where I link different approaches.

equals, both striving for new self-insight as well as insight into their own and each other's life worlds. In any practice community there will be differences in 'learning conditions', but none of the parties in the practice community has a monopoly on knowledge, for example in terms of being able to determine the validity of certain world views or solutions. Knowledge will always be a shared product, although the participants may have different shares in its production. Thus, in my opinion, describing the coaching dialogue as either symmetrical or asymmetrical is unhelpful – also when I consider my own previous position (Stelter, 2002a). Describing coaching as an asymmetrical dialogue has been the common assumption in the coaching literature, but here it is being replaced by a more dynamic understanding (see also Hede, 2010). Coaching can be viewed as a co-creative and collaborative process where both parties can be defined as *equal parties and experts* within their respective domains (see also Anderson, 2007a), and where they can enrich each other's self-perception and world views within the framework of the conversation.

I consider the following dimensions crucial to an understanding of theories about situated learning (see Lave & Wenger, 1991; Wenger, 1998) and collaborative practice (Anderson & Gehart, 2007; Paré & Larner, 2004) and for the concretization of these theories in the coaching dialogue:

- Knowledge and learning are relational and situative in character; for example, knowledge and learning can emerge in the interaction between the coach and the coachee, where the coachee's life world is included as the special context of the conversation: specific persons, the concrete social and physical environment, structural conditions, different positions, special and possible divergent stories.
- Learning is an inherent part of the social practice that the coach and coachee(s) create together. Thus, learning is not necessarily a planned activity but may be part of many types of collaborations. The dialogue that the parties create forms the basis of developing both their shared and their individual understanding in relation to the topics and situations that are addressed in the dialogue.
- Person, action and context mutually constitute each other in the concrete social practice. The coachee is not perceived as a person with stable characteristics, independent from his or her actions and from the social relationships that the coachee includes in the conversation from particular contexts and situations. The coachee's actions are shaped in relation to the possibilities that the social and physical environment make available and allow. Coach and coachee(s) create their world *together* through the dialogue that unfolds between them. At the same time, other social arenas are also invited into the dialogue as part of the coachee's world.
- Coach and coachee(s) are both *legitimate peripheral participants*[8] in their community of practice. They have made a mutual contract, where they strive

---

[8]The concept comes from Lave and Wenger (1991) and describes the situation where none of the participants in the (learning) situation has a knowledge monopoly. Both parties can learn from the situation, regardless of their starting point.

to inspire each other, and where the coachee has a special set of expectations for the direction and purpose of the conversation. Even though the coach may occupy a special role in the dialogue, based on his or her professional expertise in coaching and psychology, neither party can claim a central position with regard to the knowledge and learning that takes shape in the dialogue. The coach or the coaching educator, treatment professional or leader cannot know what the other should learn, as the concrete situation that is discussed in the coaching dialogue will be perceived differently by the different participants. The different positions and perspectives that can be adopted in relation to the situation make it difficult to define a clear objective or goal for the conversation from the outset. It is important to go with the flow of the conversation and to remain attentive to what unfolds through the participants' social practices and dialogues.

• Participation in the social practice of the coaching dialogue thus always implies a reflection process, a 'negotiation' of meanings in relation to the situation that the individual is involved in. Coach and coachee(s) enter into the situation based on their own perceptions and experiences, which influence their personal meanings in relation to the events and situations that are addressed in the conversation (the experiential perspective). These (individual) perspectives on the situation and the events are brought into the dialogue, where meanings are developed further in the dialogue. Coach and coachee(s) become co-learners in a process of expanding their shared understanding in relation to the topics that are addressed in their dialogue.

• The coach acts as a partner in the dialogue, not as an expert on the topic. The coach's expertise lies instead in creating conditions for the coaching conversation that facilitate and promote the development of the collaborative relationship and the emerging learning and knowledge community. This collaborative process requires an ongoing interaction among all the participants in the community of practice. An optimal learning and coaching environment requires that the dialogue partners speak *with* each other rather than *to* each other and *about* something. The English communication researcher John Shotter (2006) speaks of 'withness thinking' instead of 'aboutness thinking'. From a systemic point of view, one would say that the dialogue takes its point of departure in the reflection domain and invites a variety of reflection perspectives in. Coaching focuses on multiversality, i.e. the inclusion of multiple voices and local truths in the dialogue. Thus, coaching becomes a process of shared meaning-making. This perspective becomes even more visible when coaching is a group or a team process.

• This collaborative dialogue not only generates new knowledge; the dialogue also affects the individual participants' identity and self-concept. Shared learning and the collaborative coaching practice facilitate personal and social developmental processes. In this process, the self appears clearly relational, as constituted by the relationships and conversations that have unfolded between the coach and the coachee(s).

2.3.3   Summary: Coaching and Learning: Between Subjective Experiences and Collaborative Dialogues

Above, I have outlined two learning approaches where the coach takes his or her point of departure in (1) the *individual's subjective experiences* in relation to specific situations or (2) the *collaborative dialogue* that unfolds between the coaching parties. Previously, these positions were not considered very compatible in an epistemological sense, but that has changed over the past couple of decades. The gap between (1) the phenomenological-experiential practice and (2) the social constructionist collaborative practice appears to be narrowing. A growing number of psychotherapy approaches, from psychodynamic to systemic-relational directions, are developing mixed forms, where different traditions fuse. As a reflective practitioner,[9] the coach must be aware of the points of departure he or she chooses in the given coaching situation, and how the two perspectives mentioned above can be integrated into the ongoing dialogue between the participants in the coaching process. Learning will always have (1) a sensory-aesthetic dimension, where the coachee is encouraged to focus on specific experiences and situations, and (2) a social dimension, where the coachee learns in interaction with others (Stelter, 2008b). Both learning dimensions rely on dynamic circularity, where the individual interacts actively with both the concrete perceived situation and the significant others who are either present in a concrete, physical sense or in the sense of their influence on the individual's thoughts and actions.

In the following and final section in this chapter, I address coaching in the perspective of organization and leadership theory and thus introduce a specific context where coaching has seen very widespread use. I am aware that this choice narrows the field. I assume, for example, that coaching will see massive growth in relation to treatment, disease prevention and the promotion of healthy living.

2.4   Coaching in the Theoretical Perspective of Organization and Leadership

Coaching has become very widespread in management and organization development. On the one hand there is the *coaching-inspired leadership style*, where the leader – in some form – wants to act as a coach or as a coaching-oriented leader. In a survey headed by the author in 2009 (Wittrock, Didriksen, & Stelter, 2009) 30 % of the surveyed HR-managers state that their managers have received coaching training, and some 20 % state that coaching is part of their company's leadership training.

---

[9] According to Jarvis (1999) and Lane and Corrie (2006), among others, the reflective practitioner always develops his or her knowledge based on two resources: (1) Research-based evidence and academic theory and (2) his or her own subjective theories that emerge on the basis of reflections on one's own practice. More about that in Chap. 6.

On the other hand, managers also use coaching to *reflect on their own leadership practice*. The reason why coaching has this role in management will be discussed in the following: The practice field of management and leadership has undergone significant changes in the past few decades; leading a company or an organization means leading others to self-management (Helth, 2009a; Ladkin, 2010). Like so many other authority figures, managers/leader have lost their knowledge monopoly, and in many cases the ultimate professional expertise is no longer a part of their leadership role. Where managers/leaders were previously assigned their role and automatically received respect by virtue of their position, which was often due to their expert knowledge, today's managers are faced with the challenge of achieving personal authority and have to manage their role in a new way. Managers need to earn the trust of the people they lead. They have to earn their leadership position. In this sense, management has undergone *a shift from being role-based to being person-based*. Managers/leaders therefore need entirely new competences and action strategies. In the future, the manager's/leaders ability to handle dialogue will be an essential qualification parameter.

2.4.1 Leadership Is Dialogical and Involving

In order to earn the trust of their staff and gain insight into the employees' perspectives on the organization and their work, managers/leaders should be invited to generate dialogue on different levels in the company. Dialogue enhances understanding among the parties and builds a sound foundation for cooperation. There is a need to overcome traditional leadership and control thinking. Managers have to ensure support for the company's basic idea, not by exercising control but by persuading and by building a sound common and collaborative foundation (Hansen, 2009; Helth, 2009b). The manager/leader has to promote a sense of community and support and a shared sense of identity in the organization. The English management researcher Ralph D. Stacey (2007) underscores the ability of narratives – and thus the communicative element – to describe the nature of the organization and to contribute to the organization's ongoing development:

> Ask people in an organization what it is all about and how they come to do what they do and they tell you a story. Ask them what the strategy has been and they tell you a story of expansion, acquisition, downsizing, or whatever. In an ordinary, everyday way, therefore, strategy is a narrative of identity co-created by people in an organization (p. 375).

Leadership, organizational development and cooperation are a process of co-creation and coordination around meaning, where all the parties seek to relate to and approach each other. The manager/leader is tasked with making the employees work together and should also strive to become 'part of the team'. The manager/leader should create results through negotiations with all relevant involved parties. In this process, the focus is not only on strategy and concrete tasks; to some extent, the manager's and the employee's person and identity are also up for negotiation – in a process that integrates leadership and organization development, and where the goal becomes to develop the *relationally created organization* that the Danish leadership research practitioner Poula Helth (Helth, 2009b) speaks about. At the same time, it is essential not to ignore the built-in dilemmas and conflicts of interest in this negotiation process. Management and staff have different agendas: Leading and being led are always framed by a particular power constellation, which the parties have to address, and which also needs to be articulated in concrete negotiation situations. Leadership therefore has to strive for legitimacy. Staff loyalty cannot be taken for granted.

2.4.2   *Leadership Means Managing Complexity*

Both managers and staff have to deal with the growing degree of complexity that generally characterizes our working life, organizations, companies and societies: The systems theory concept of *contingency* offers a good way of describing this particular challenge. The German systems theorist Niklas Luhmann (1995) describes the concept as follows:

> Complexity ... means being forced to select; being forced to select means *contingency*; and contingency means risk. Every complex state of affairs is based on a selection of relations among its elements, which it uses to constitute and maintain itself. The selection positions and qualifies the elements, although other relations would have been possible. We borrow the tradition-laden term 'contingency' to designate this 'also being possible otherwise'. It alludes, too, to the possibility of failing to achieve the best possible formation (p. 25; my italics).

The concept of contingency describes the impossibility of finding clear-cut solutions. Leadership is about dealing with this contingency and living with the permanent impossibility of achieving clarity, safety and certainty. Today, much more than before, we have to learn to live with the risk of being wrong. One strategy for handling contingency is to be in and appreciate the permanent space of reflection. In this connection, The Danish leadership researcher Bettina Rennison (2009) speaks of *reflexive leadership*, where the goal is to move away from a state of "an operational closed stance to a self-observing reflexivity, where the management system observes its own way of thinking and acting" (p. 123; translated for this edition). One has to be able to adopt a meta-position, *taking a reflexive stance to one's own self-reflexivity*. In order to achieve depth and new perspectives in relation to developing a greater capacity for self-reflection, it may be helpful for a manager to see a coach or to be part of a coaching-oriented leadership network. Reflexive management is always *second-order management*. Helth (2009b) describes the reflexive leader as someone who can simultaneously adopt a participant's and an observer's position while also maintaining an ongoing inner dialogue with him/herself. The special challenge lies in seeing the situation from different angles. The manager has to be able to include the different voices and positions that exist in the organization in relation to any concrete situation, task or event. The manager has to embrace *polyphonic leadership*, which involves the ability to see and articulate different voices and to shift between different positions and competence profiles. Thus, leadership now has a much less hierarchic orientation than it once did, and the manager has to live up to much higher demands for self-creation, multi-disciplinary approaches, negotiation and responsiveness (Pedersen, 2001). In order to promote success and development for the organization in this hypercomplex situation, good leadership has to promote the employees' capacity for reflection and provide them with optimum conditions for development and learning with regard to their professional as well as their social and personal competences.

At some point, however, handling complexity and contingency requires clear and visible leadership. A permanent openness to the many potential choices is not exactly what is expected of a good leader. A lack of leadership can lead to uncertainty and ultimately produce stress among the employees (Brandi & Hildebrandt, 2008; Hildebrandt, 2003). Offering direction and taking the lead are characteristics of good leadership and personal agency. Kjerulf (2008) defines personal agency in leadership as the ability to translate intentions into action; he adds,

> Translating ideas and intentions into action requires … five properties in a person. Your self-insight, your individual background and your emotional capacity form the spokes in the wheel of agency, while your ambitions tie the spokes together and set the wheel in motion. The stronger the ring of relations that surround the wheel, the more merrily it spins, and the fewer punctures it has (p. 21; translated for this edition).

2.4.3 Personal Leadership and Value-Oriented Action

If leadership is a sea voyage under varying weather conditions, leadership must have certain fixed points to navigate by. The leader must provide direction. A growing number of management theorists are convinced that values can serve as an anchor and a guideline for the individual manager's (and employee's) actions, and thus help keep the organization on course. Values are expressed through the leader's agency (Kirkeby, 2006b, 2007). From an analytical perspective, Knudsen and Thygesen (2009, pp. 77 f.) mention four areas where values can come into play as a form of framing discourse (see also Thyssen, 2009):

1. *Branding the organization*, i.e. creating a credible image with reference to the citizen/customer as someone who has a choice among competing offers.
2. *Controlling the organization* by means of values, so that citizens or customers encounter a uniform stance in their contact with the organization.
3. *Building a community*, where the values serve to create a community with reference to citizens or customers as co-creating stakeholders.
4. *Providing licence to criticism*, where the values help create a developing culture.

In the understanding that has been presented here, values have a meaning that is closely related to thinking and action. Values provide a basic orientation that reflects our ethical-interpersonal foundation. Values frame the purpose and goal orientation of actions (Stelter, 2009a), thus expressing the intentional orientation of our actions and giving our actions legitimacy. Values provide bearings, generate agency and provide a space to manoeuvre where the actor's personal authority is expressed, and where decisions rest on an ethical and authentic foundation. Values differ from rules and are generally characterized by being categorical, inflexible and often unreflective. Values represent the meaning-making and meaningful in our actions and thus reflect our professional and personal identity. Kirkeby (2000, p. 72) speaks about norms and values as "the explanatory setting of our actions." "Leadership is the name of the movement whose fixed point is the right moment and the right mood (p. 74)," he concludes. Values often reflect the implicit aspects of our actions and are thus not always clearly articulated. Kirkeby (2000) says that leadership as a function approaches our understanding of social competences – competences that concern (1) the organization itself, i.e. the ability to encourage and engage employees, (2) the customers, by creating a coupling between needs and the company's technical reality, and (3) the rest of the network, including suppliers, consultants, trade unions and shareholders. In his understanding (Kirkeby), the leader's value-based actions are rooted in certain virtues; he mentions the following six virtues:

1. *eubolia* = good deliberation skills, the ability to see things in a new light, resourcefulness
2. *euphoria* = expression of unambiguous engagement; sense of reality, the ability to lead
3. *hypomoné* = the capacity for patience, self-restraint, letting things speak
4. *prolépsis* = related to imagination, prediction, the ability to anticipate
5. *maieutics* = midwifery: letting the people under one's leadership find their own motivations for the things they do
6. *epibolé* = a form of embodied intuition

Kirkeby (2000) points out that these virtues are not values in the sense of being 'operationalizable' criteria; they unfold in the individual as a mood or a form of 'attunement' capable of defining the person as an individual who stands for something special.

Acting on the basis of values is thus not the same as value-based leadership. The two Danish organizational consultants Thorkil Olsen and Dorthe Lund Jakobsen (2006) express their experience and their critical reflection on value-based leadership in the following comment:

> The risk, as viewed from our perspective, is that value-based leadership inadvertently creates a potentially unethical practice and leadership practice where the basis of power and decisions is concealed from the actors in the organization. Oh, yes, and huge amounts of time and money continue to be invested in value activities. In our opinion, most organizations would be better off giving it up. One might even say that values are not something that can be made the topic of decisions. The values we share in some sense or another are embedded in our language as meaningful actions within the framework of a given culture (p. 52; translated for this edition).

Based on this reflection, value activities become more of a personal developmental project for the individual manager than a project for the entire organization.

2.4.4   Coaching in a Leadership Context

Based on these reflections and theoretical concepts on leadership, I will now discuss which functions coaching may serve in relation to leadership and organization development. Coaching can be applied either as an approach to a dialogue, where the manager chooses to talk with a coach, or the manager may include inspiration from coaching and its methods in his or her own leadership practice. In the following, I present three different ways of using coaching in a leadership context:

1. *Coaching as a reflective space for the manager*: Since leadership is, in part, about managing complexity and contingency, and since leadership also involves demonstrating value orientation in action and words, it is essential for managers to have an opportunity to engage in conversations where they take the time and the chance to reflect more deeply on their interactions with others and their relationship with the organization's challenges and developmental perspectives without necessarily having to focus on specific tasks and preferable solutions. This form of conversation may, for example, involve an executive or management coach who has no other involvement with the company. Working with an external management coach lets the manager find the time and the space to develop the necessary trust and confidence that is a key condition for conversation and reflections. That gives the manager the freedom to step back from the pressures of day-to-day events and find a calm space to reflect (O'Broin & Palmer, 2010).

   As an additional possibility I would like to mention *group coaching for managers*. Here, managers from various organizations and companies meet with a coach with the purpose of creating a shared reflective space in order to develop their personal leadership, focusing on specific organizational and personal challenges in the workplace. Here too, it is crucial that the participants develop mutual trust if group coaching is to serve as a free space for mutual development.[10] The overall ambition in leadership coaching is to promote the manager's capacity for value-oriented agency. Therefore I will focus especially on the development of leadership virtues. Reflecting on one's own virtues continually strengthens the manager's agency. Coaching thus becomes more of a Bildung project and less a process of putting out brushfire, where the coach simply helps the manager find answers and solutions to urgent organizational challenges. The management coach should not be reduced to a trouble-shooting consultant but should work as a dialogue partner, engaged in developing the manager's personal leadership. Developing leadership competences means focusing on culture, context and the interpersonal dimension in the coaching

---

[10]The former head of AS3-Work & Care Tina Post Aagaard mentioned to me that many managers have difficulty abandoning their focus on personal self-presentation and the efforts to brand the company and their own leadership skills (personal conversation on 29 June 2010). Therefore it is crucial to create a shared contract where all participants agree to use group coaching as a space for development characterized by maximum openness. Aagaard also mentioned that group coaching can be combined with individual sessions.

conversation. The process should help managers discover what is meaningful in their leadership practice, what they stand for, what they are passionate about and what is helpful for them personally as well as for the organization and the staff. In addition, there should be a focus on the normative aspects of human practice. To quote Ole Fogh Kirkeby, the central maxim and purpose of coaching is "prove oneself worthy for the event," i.e. for the coach to help the manager/leader "learn from important events" (Kirkeby, 2008, p. 271; translated for this edition). By reflecting on these events, managers can explore the meaningful and value-bearing aspects of their leadership – in light of the organization's visions and mission, staff well-being and development and the relationship to the environment, customers and business partners.[11]

2. *Coaching as a tool for staff development*: As discussed in *Coaching Barometret 2009* (Wittrock et al., 2009), a growing number of managers are interested or trained in using coaching as part of their leadership practice. It is also my personal impression that many managers are interested in acting as a coach or a coaching-oriented manager in some form.[12] Further, a survey from Danish consultancy firm *Væksthus for Ledelse* (2005) highlights *relational understanding* as a key dimension of good leadership – a competence that can unfold in the framework of coaching or coaching-inspired leadership practices.

Despite these facts, I want to once again draw attention to the challenges and potentially unfortunate consequences of acting simultaneously as a manager and a coach. Leadership implies a position of power, which should not be allowed to influence or overshadow the coaching relationship. How can this dilemma be resolved or at least be minimized? What opportunities arise when coaching is included in leadership? In an effort to address this dilemma, one might focus on coaching contexts and various forms of coaching activities. I see the following opportunities for the use of coaching:

- One opportunity presents itself when an employee comes to the manager/leader expressing an interest in receiving coaching. This presupposes that coaching is a recognized and widespread dialogue form in the organization. Such a request requires, for example, that the employee trusts the manager and that the employee wants to discuss a topic that he or she feels is 'suited' for a coaching conversation with the manager.
- Another potential context for coaching is the annual staff development conversation. The manager should proceed with caution, however, and remember to ask whether the employee finds a coaching approach acceptable in this

---

[11] Read more about Kirkeby's understanding of the event and the concept of influence inregard management and leadership in Kirkeby (2000).

[12] Since 2009 I have been responsible for the module *"Det personlige lederskab and dialogisk coaching"* (Personal leadership and dialogical coaching) in the programme for Master of Public Governance, which is offered in a partnership between Copenhagen Business School and the University of Copenhagen. This module has clearly demonstrated the interest of participating managers in being able to apply coaching in some form.

context. Coaching is appropriate in situations where the employee is open to exploring new developmental opportunities, and where the manager also has a sincere interest in hearing about the perspectives that the employee sees, for example in a particular future context.

- A third opportunity would be when the manager is engaged in a conversation with the employee where the purpose is exclusively to offer value-related coaching – focusing on the meaningful aspects of the job, aspirations, dreams or goals. Kirkeby (2009) speaks of *protreptics* in this context. The manager might ask, for example, "What does your involvement in this task say about what you appreciate, and what you strive for? What do you hope to accomplish? What does this task mean for you and your work?" One should always avoid taking the employee by surprise. The manager is therefore encouraged to invite and propose a contract – in the form of a brief dialogue about the special format and potential of coaching. And the employee must have the inviolable right to reject the offer without fear of negative consequences. Here, again, it is the manager who has to prove him/herself worthy of the coaching occasion.

3. *The coaching-oriented manager as an organizational and team developer*: The manager can also serve as a coach or, more aptly put, as a coaching-oriented manager, in organization development, especially on the micro-level, for example when management and staff have agreed to improve (team) cooperation and well-being, improve working processes or plan future projects. The precondition for engaging in coaching-oriented leadership is that (1) the situation is not conflict-ridden, and (2) the manager has to state explicitly when speaking from a management position whether he or she is speaking as a coaching-oriented manager or from a management position (see Søholm, Storch, Juhl, Dahl, & Molly, 2006). A good example of the coaching-oriented manager is offered by the Danish consultants Thybring, Søholm, Juhl, and Storch (2005) in their description of team development conversations; they consider it a very appropriate approach when the team wishes to address special challenges, carry out self-evaluation, plan the goals or tasks for the coming year or perform a *team check-up*, for example within the following six categories: goals, results, management, cooperation, learning culture and relationship with management. As a key condition, the authors highlight the following principle: *Manage the conversation without controlling the content*! In that connection, here are some essential guidelines for the coaching-oriented manager:

- Clearly mark in which capacity you are speaking (manager as process facilitator or as MANAGER).
- Mark the stages in the conversation (for example: 'I think we have heard all the points of view, the next step now is … ').
- Summarize during the process in order to develop a clear image of where the team is at.

- Ask bridging questions (for example: 'What are the common features in what we have talked about so far?', 'Which of the things the others have pointed to do you find inspiring?').

2.5   Closing Remarks

The purpose of Chap. 2 was to offer a general theoretical perspective and some insights into the origins and development of coaching that rise above concrete coaching practice. In my assessment, it is essential to position coaching as a practice field and as part of an abstract-theoretical universe. Under no circumstances should coaching be reduced to a technique. Therefore it was important for me to demonstrate how the coaching dialogue springs from our societal challenges, how coaching forms the basis of an entirely new approach to learning, how coaching can facilitate self-reflection and identity development, and how coaching offers an essential contribution to leadership development and personal leadership. By outlining this general foundation I also hope to contribute to the theoretical evidence of coaching practice. According to Stober et al. (2006) it is crucial for a broad understanding of the concept of evidence to include coaching-specific research and research from related disciplines as well as one's own expertise and an understanding of the coachee's characteristics.

Coaching has developed as a research and practice field, and that is an important condition for the development of coaching as a dialogue form and profession. Coaching has become fairly diverse. More and more versions of coaching have emerged and been presented in books and countless courses and education pro-grammes. Differences between coaching approaches are ideally motivated by differences in the theoretical basis of the coaching intervention (psychodynamic, cognitive, philosophical, systemic etc.), but it is not uncommon to highlight differences for branding purposes, where coaching providers attempt to stand out from the competition. A key goal for me in this chapter has been to describe how coaching is anchored in dominant societal phenomena concerning social change, identity, learning and leadership. To some extent, this general social science basis also frames the format of coaching and coaching psychology in theory and practice. The next two chapters offer a basic introduction to approaches that I consider indicative of the future development of the profession.

Chapter 3
Intervention Theories in Coaching and Coaching Psychology

In this chapter I offer some general thoughts on coaching as a special dialogue form with a focus on relational and co-creative qualities as the main ingredients of the conversation. Following that, I address three key basic intentions that the coach can apply in relation to the coachee. I highlight coaching in a reflective perspective as a third-generation approach to coaching. The coach's basic intention has a crucial impact on the format of the conversation.

In the central section of the chapter, it will be clear how particular basic intentions are reflected in the presented approaches to coaching and coaching psychology.

3.1 Coaching as a Special Dialogue Form

Coaching is a dialogue form that provides a special framework for developmental and self-reflective conversations – conversations that one otherwise would not have, because they are based on certain premises and a certain stance from the participants. Dialogue and conversation are used more or less synonymously here. In the present context, dialogue should be understood as a conversation where the participants explore each other's assumptions, thoughts, opinions and perceptions of the world. Dialogue differs from debate and begins where discussion ends (David Bohm, 1996). In a dialogue, one does not attempt to persuade the other but instead seeks to listen and accept differences in perspectives that may enrich one's own position. These basic conditions make it possible to create quality in the conversation and to achieve positive outcomes. The philosopher Mikhail M. Bakhtin (1895–1975) highlights the fundamental importance of dialogue for people:

> To live means to participate in dialogue: To ask questions, to heed, to respond, to agree ...
> In this dialogue a person participates wholly and throughout his whole life: with his eyes, lips, hands, soul, spirit, with his whole body and deeds. (quoted from Gergen, 2009a, p. 250)

In the following, I will explore the qualities of the dialogue and present selected theories that shed light on the dialogue as a conversation phenomenon, and which examine the manifestations and qualities of the dialogue.

R. Stelter, *A Guide to Third Generation Coaching: Narrative-Collaborative Theory and Practice*, DOI 10.1007/978-94-007-7186-4_3,

3.1.1 Martin Buber and His Understanding of the Genuine Dialogue

Martin Buber (1878–1965), an Austrian-Israeli theologian and one of the world's leading 'intersubjectivity philosophers', considers dialogue a fundamental meeting between two people with the goal of creating a connection and a relationship in order to understand oneself and the other on a profound existential level. He views the dialogue as an event where each participant holds the other in mind, with his or her present and specific ways of being, in order to imbue their relationship with reciprocity. Buber (2004) describes it as follows:

> Through the *Thou* a man becomes an *I*. That which confronts him comes and disappears, relational events condense, then are scattered, and in the change consciousness of the unchanging partner, of the *I*, grows clear, and each time stronger. To be sure, it is still see caught in the web of the relation with the Thou, as the increasingly distinguishable feature of that which reaches out to and yet is not the *Thou*. But it continually breaks through with more power, till a time comes when it bursts its bonds, and the *I* confronts itself for a moment, separated as though it were a *Thou*; as quickly to take possession of itself and from then on to enter into relations in consciousness of itself. (p. 44)

According to Buber, I-Thou is a *primary word*: I and Thou are each other's prerequisites and thus mutually dependent or co-dependent. The I is created in the relationship. *I-Thou* expresses a fundamental relationship and characterizes the *world of relation*, whereas *I-id* (*I-it*) is the primary word for the *world of experience*. I-Thou relations describe the close relationship with another human being, while I-it relations describe the relationship with another human being in his or her function or role. Buber defines his dialogue concept by describing what the dialogue is not. Verbal communication between individuals, according to Buber, can take on one of the following three formats: (1) the *monologue*, a camouflaged dialogue, where one party simply talks without having any real interest in establishing a relationship with the other, (2) the *technical dialogue*, where one party conveys information and facts to the other, and (3) the *real and genuine dialogue*, where each dialogue partner bears the other in mind, and where everybody strives to establish a living, mutual relationship with each other. In the genuine dialogue, the individual constitutes both him/herself and the other. In a dialogue one person contributes to creating the other; through the dialogue meaning and authenticity are created for the individual, and one comes into being through the other. Buber (1999) expands on his perception of the genuine dialogue as a basis of a professional psychological conversation as follows:

> Every speaker 'means' the partner or partners to whom he turns as this personal existence. To 'mean' someone in this connection is at the same time to exercise that degree of making present which is possible to the speaker at that moment. ... But the speaker does not merely perceive the one who is present to him in this way; he receives him as his partner, and that means he confirms this other being, so far as it is for him to confirm. (pp. 85–86)

The relationship can thus be considered the cornerstone of personal meaning-making and self-comprehension. Through the dialogue, the dialogue partners co-create each other, just as their mutual relationship is created through dialogue. Thus, Buber's concept of the dialogue can be considered essential to any deeper relationship, the type of relationship that should be developed between coach and coachee. The genuine conversation between coachee and a listening and relation-building coach lets coachee (and the coach) learn something new about him/herself and thus develop and grow as a person and a professional.

3.1.2 Pearce & Cronen: Coordinated Management of Meaning (CMM)

In the following, the dialogue will be presented as a *performative act* by two or more parties. Pearce (1994) defines dialogues or conversations as "forms of conjoint actions, that is, as makings and doings" (p. 203) and relations as "a set of patterned linkages in which two or more objects are constituted" (p. 203). Relations are created through the dialogue and in the concrete practice that the parties are involved in. Viewing the coaching conversation as such a performative act implies that both the coach and the coachee present themselves through the specific conversation, which helps establish their relationship and allows them to appear in a particular way, perhaps a new way. The coach carries the main responsibility for establishing a foundation for the coachee's developmental process. The dialogue has its own dynamic, where all activity takes place within the co-creative community.

The task is to coordinate actions and meanings in a specific dialogue situation. Pearce and Cronen's (1980) theory about *Coordinated Management of Meaning* (CMM) can be included here to shed light on the basic anatomy of the coaching dialogue. The CMM theory is helpful for describing how people (co-) create their own social worlds and realities through conversations and action. According to Pearce and Cronen, individuals, for example a coach interacting with a coachee or a coaching group, act on the basis of their perception of the situation and on the basis of certain rules that enable them to act appropriately and purposefully. In this sense, the coaching dialogue enables new possibilities, because this safe conversation space lets the parties experiment with their thoughts and consider new ways of acting. The coaching dialogue offers an opportunity to test *new forms of logic in relation to meaning and actions.*

By incorporating the CMM theory, the coach can cooperate with the coachee on (further) developing the coachee's meaning universe. According to the CMM theory, the format of the coaching dialogue is framed by certain rules: *Constitutive rules* are rules of meaning, which the parties use to interpret an event or a message in a particular way. *Regulatory rules* are rules of action that help the parties respond and relate appropriately in the situation. In a coaching process, the coach can draw attention to these rules and their action consequences and make them the subject of reflection, perhaps in a new light, in order to enable the coachee to act differently, for example in critical or stressful situations. The coachee can consider how these rules lock him or her into certain situations or contexts, and what it will take to act differently. The following three concepts illustrate the relationship between communication, events and objects in the social world. These concepts are thus constitutive for the meaning-making process that, for example, the coaching dialogue enables (cf. Pearce & Cronen, 1980):

- *Coordination* directs our attention to the ways in which our actions intersect and create patterns that include and characterize events and objects in our social world, and which are constructed through the activities that the participants have contributed. The central aspect of the theory is thus a focus on relationships and patterns rather than a focus on the individual. The coach can help shed light on these relationships and patterns in the coachee's personal and working life, and this awareness can facilitate and initiate new ways of action in future situations.
- By focusing on *coherence*, coach and coachee draw attention to stories and narratives that help make sense of the coachee's life. Creating coherence and making sense are a fundamental part of human life, and stories are a key element in this process. The coachee is constantly shaping stories about such things as his or her individual identity, the collective identity of his or her workplace, the surrounding world and the facts and actions that shape the coachee's world. The coach can help the coachee draw these stories into the light and expand on them, for example by initiating change by moving or shifting the focus in the stories. Such a shift can be achieved by moving from a language that is focused on flaws and shortcomings to an appreciative language, by moving from a focus on problems and the past to a focus on possibilities and the future or by moving from an individual focus to a social and relational mindset. This lets persons, groups or teams eliminate unhelpful blockages in their world views and move forward toward new horizons.
- The *mystery* concept is used in the theory to remind us that there is more to life than day-to-day existence. Pearce and Cronen (1980) are convinced that reducing one's perspective to day-to-day events is a mistake. The term *mystery* directs our attention to the fact that our world is much larger than the stories and narratives that pretend to offer a full description of our lives. Pearce and Cronen point out the importance of reflecting on – and questioning – any pattern and any relationship. It is also helpful to address any form of social organization or pattern and to ask how they were created, and how we can create something that is different, perhaps better.

The fundamental goal of the CMM theory is to create a better social world. This world can be achieved if we recognize differences and strive to understand each other better. An important element in this approach is to enhance the awareness of the communication patterns we contribute to – individually and in relationships. We can challenge these communication patterns, for example, by facilitating the development of alternative stories of a more uplifting and inspiring character or by asking circular questions. A successful coaching dialogue can enable us to develop new – and perhaps more constructive – stories that in turn enable the coachee to create change and positive renewal in his or her life and work.

3.1.3   Harlene Anderson and Her Understanding of Collaborative Language Systems

In cooperation with the late Harold Goolishian, Harlene Anderson has developed an understanding of dialogue processes in therapy that she calls *collaborative language systems approach* (Anderson, 1995) or simply the *collaborative approach* (Anderson, 1997). Her approach goes a little farther, as she underscores the alliance that is forged between the therapist (here: the coach) and client (here: the coachee). In a therapy context she describes the post-modern approach to the dialogue as "a language system and a linguistic event in which people are engaged in a collaborative relationship and conversation – a mutual endeavor toward possibility" (Anderson, p. 2). I will now apply this dialogue concept to coaching and the intervention in coaching psychology. With inspiration from Anderson's thinking, which is strongly influenced by post-modern thinking and social constructionism, the coaching dialogue can be viewed as a process of relational knowledge production and as an opportunity for the coachee to acquire greater self-comprehension and self-insight; something that is achieved exactly through the verbal discourses that the coach and coachee are mutually involved in. The coaching dialogue can be viewed as a shared process of exploration, where the therapist/coach and the client/coachee explore the world together, thus creating a conversation partnership. In my assessment, the underlying philosophical position that Anderson (2007a) describes for her therapeutic work is also an appropriate basis for the collaborative and co-creative practice in coaching (psychology): Coach and coachee are both viewed as experts and as dialogue partners, and they are both involved in the shared production of meaning and knowledge that takes place in the reflective process of development, learning and transformation in the coaching dialogue. The coach should be seen as the *generous listener* (Stelter & Law, 2010), who seeks to expand on the coachee's contributions to the dialogue. In the effort to be a generous listener, it is helpful for the coach to *wonder naively*, that is, to be *curious*[1] and non-judging, not least in relation to his or her own positions or world view, and to remain open to new interpretations in relation to the topics that come up in the dialogue.

3.1.4   The Relationship as a Central Focus of the Coaching Dialogue

The three theories that have been outlined here illustrate how crucially important the relationship is for the coaching dialogue. Buber's understanding focuses squarely on the existential dimension of the dialogue. The individual is created and can

---

[1] 'Naively wondering' is a much better description of the state of being that I strive for as a coach than the word 'curious'.

only understand him/herself through the dialogue. The Thou is the precondition of the I and thus of self-awareness. Translated to the context of the coaching dialogue, that means that the coachee needs the coach's contributions to approach self-comprehension and develop meaning in relation to his or her own experiences. At the same time, the coach can help develop and renew the coachee's identity, experiential space and agency through the way he or she conducts the dialogue. The relationship is not merely fertile soil but a fundamental necessity for the coachee's existential development.

Anderson, Pearce and Cronen base their dialogue concept on a social constructionist paradigm. These authors do not focus on the existential meaning of the relationship but on the co-creative practice and the shared meaning production that the dialogue enables. The decisive factor for the developmental potential of the dialogue is what develops *between* the parties, not in the individual. This dialogue concept clearly assigns the coach an active role, especially when considering Anderson's concept of the dialogue as a *collaborative* practice. The coach is not merely a facilitator for the coachee. At times, the relationship between the parties can become a symmetrical relationship, where the coach reflects actively on general human aspects and value perspectives that come up in the conversation. The more clearly the coach presents his or her reflections, the more pronounced the production of new meanings and stories in the dialogue between the parties. The stories ultimately enhance the coachee's capacity for finding new ways and possibilities of action outside the space of the coaching dialogue.

3.2 Basic Intentions in the Coaching Conversation

The coaching literature has come to include an almost overwhelming number of intervention theories and methodologies (Cox, Bachkirova, & Clutterbuck, 2010; Palmer & Whybrow, 2007; Passmore, Peterson, & Freire, 2012). Some approaches have developed within the field of coaching itself (e.g. the GROW model), but most have originated within psychology and psychotherapy (e.g. gestalt, existential, cognitive-behavioural, solution-oriented, positive psychology, narrative approaches). In psychotherapy research, we see growing interest in the 'common factors' – factors independent of therapy form – that can be viewed as crucial for therapeutic success (Wampold, 2010a, b). For example, there is research evidence that the presence of such factors as empathy, positive attention and congruence/authenticity on the part of the therapist have a crucial impact on the client's benefit from therapy. Despite the lack of research evidence in the coaching field, the kinship between psychotherapy and coaching may justify the assumption that 'common factors' also apply to coaching.

To move the narrow focus away from coaching approaches and techniques and toward a more general differentiation of coaching I invite the reader to reflect on a structural categorization of the main forms of coaching into three *generations*. These categories will be used to describe the progression and development of coaching practice over time. First-generation forms are the oldest, while the latest are relatively new and reflect the most current trends in coaching and coaching psychology. I am aware that all three generations continue to be in use by coaching practitioners today. In all likelihood, the three generations will continue to co-exist, just as individual coaches or coaching psychologists will mix different generations in their practice. However, I want to point out that moving toward third-generation coaching can be considered the most sensitive response to the new demands for self-reflection and self-reflexivity that society places on individuals, and which were described in the previous chapter. As a criterion for distinguishing between the three generations I use the basic intentional orientation of the coach and coachee in their conversations, which to some extent are determined by the coach's theoretical foundation and position. The main focus, however, will be on the coach's *intentional orientation* rather than on the coach's theoretical position, although the two are of course related.

3.2.1   The Three Generations of Coaching

In the following, I present three general perspectives on coaching – fully aware that this is a simplification of the wide range of approaches in coaching and coaching psychology (see Passmore et al., 2012). Nevertheless, this coarse structure may help clarify how coaching can be characterized in relation to the coach's basic ambition and goals for the conversation. Generally speaking, the three generations of coaching can be characterized as follows:

Coaching in a problem and goal perspective: First-generation coaching includes sports coaching (Gallwey, 1974; Robinson, 2010), the GROW model (Whitmore, 2002),[2] NLP (O'Connor & Lages, 2004) and, to some extent, psychodynamic coaching (Sandler, 2011) and cognitive-behavioural coaching (Palmer & Szymanska, 2007). The main perspective of the intervention here is to help the coachee address his or her particular challenges and problems in order to achieve specific goals and develop action strategies. For example: I want a new job – how do I accomplish that? Or: I would like to lose 10 kg – how can I do that in

---

[2]The GROW model is divided into the following four stages: (1) *Goals*, with a focus on such questions as, What should we talk about? What is the reason you bring that up? What do you hope to achieve with our conversation? (2) *Reality*, with a focus on such questions as, What is the status quo for the current situation? What happened – who did what? How often does the problem occur – and how? What have you done so far? (3) *Options*, with a focus on such questions as, What can you do to change the situation? What options do you see? What are the pros and cons of those possibilities? Which solution is more appealing to you? and (4) *Wrap-up* (action and closure), with a focus on such questions as, What is the next step? When will you do what? What are your success criteria? What might get in the way?

the shortest amount of time? In first-generation coaching the coach risks slipping
into the role as expert or as the most knowledgeable in the relationship, which
ultimately goes against the basic principles of coaching.

Coaching in a solution- and future-oriented perspective: Second-generation coaching includes systemic and solution-focused coaching (Berg & Szabo, 2005;
Moltke & Molly, 2010; Stelter, 2002a), Appreciative Inquiry coaching (Orem,
Binkert, & Clancy, 2007) and positive psychology coaching (Biswas-Diener,
2010; Biswas-Diener & Dean, 2007). The main goal and intention in this
generation of coaching approaches is to generate positive future scenarios with
a strong focus on existing resources and strengths that the coachee already
possesses, and which the coachee should be able to build on. The conversation is
focused on possibilities and preferred futures rather than previously experienced
challenges and problems. It tends to set up less narrow goals than first-generation
coaching. The coach's interest and intention in the dialogue is to work with
the possible (or already established) solutions and to focus on potential future
scenarios and on strengths and qualities in the coachee that the coachee has
previously been unaware of.

Coaching in a reflective perspective: Third-generation coaching includes narrative
coaching (Drake, 2007, 2009a; Nielsen, 2010), narrative collaborative coaching
(Stelter, 2012; Stelter & Law, 2010) and protreptic or philosophical coaching (Kirkeby, 2009). Third-generation coaching is a further development of
approaches from second-generation models and theories. It involves a shift,
however, in the coach's basic orientation and relation to the coachee. First-
generation and especially second-generation coaching are characterized by a
clear asymmetry between coach and coachee. The coach's basic position is to
be neutral and not-knowing and to avoid being directly engaged or involved in
the coachee's challenges. A third-generation coach will place a higher emphasis
on being a *fellow human being*. In certain stages and situations, the coaching
conversation will be a *genuine dialogue* between two human beings (cf. Buber,
1999), where the coach, for example, shares his or her considerations and
reflections with the coachee in order to serve as a witness and a co-creator
in the dialogue. The coaching conversation can be described as a co-creative
and collaborative process, where the coach and coachee are both experts in
their respective domains and, at the same time, not-knowing at the beginning
of the conversation. The knowledge that is generated emerges *between* them
in a dialogue process that gives rise to something new for both of them.
As a prominent feature, the coaching dialogue revolves around values and the
meaning-making aspects of life – aspects that are especially central in people's
lives – thus inviting both the coach and the coachee into a reflective space that
transcends everybody's life and its challenges. The coach and coachee act as
philosophers, their reflections sometimes shedding light on the big questions in
life. Both take a wondering stance to essential human, existential and often value-
oriented issues, and together with the coach the coachee explores new ways of
understanding his or her existence and life.

This categorization aims to provide a general orientation. In a coaching process, the competent coach can mix approaches to some extent. A key aspect is the coach's awareness of the *intentional focus* during the conversation, which this categorization draws attention to. However, I would also like to shed light on new trends and developments in coaching. Here I am convinced that the trend will be toward a greater focus on the *reflective perspective* that characterizes third-generation coaching, and which is the coach's *basic intentional orientation* in this form of coaching. My conviction is based on considerations and conclusions that were presented in the first part of the book. Based on (1) the changes in society (globality, hypercomplexity, late-modern reflexivity), (2) the major challenges to the self (patchwork identity, demands for self-reflexivity), (3) the permanent demands for learning and self-development and (4) the new requirements for personal leadership, it is easy to envision moving in a direction where coaching increasingly offers a space for reflection that lets the coach and coachee act as collaborative partners in a space that offers development opportunities for both parties.

The subsequent presentation of basic theories and methodologies (see Sect. 3.4) represents a special selection that forms the basis of *second- and third-generation coaching*. The theories were selected on the basis of certain shared basic assumptions, all based on a post-modern view of science and cognition.

3.2.1.1 Shared Basic Assumptions in Coaching

Most approaches and theories in second- and third-generation coaching have a shared ontological and epistemological foundation,[3] which is only outlined here, since the theories differ on a more detailed level. I am going to address four key basic assumptions that underpin these theories, and which have a direct impact on coaching practice:

- *Hermeneutic constructionist assumption:* As humans, we acquire the world by means of interpretations that will always depend upon the time, culture and context we live in. This assumption enables new possibilities: Our interpretations of the world are not static but open to revision; for example, one may move from a negative to a positive interpretation. This basic assumption is in contrast to realism, which views reality as something that has an objective existence, which is built on regularities, and which can be studied by means of observation. In hermeneutic and social constructionist thinking, on the other hand, there are no final and universal truths. Here it is considered more interesting to examine how individuals arrive at their interpretation of the world than to strive for certainty or a position that remains valid over time.

---

[3]Ontology is the theory of the specific and (inherently) required conditions for being, i.e. for the existence of the world or the subject. Epistemology is the theory of human knowledge and understanding, its conditions, possibilities, nature and limitations.

- *The relational assumption*: The individual is created and shaped by contexts and relations rather than by internal factors that could be called the individual's stable *character features* or *nature*. The theories addressed here view human 'qualities' as social constructs or as the result of dynamics in social systems. A person may thus have very different manifestations depending on the context, he or she is in, and individuals may adopt a variety of *positions* depending on the social context.[4] In practice, the coach or the coaching psychologist will, for example, address how the coachee appears in many different ways, and how the coachee's self-presentation alters depending on the current relationship – rather than searching for an 'inner I'. This basic assumption is in contrast to essentialism, which can be described as the ontological position where everything has an essence that characterizes a given reality. In personality psychology, the essence may for example be described as the personality core, which irrefutably defines and explains the person and his or her behaviour.
- *The negotiation or interaction assumption*: The context and the way in which we talk about ourselves, others and the world we live in have an influence on our understanding of the world. Language is involved in creating the context, and the context invites certain actions and a particular language use. The individual does not independently decide how the world is shaped, but the interaction with a concrete social context in a given culture does invite certain possible actions and shapes the world in a particular way. At the same time, however, the individual also co-creates his or her world: through actions and the way in which the person talks about things and with others. There is an interaction between individual and context that holds possibilities for change and development. The individual thus engages in negotiations with others, and this process of collaboration and co-creation is fundamental in shaping a reality for the involved parties. A narrative collaborative coach or coaching psychologist will focus on the coachee's social negotiation practices and invite reinterpretations of reality that can lead to new future negotiation strategies.
- *The contingency assumption*: The world is hypercomplex and invites a multitude of interpretations. There is no causal and linear logic that explains human and social life. One cannot claim that a given action, A, will always lead to a particular result, B. We live with an experience of contingency, which means that our perception of reality can and must change continually. The social life is a complex and multi-dependent entity where many factors play in, and many reality perceptions meet. The explanatory logic is characterized by chaos and varying dynamics, and at best, we may arrive at an abductive analysis that attempts to offer a probable explanation based on observations or situated conditions. *Circular logic*, which was developed in systemic theory (Tomm, 1988), introduces a new way of dealing with processes of communication and development by looking at the complexity of interpersonal interactions (see also

---

[4]The term *position* is used, a much more dynamic and less fixating term than the traditional concept of *roles*.

Hieker & Huffington, 2006). In circular logic, the cause is simultaneously the effect. We create the conditions that we observe, and vice versa. No single description of the situation can ever be final; any description is always open to interpretation, the opening created by including multiple observer perspectives. This lets us understand our life contexts anew and ultimately allows us to be involved in shaping new life conditions.

For a coach, coaching psychologist or consultant, these assumptions can form the basis of a mindset and an approach where we move ourselves and our clients away from an ambition of solving problems and into new positions where we *view 'reality' from different angles* and thus create the conditions for a collaborative process that aims for new and temporary understanding of reality. When *problem-solving* was attempted under influence of the realist paradigm, the aim was to *identify the cause* by understanding what things *were really like*. The tendency was to assume that there was a truth and an underlying cause of the undesirable state of affairs, for example a conflict or the lack of motivation in a group. The problem-solving logic was based on a causality perspective and a desire to *control conditions* in a way that *solved* the problems. The (hyper) complexity of the social world rejects the problem-solving logic, which also characterized first-generation coaching. In the new post-modern logic, the point is (to some extent) that we have to learn to live with uncertainty in all areas of life. With this capacity for tolerating uncertainty as my platform I aim to create a basis for focusing on the concepts of *self-reflection, value work* and *meaning-making* in various social arenas (e.g. work or family life). These three concepts should underlie the thinking of the coach, the coaching psychologist or the consultant, as illustrated in the following presentation of intervention theories and methodologies (in Sect. 3.4), all of which share the four basic assumptions outlined above.

3.3   The Coach's Basic Orientation

In the following, I will review some key premises of the form of coaching intervention that supports the coach's and coaching psychologist's intentional focus on creating a reflective space and thus belongs within the framework of third-generation coaching:

- It is not an approach that promises to deliver a simple solution or a quick fix. In our complex world, that is often difficult to achieve by means of coaching.
- The approach has to make room for the coachee's *self-reflection*. Here, an overriding and often philosophically anchored value orientation often plays a key role. Clarifying values may be an objective in itself as a developmental orientation or as a basis for a more clarified goal perspective and possible 'solutions' to pursue.
- A coaching process is often a short-term intervention. In order to achieve a long-term effect the coachee has to engage in a *process of self-Bildung*. That can easily

become a life-long developmental project where coaching only sometimes serves as a dialogue partner, and were the individual develops continually in interaction with relevant others.

With the inclusion of findings from psychotherapy research I will mention two additional conditions which I also consider important for a successful coaching intervention:

- The coach's essentially appreciative and uplifting basic orientation can be considered a fundamental condition for the coachee's positive (self-) development. It is essential to support the coachee's strengths, resources and personal agency (see Bohart & Tallman, 2010, who highlight these dimensions in relation to psychotherapy).
- In everything that we do as coaches, we should remember one essential aspect: Ultimately, it is the coachee who creates development and progress in coaching. In relation to psychotherapy Bohart and Tallman (2010) expresses it as follows:

> In short, it is the client, more so than the therapist or technique, who makes therapy work. ... Clients are not submissive recipients of an intervention. They actively operate on therapists' inputs, transforming bits and pieces of the process into information and experience which, in turn, are used to make change occur. Their effort, involvement, intelligence, and creativity enable them to accommodate and metabolize different therapeutic approaches and achieve positive outcomes. (pp. 94–95)

The Danish clinical psychologist Ken Vagn Hansen (2010) has offered a very broad definition of psychotherapy, which in my interpretation also highlights what is created *between the parties* in therapy. I will use this definition as my point of departure in describing the relationship between coach and coachee. Let us first take a look at Hansen's definition[5]:

> If we look at psychotherapy in what I consider its most complex form, psychotherapy is a *life between two people*, and precisely because there is a *life*, it involves both parties' outer and inner world and the interaction that develops between them. Psychotherapy is a meeting between two people, a therapist and a client, that is continually aimed at creating an optimal life between them. Both parties contribute to the life that unfolds every time they meet. The therapist is presumed to have sufficient emotional and cognitive competence that he can stay alive, healthy and alert in the meeting with the client and thus constantly strive to complement the client's inadequate capacity for being alive. Therapy is initiated because the life that unfolds in their meeting is not optimal, and it is concluded when that has been achieved. (p. 17; translated for this edition)

The difference between therapy and coaching, as I see it, is that the coachee essentially *cannot* be attributed any 'inadequate capacity for being alive', as Hansen puts it. Coaching is used more as a means of self-development and relational development and hence does not necessarily stem from a sense of emotional or

---

[5]I am aware that Ken Vagn Hansen represents a new direction in the psychoanalytic therapy tradition: relational psychotherapy. The psychoanalytic tradition is not included in my work as a coach. In my linguistic 'transformation game' I use the relational character of the definition and transform it with a focus on reflection, which I wish to highlight as the main intention in coaching.

existential suffering. Thus, coaching focuses less on the coachee's basic capacity for being alive, as that it not typically what the coachee is seeking help for. I have based my development on third-generation coaching on the following basic assumption: The coachee seeks coaching due to a lack of clarity in relation to specific challenges in his or her work and private life, where the coachee wants greater insight, understanding and a new perspective, goals that are generally pursued through a process of *reflection* that ideally involves both parties' inner and outer life. With this as our basis we can now describe the basic intention for third-generation coaching as follows:

> Coaching is reflection between two people, and precisely because it is reflection, it involves both parties' inner and outer life as well as the interaction that develops between them and their mutual reflections. Coaching is a meeting between two people, a coach and a coachee, which is continually aimed at creating optimal reflection between them. Both parties contribute to the reflection that develops every time they meet. The coach is presumed to have sufficient reflection competence that he can remain reflective in the meeting with the coachee, thus constantly striving to complement the coachee's inadequate competence for being reflective. Coaching is initiated because the reflection in their meeting is not optimal, and it is concluded when that has been achieved.

In order to show sufficient reflection competence and to remain reflective in the meeting with the coachee, the coach should maintain focus on two essential basic orientations:

- The capacity for a shift in perspective
- The situation-specific perspective

3.3.1 Shifts in Perspective as an Essential Developmental Orientation in the Coaching Dialogue

The capacity of the coaching conversation to enable the coachee to achieve a *shift in perspective or a perspective transformation* and to *see reality in a new light* can be considered a key to generating development and reorientation in relation to the challenges that the coachee experiences in his or her private life or work. The coachee's perspectives on him/herself, specific contexts, certain tasks or other people contribute to the development of certain perceptions of the reality that the coachee lives in. These perceptions become part of the coachee's overall picture of reality, a reality that manifests itself in certain stories which the coachee has about him/herself and his or her past, abilities, family, workplace and co-workers and everything else that matters in the coachee's life. These life constructions and stories can be uplifting and life-affirming, but they may also have a form and a content that restricts the person and poses a barrier for the coachee's or the organization's further development or for a *good life* overall. Any perspective is associated with a particular observer position (Tomm, 1988, 1989, 1998). The coach's questions help the coachee adopt a variety of observer positions. The coach's main intention in conversations with the coachee is to incorporate new perspectives and to invite the coachee to adopt new observer positions and perceptions of the situation. These

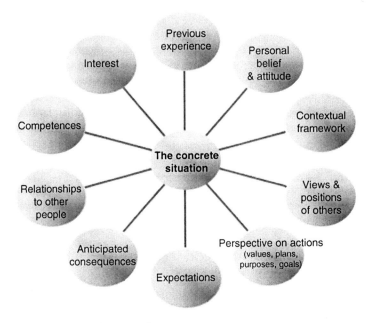

Fig. 3.1 The situation-specific perspective

shifts in perspectives or perspective transformations are the basis of transformative learning processes (cf. Mezirow & Associates, 2000; Illeris, 2004; see also Chap. 2, Sect. 2.3.), and they help the coachee engage in development and reorientation processes.

In the later presentation of various coaching approaches and in the application-oriented chapter I follow up and continually examine how the theories and methodologies presented here help initiate a shift in perspective.

3.3.2   The Situation-Specific Perspective

The individual understands the world through interactions with specific environmental contexts. Person and environment are best described as co-dependent and inseparable. We only sense and understand our world by acting in it or by imagining concrete acts in a given situation (Stelter, 1999). In my understanding of coaching, therefore, it is fundamentally essential to focus on specific situations, and I consider this focus paramount for successful reflection processes. This situation-specific perspective is the basis of the coachee's concrete and specific involvement in the context, which in turn enables a shared reflection focus for the coach and coachee (see Fig. 3.1).

The situation-specific perspective helps establish a *context* that both the coach and coachee can refer to. The *situation-specific* perspective is an absolute requirement for viewing the world from a specific observer position. As I will demonstrate in the example below, the situation-specific perspective initially focuses on the person's life world. Life world is a concept from the tradition of existential phenomenological theory (Husserl, 1931; Merleau-Ponty, 2012), which captures the individual's everyday understanding; this understanding is partially embodied and thus pre-reflexive, that is, unarticulated. The coach focuses on situative aspects and thus helps the coachee verbalize the things that are often rooted in habits and action routines. The ability to dive into the coachee's life world or everyday reality is facilitated by the coachee's insights and in-depth and experiential examination of the situation's complexity.

Here, the coach's ability to ask the right follow-up questions plays a crucial role. These questions (1) add depth to the perspective and thus enable new insights and (2) enable new and additional perspectives in relation to the person's understanding and interpretation of the specific situation.

Let me offer an example that clarifies the difference. We will focus on '*previous experiences*'. In the case, the coachee talks about his *difficulties with being frank with other people*.

- As a first step, the coach and coachee may investigate a specific situation, perhaps ideally concerning the near past, a possible future or a desirable situation that the coachee is asked to imagine. In relation to the selected situation, the coachee is asked to exemplify and specify his experiences. This gives the coach an initial understanding of the situation. It also helps the coachee 'tune into' the situation.
- In the next phase the coach will ask questions from a different angle in order to allow the coachee to immerse himself in the situation and bring out new facets through an in-depth description of the situation. This descriptive approach may form the basis of a more profound or renewed understanding of the situation.
- In the final phase, the coach deliberately tries to initiate a new orientation. Here the coachee moves away from the immediate everyday experience and addresses the situation or the issue it pertains to from an expansive perspective. To do this, the coach may, for example, ask circular questions ('What does your close colleague say about your way of communicating?'), focus on positive exceptions ('Do you recall a situation where you felt that you were communicating frankly with another person?') or focus on the coachee's strengths ('Where do your strengths lie in your communication with others? Are there particular situations where it has proved to be an advantage to communicate the way that you are doing now?').

The final point of the example anticipates many aspects, especially with regard to my description of the possible questions that might be asked in the final phase, where the emphasis is on reorientation and on developing an expanded perspective. The reader will gain a deeper understanding when the various intervention theories have been presented. In the example, I selected one dimension in the situation-specific perspective: previous experiences. Other dimensions are indicated as circles in the figure. These dimensions are not the only ones, but they will probably be important focus points for the coachee's situation-specific exploration, although they should not be seen as exhaustive. The reader is hereby invited to add further dimensions to the figure.

3.4   Basic Theories and Their Role in Coaching

Despite the importance of the coach's basic intentional orientation, the coachee's necessary engagement in the conversation and the fruitful interaction between coach and coachee as conditions of the overall success of the coaching process, we should also consider the coach's basic theoretic platform as a condition for a well-founded coaching practice. By linking theory and practice, the coach or coaching psychologist will be able to act as a reflective practitioner (Schön, 1983; see more on this topic in Chaps. 6 and 7). It is important to strike a good balance between theoretical understanding and practical effectiveness. Over time, this balance between professional experience and the ability to incorporate theoretical reflections will develop into a complex competence that defines the reflective practitioner. Schön describes this professional competence as follows:

> The artistry of a practitioner ... hinges on the range and variety of the repertoire that he brings to unfamiliar situations. Because he is able to *see* these *as* elements of his repertoire, he is able to make sense of their uniqueness and need not reduce them to instances of standard categories. (p. 140; italics in original)

In the following, I present a selection of basic theories and approaches to coaching, many of which have been tested in a psychotherapy context, in other forms of developmental conversations and, during the past 10–15 years, in coaching and coaching psychology. The theories were selected based on the following key criteria: The presented theories should prepare and especially *support third-generation coaching*, i.e. they should support a working perspective where the coach very much acts as a *fellow human being* and a genuine conversation partner for the coachee (cf. Buber, 2004), and where the coach or coaching psychologist can also share his or her thoughts or reflections with the coachee and thus act as a witness and co-creator in the dialogue. In this framework, the coaching conversation becomes a co-creative and collaborative process, where the coach and coachee are on equal footing as experts and as not-knowing, and where the dialogue is focused especially on self-reflection, values and meaning-making. Third-generation approaches are not a clearly defined area, however, but based on traditions and methods that have emerged as part of the approaches of previous generations. The theories that are described in the following are well established in coaching, coaching psychology, psychotherapy and other counselling contexts and form the basis and a precondition for the development of third-generation coaching.

The following theories and methodologies will be presented:

- *The systemic-social constructionist universe:*
  - Development of systemic theory
  - Systemic theory and practice
  - From systemic thinking to a focus on social construction processes and collaborative practice
  - *Social constructionism*
    - Solution-focused theory and practice
    - Appreciative Inquiry (AI) theory and practice
    - Narrative theory and practice
    - Collaborative theory and practice.

I supplement the presented theories and methodologies from the systemic-social constructionist universe with a selection of theories that may be viewed as an extension of the appreciative perspective or an expansion of social constructionist-narrative approaches to coaching.

- *Additional theories and approaches:*
  - Positive psychology – a focus on strengths
  - Experiential and emotion-focused approaches
  - Mentalization-based approach

3.4.1 The Systemic-Social Constructionist Universe

In several publications (e.g., Tomaschek, 2006) and in the coaching profession, the systemic-constructionist/constructivist universe is often considered a single coherent theoretical universe. In recent decades the gap between the two has diminished. In the following, however, I seek to clarify some fundamental differences.

Before presenting the systemic approach I would like to share some impressions with the reader: The word *systemic* has, strictly speaking, become slightly misleading, as most researchers and practitioners have now moved away from the closed cybernetic and autopoietic perception (e.g. Maturana & Varela, 1980) that forms the basis of constructivism and have moved gradually toward a dynamic social constructionist theory foundation.[6] In the following presentation I have chosen to

---

[6]According to *Psykologisk pædagogisk ordbog*, a Danish dictionary on psychological and educational terminology, 'constructivism' is defined as the perception that human cognition and knowledge are an interpretation, i.e. a construct that is based on sensory impressions that are processed in the framework of cognitive contexts, e.g. cognitive structures that pose certain restrictions. Piaget, for example, is a constructivist. He describes the cognitive context as a 'cognitive schema' and describes two fundamental cognitive adaptation skills: *assimilation* as the incorporation of the environment and adaptation to the existing cognitive schema, and *accommodation* as a modification and expansion on the existing cognitive schema, which lets the

present the systemic thinking in its original version, as it still has value – in practice; especially in relation to the use of circular questions. In the Scandinavian literature (see e.g. Moltke & Molly, 2010) there is often a tendency to combine systemic and social constructionist thinking into one without informing the reader of the basic epistemological differences between the two schools of thought.[7]

In the following presentation I shall be keeping constructionist and constructivist theory separate in order to convey the underlying epistemological differences. It is essential to have a clear understanding of one's theoretical foundation to properly address and engage with the possibilities and limitations of the respective theoretical frameworks. In actual coaching practice, however, these epistemological differences often play a less significant role. Here, the systemic approach is reduced to a methodology of inquiry. The social constructionist approach has taken over the field as the dominant epistemological basis.

3.4.1.1 The Development of Systemic Thinking

System theory is an interdisciplinary conceptual framework that is used in sociology, psychology and organization theory but also in biology and engineering. Systemic theory has been applied in psychological practice because therapists working in a psychoanalytical framework have been under growing pressure to make their work more efficient and less costly, especially with regard to services for troubled families. The systemic approach in psychotherapy dates back to the so-called Milan school.[8] The Milan school began its work in 1967 and underwent a number of phases that reflected an ongoing development of their methods, often initiated by new publications from leading (systems) theorists such as Bateson.

In the past decade, systemic thinking has become very widespread in coaching (Cavanagh, 2006; Stelter, 2002a) and organizational consultancy (Hornstrup, Loehr-Petersen, Madsen, Johansen, & Vinther, 2012). The central position of systemic

---

individual develop new behaviours. A radical variant of constructivism was developed by von Glasersfeld (1995), who defines the interaction between the sensing person and the environment as a closed circuit. To describe this notion Maturana and Varela (1980) use the term *autopoiesis*, which will be defined later in the text. *Constructionism*, on the other hand, does not focus on a cybernetic and autopoietic understanding but sees human development, cognition and learning as the result of relations with other human beings. Gergen (2009b) expresses this relational perspective with a rephrasing of Descartes' famous statement, which now becomes *Communicamus ergo sum*: We communicate, therefore I am.

[7] I have been confirmed in my perception in conversations with Kenneth Gergen. He clearly rejects the epistemology of systemic thinking. In his eyes, the systemic theory is stuck in the system entity and its autopoietic character, just as psychodynamic theory and *personality* psychology have locked into the concept of personality with its stable character features. The strength of social constructionism lies in its distance from any form of entity. Instead, it takes a dynamic view of what happens between and among people – in the relationship.

[8] The systemic approach was developed in part by a group of Italian family therapists from Milan, a tradition that found special recognition in Denmark. An excellent overview of the development of the Milano School has been presented by Tomm (1984, 2004).

thinking in developing organizational and conversation practices stems from the following key reasons:

- Meets growing demands for efficiency, also with regard to duration/number of interventions.
- Liberates the process from an individual focus and enables a look at the system (individual, group, organization, society) and the interactions among the parts.
- Allows for a multi-perspective and for divergent interpretations of the same phenomenon and thus invites rethinking and new impulses for developing the system.
- Has created a methodology involving strategies and inquiry techniques that are considered appropriate for initiating change processes in individuals or an organization – methods that can also be applied in third-generation coaching.

The systemic approach to coaching and organizational development is based on systems theory, which examines social systems (e.g. an organization, a family, a working relationship) and the interdependence among the individual components of the system. According to Ludvig von Bertalanffy (1901–1972), the founder of general systems theory, a system is a set of interrelated elements (Bertalanffy, 1981). The elements of a system create and maintain their identity through a process of mutual interaction. In this understanding, systems theory focuses on communication and interactions among the components rather than the individual component (the individual) in itself: A system is more than the sum of its parts, and exploring the interactions in a system is considered more important than studying the individual parts; for example, conflicts will be examined by focusing on the workplace as a system rather than labelling a given employee as 'problematic'. In a systemic perspective the attempt is to avoid a linear, reductionist mindset and move toward what Bertalanffy called 'perspectivism', a stance that acknowledges that as humans, although we know that there is a reality out there, we can never make objective statements about this reality. We are limited by our own perspective, but according to Bertalanffy all perspectives are essentially equally valid (see also Tomm, 1998).

In the course of the 1970s, cybernetics and constructivist ideas from Gregory Bateson (1972), Paul Watzlawick (1978), Humberto Maturana (1978) and others have been incorporated into the understanding of communication and therapy. Cybernetics, a cross-scientific approach to regulation and control, deals with information, communication and (self-) regulating systems. Constructivism assumes that reality is constructed by the observer from his or her perspective on the specific environmental situation (= autopoiesis).

Bateson

Although the English thinker Gregory Bateson (1904–1980) was a trained biologist and anthropologist, he has rightly become a leading figure in the field of psychology (Bale, 1995). Bateson's book *Steps to an Ecology of Mind* (1972) with its complex thoughts about (meta-) context, (meta-) communication, relationships between map and landscape, logical categories and cybernetic epistemology (Bateson, 1979; Nechansky, 2008) led systemic practice to its three fundamental principles: hypothesising, circularity and neutrality (originally in the field of family therapy, see Selvini-Palazzoli, Boscolo, Cecchin, & Prata, 1980; Cecchin, 1987; more on that later in this section). Bateson's thoughts on information, context and communication may be the most crucial in this development. Bateson (1972) has also clarified the difference between linear and circular thinking, which becomes essential in relation to possible forms of inquiry.

Information, according to Bateson, is "any difference which makes a difference" (Bateson, 1972, pp. 381, 453). He considers this definition crucial for analyses of systems and their organization; it implies that it is perceived differences that activate a system and are capable of producing change. The context is the setting in which a message occurs, and as such it categorizes the message. The context also defines the meaning we attribute to the message. Thus, if the context is too unclear to us, we fail to grasp what is going on; we become insecure and may find it difficult to act. According to Bateson this involves several layers of contexts: the immediate context and the (theoretically speaking) endless number of meta-contexts. Each context is influenced by the next larger context, and if there are discrepancies among them, the result may be conflict and action dilemmas for the involved parties, which Bateson (p. 245) called a *double bind* in connection with his research on schizophrenia and communication. In fact, communication is crucial for our overall being in the world: Our communication *is* our relationship with the world, says Bateson.

Watzlawick

Paul Watzlawick (1921–2007) also worked on human communication, and like Bateson he is focused on communication and interaction in relationships among the parts in a system. He emphasizes that 'one cannot not communicate', i.e. all behaviour is communication, and all communication influences behaviour. Every statement in a communication reflects an interpretation of the previous statement and relates to it, for example by rejecting or accepting it. This constant feedback flow produces patterns of interaction sequences, which the involved parties make sense of (Watzlawick, Jackson, & Beavin, 1967).

Maturana

According to Bateson, the Chilean neurobiologist Humberto Maturana (born 1928) addresses the same type of epistemological issues as Bateson, and his ideas have had a significant influence on systemic (family) therapists of the Milan School (Boscolo, Cecchin, Hoffman, & Penn, 1987) as well as on the development in Scandinavia (Ravn & Söderqvist, 1987).

This includes Maturana's ideas about autopoietic and structurally determined systems: Autopoietic systems are self-referential, i.e. they create themselves by virtue of their own inner movement and structure. Thus, Maturana presents a constructivist point of view where all knowledge and cognition arises in the individual him/herself: We construct our own reality. Because we perceive the world from the basis of our own inner structure, as humans we are incapable of recognizing an objective truth, which leads to the existence of many versions of reality. Ultimately, Maturana speaks of closed systems with a circular organization, but he still presents a possible connection: Individual structures can interconnect by means of *structural coupling*. Maturana believes that all individuals do their best and cooperate from the point of view of their own logic and perceptions. However, he also claims that man is not obedient. A system can only act, interact and change in ways that are in accordance with its own structure, i.e. in ways that the system itself perceives as meaningful. Hence, Maturana views instructive interaction or good advice as an impossibility; everybody decides for themselves what they are willing and able to connect with. When that happens, it is through language that we as human beings are able to interconnect and coordinate our actions. We can connect with the other person's logic and try to explore and understand what is meaningful for the other. That is how we create reality together (Maturana, 1978; Maturana & Varela, 1992).

After this presentation of the fundamental theorists I will now describe some of the key theoretical constructions/principles in systemic theory and practice.

3.4.1.2 Systemic Theory and Practice

Systemic thinking has initiated a fundamental move away from an essential and intrapsychological point of departure, where the focus is on psychological processes in the person, and toward emergent and constructivist thinking: No concept or phenomenon has any fixed meaning (essence thinking) in itself; instead, meaning is created as the result of a semantic construction process (emergence thinking) (Luhmann, 2006). In extension of this point, a systemic practitioner, in contrast to, for example, a psychodynamic practitioner, will avoid describing the individual by means of a label that characterizes the individual as pathological or as the bearer of the problem. Instead, the focus is on the context and the mutual relations in the contexts and settings where the problem behaviour is expressed (in a therapeutic context, see Boscolo et al. (1987). In coaching, see e.g. Tomaschek, 2006).

As systemic practitioners (therapists, coaches, organizational consultants) will view themselves as part of the system, from a systemic perspective they will never seek to occupy an objective position outside the topic of their investigation. The goal is not to achieve change in a particular direction but to create a space for change. Based on the presented systems theory literature I will now present the basic assumptions that originally formed the basis of the systemic approach to coaching, and which still offer a perspective on reality with an associated practice:

1. *A system (e.g. a relationship, a team, an organization) is always moving between stability (homoeostasis) and change (transformation).* It would be

an illusion to think that the system can be preserved in a state of permanent stability. There will always be external influences (e.g. a financial crisis that affects the demand for services/products), internal influences (e.g. dissatisfaction with management) or merely a dissatisfaction with the state of affairs (e.g. in a romantic relationship) that has the potential for destabilizing the system. In some situations, change will be a necessity for the survival of the system. The assessment of change versus stability will differ greatly with the various actors' perspectives on the situation: Change may be liberating or a source of anxiety or even chaos; stability may feel safe and secure, but it can also lead to a profound sense of boredom. However, the system always strives to re-establish the stable condition, homoeostasis, even in case of unsatisfying states, which tend to lock the parties into unproductive patterns, for example in relationships between co-workers. Here, a systemic coach might ask, 'What makes you hold on to what you two have in your relationship?' With this question, the coach seeks to explore the meaningful and stability-ensuring aspects of the relationship between the two co-workers.

2. *A system is an entity that is structured through feedback.* Cybernetic thinking distinguishes between two types of feedback. The traditional and simple form of *first-order feedback* is the type we know from a radiator thermostat, for example. The purpose of the thermostat is to maintain a constant pre-set room temperature of 20 °C. It reacts by only letting hot water into the radiator once the room temperature drops. Thus, the thermostat maintains stability in the system, homoeostasis (= room temperature of 20 °C). *Second-order feedback* is more sophisticated. If we stick to the example, the thermostat would be 'reflective', that is, able to assume certain premises for its actions. This type of technical solution already exists in simple versions, for example in dishwashers, which measure the amount of dishes in the machine and adjust the amount of water accordingly. But now for social practices: What role do these forms of feedback play in social systems or in learning and development? Let us look at an example of how the system of a 'relationship between a teacher and a 'misbehaved' boy' is shaped and maintained through first-order feedback: The student 'disrupts' the classroom activities, and the teacher reprimands him. Over time, the student discovers that this form of disruption finally gets him the attention that the teacher otherwise does not give him. This sets up a system context, a pattern, between the teacher and this particular student. Based on the same thinking, the two organizational psychologists Argyris and Schön (1978) introduced the term *double-loop learning*. Here, individuals or organizations question the fundamental assumptions, norms and values that usually frame their actions in order to be able to handle challenges in new ways, based on new premises. The teacher in the example would then view the student differently, for example by noticing the student's need for more attention, which he currently only receives by 'misbehaving'. Double-loop learning generates perspectives that are inconceivable in traditional (single-loop) learning, because

it gives rise to entirely new conditions as the basis of a process of development and learning. Double-loop learning is especially important when organizations have to make careful decisions under rapidly changing and often uncertain conditions.

3. *Feedback develops patterns over time.* In the example above, a pattern has developed between teacher and student. This pattern is maintained as a result of stable and recurring feedback mechanisms. If the teacher were to engage in coaching in order to reflect more on her relationship with this student, the coach would seek to initiate a second-order feedback process in order to break up the pattern and thus create a basis for a new relationship between teacher and student. For example, the coach might ask the teacher, 'What would it take to alter the premises of your mutual relationship?' The teacher would then be able to see through the pattern that frames their actions. A new perception of the situation – new premises for the interpretation – would enable a new pattern. The teacher might, for example, offer the student a different kind of attention, including him in the classroom activities in a new and more constructive way.

4. *Identifying a pattern introduces the concept of an observer of the pattern. A pattern only exists if someone orders the event in a particular manner.* By attributing a certain understanding, meaning and pattern to a situation and event, the observer defines the situation and the event in a particular way. Situations and events *do not* have any specific character per se. By virtue of his or her interpretation, the observer creates a situation with a particular pattern.

5. *Concepts such as 'problem', 'difficulty' etc. describe an interactive process between the observer and the observed. If the parties interact they form a system, and their actions become meaningful to a larger system around them.* To discuss the two latter assumptions I will return to our classroom example: When the student first addresses the teacher, it is the teacher who, from her observer perspective, describes the situation as 'disruption' and the student's behaviour as 'problematic' and as 'misbehaving'. This description of the situation and the emerging relational pattern between the teacher and the student only offer one perspective on the situation, one specific way of interpreting events. A pattern emerges because the observer (in this case the teacher) repeatedly interprets a particular event involving the student in the same way. In systemic thinking, we are therefore very aware of the labels we attach to people, or which the coachee and conversation partner attaches to him/herself and others. A label locks the person (in this case the student) into a particular position. A label is a description from a particular observer perspective. This understanding leads to the following assumption:

6. *The key aspect of a 'problem' is to understand the underlying meaning behind the interaction between the 'bearer of the problem' and the surrounding system.* Therefore, change is only possible when the parties are willing and ready to view situations and persons from other angles and thus break away from the observer perspective that framed their description of the situation and events in light of a particular pattern (shift in perspective; see Sect. 3.3.1).

7. *A pattern forms a context, and the context forms the basis for events and actions to take on meaning.* A context develops because the observer attributes a particular meaning to the event. For the teacher, the meaning develops as follows: I have a responsibility for the whole class. There has to be order in the classroom! I can't have Peter (the student) interrupt and disrupt things all the time. I have to make sure that he learns to behave. For Peter, the context is undoubtedly different. He has his own observer perspective on the situation. Perhaps he interprets the context as follows: I don't understand why the teacher is always giving me a hard time. I should be allowed to say something too. I think she's stupid. She has her favourites who are allowed to do whatever they want. As soon as I want to say something, she yells at me.

8. *Meanings have a hierarchical structure.* Our example illustrates the hierarchical structure of meaning. From the teacher's perspective the hierarchy is as follows: The teacher feels that she is an agent for an essential institution in society. She feels an obligation to society and a responsibility to the students. She has a mission: The school operates by means of the education she provides, and the students have to adapt. This overriding level can be described in the framework of concepts such as culture, society, convictions and religion. The teacher's perception and conviction clearly affects her view of Peter's actions. It affects the *relationships* on the second level of meaning and ultimately also the *individual action* on the third level: her actions toward Peter. The three levels of meaning mutually condition each other. Culture and convictions condition relationships and the individual's concrete behaviours, and conversely, individual acts also affect relations and ultimately the culture in which the individual lives or works.

9. *Acts and context are in a mutual circular relationship. A particular act emerges or is initiated as an attempt at creating a new relationship or a new pattern.* We act because we have particular perceptions or convictions in relation to the context (cf. the teacher's convictions about the role of the school in society), and on the other hand, our perceptions are either supported or challenged by the feedback we receive on our actions. Furthermore, individual acts and the way in which we speak to and about each other can also affect our surroundings, and they can be viewed as an attempt at initiating change in certain relationships and contexts. This perspective is essential in legitimizing the work that coaches or organizational consultants do with their clients and customers.

10. *The objective of the coaching conversation is to enable the individual/ organization to view the challenge or the problem in a new and different manner.* The coach will structure his or her work with individuals or groups around initiating a shift in the observer perspective of the individual or members of an organization in relation to a specific focus area. This shift in perspective is a fundamental condition for being able to see selected contexts and relationships in a new light. The coach or organizational consultant can initiate change for example by asking circular and reflexive questions (more about that later) that influence the participants' perceptions and actions. In systemic terms, this helps bring about a 'new context', i.e. a different perception of the context.

The Three Basic Principles of Systemic Practice: Hypothesizing, Circularity and Neutrality

According to first-order cybernetics, systems can be understood independently of the observer. The focus here is on the 'observed system' and its (mechanical) feedback processes. This thinking was criticized for neglecting human social meaning construction, and in response to the criticism, second-order cybernetics was developed.[9] According to second-order cybernetics, systems can only be understood as human constructs based on people's experiences and basic assumptions. The focus is now on the 'observing system': The coach is always a part of the system that he or she observes in the conversation with the coachee.

Curiosity is the term that the systemic family therapist Cecchin (1987) used to redefine the original term, neutrality. As a term, neutrality implies that the coach actively rejects the idea that one point of view may be more correct than any other. Thus, the coach allies him/herself with all points of view and perspectives and, simultaneously, with none of them. However, this external behaviour may be misread as an internal stance of indifference and lack of involvement; therefore, the concept of curiosity is proposed as a superior alternative. The coach should always be in a state of curiosity, which makes it possible to explore all the different points of view. In order to challenge the coachee's perceptions, the coach also assumes a position of *irreverence* (Cecchin, Lane, & Ray, 1993). From a neutral position the coach attempts to challenge the coachee's perception of reality and to ask questions that may be surprisingly and suitably disruptive for the coachee. Peter Lang[10] replaced the term curiosity with *wondering* – a state where the coach appears directly involved and engaged. Curiosity has a slightly inquisitorial negative undertone.

This basic stance of wondering is also used for hypothesizing. Hypotheses allow us to reflect on possible futures that the coach asks the coachee to imagine. Systemic hypotheses are assumptions, i.e. they are in themselves neither right nor wrong, although they will be more or less helpful. Hypotheses are based on the coach's assumption about the state of the system. Hypotheses are based on (1) the insights that the coach has reached in his or her conversations with the coachee, (2) the coach's experience with comparable cases and (3) certain psychological theories that the coach knows and finds it relevant to include (see also Tomm, 1984, 1988). The coach can use *hypothetical questions* to obtain information about whether the hypothesis can be confirmed or disproved or needs to be modified. Furthermore, a hypothesis and its underlying ideas can be used to assess the most likely new direction for the system that the coachee is a part of. The coachee is thus invited to shift his or her perspective on the system or a particular environmental situation.

---

[9]These concepts were originally introduced by the Milan School family therapists Selvini-Palazzoli et al. (1980).

[10]I heard Peter Lang speak about *wondering* at Attractor's Summer University in the Danish town of Middelfart in August 2009.

Curiosity is also an important condition for understanding circularity and the associated patterns and connections in the system. Bateson (1972) in particular has pointed to the importance of perceptual differences in human thinking. The interaction between parts of our consciousness revolves around differences. A difference is established as a result of the mutual and circular relationship among certain entities. Circularity is the notion that everything is connected to everything else, and it thus differs from a linear cause-and-effect perspective. Circular thinking means abandoning the notion of being able to control and understand events and acts in just one way. It acknowledges the complexity of the world and the multiperspectivity of possible understandings. In circular thinking, the coach and coachee are interested in a shared exploration and clarification of differences. The coach asks questions aimed at uncovering differences and similarities, patterns, habits and connections (see Hieker & Huffington, 2006). In relation to this idea, a whole range of question types and categories have emerged that are used in systemic coaching (see especially Tomaschek, 2006). That is how the interview was established as an intervention form (Tomm, 1988, 1989, 1998). According to Cecchin (1987), circularity is a technique that is applied in hypothesizing and in maintaining neutrality, because it is capable of undermining the client's 'truths'. He concludes that the three principles of hypothesizing, circularity and neutrality are closely connected and condition each other.

Circular Versus Linear Questions

Karl Tomm (1988, 1989, 1998), the Canadian family therapist and professor of psychiatry, was the key driver in the development of a set of questions that integrates circular and linear questions as well as the intentions behind a variety of question types into a holistic concept. The concept is presented in the following figure (Fig. 3.2).

The conversation may be guided by two basic intents with regard to exploring and shaping the conversation partner's reality: the *orienting* or the *influencing* intent. These two perspectives may be pursued by means of two different forms of question logic: traditional, familiar *linear assumptions* or the *circular assumptions* of systemic thinking. Linear *assumptions*, for example, operate on the underlying assumption of a time line or a cause-and-effect link. At the beginning of the conversation, the coach often aims to find his or her own orientation or to give the coachee more orientation in his or her life world. And toward the end of the conversation, the coach may offer orientation by asking what the coachee is thinking about doing in conclusion and thus as a first step toward new acts. The circular *assumptions* break with many of the qualities we are familiar with from our 'normal' way of speaking to each other. *Circular questions* allow us to explore and discover several perceptions of reality, including the realities of others in the coachee's workplace or other people's positions in relation to a particular event.

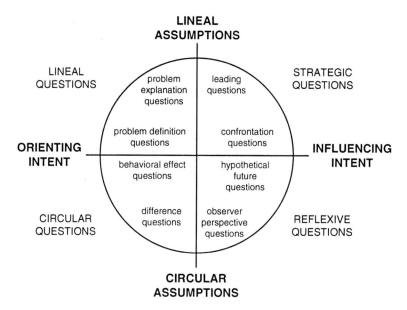

Fig. 3.2 Systemic question circle (see Tomm, 1988)

By asking circular questions, however, the coach also affects the person's way of reflecting on reality, for example through hypothetical questions that challenge a particular perception and allow for other perceptions of reality.

In coaching training, the question circle presented above has proved very helpful for structuring the coaching conversation. Although in many regards, the orthodox systemic tradition has been abandoned today, the notion of circular questions in particular has proved its usefulness.

3.4.1.3 From Systemic Thinking to a Focus on Social Construction Processes and Collaborative Practice

While systemic thinking, especially in a therapy context, was initially inspired by early systems theory and the cybernetic perceptions of systems as 'closed' and oriented toward homoeostasis and by Maturana's and Varela's (1992) constructivist ideas about the autonomy and autopoiesis of living beings, the past 10–15 years has seen a movement toward social constructionism with its emphasis on human social relations and interactions. While the systemic perspective emphasizes the individual, constructive consciousness, social constructionism focuses on consciousness as relational and considers the development of meaning a discursive process: It is no longer the structure of an individual system but rather the shared context and practice that creates meaning.

Here I think it is relevant to consider whether we are still dealing with a truly systemic framework, or whether the term 'systemic' might be misleading.[11] If, however, one chooses to focus on possible similarities, both constructivism and social constructionism essentially reject the assumption that knowledge reflects an ontological reality; instead they both claim that knowledge is a construction. Thus, both positions reject the notion that consciousness reflects reality and instead posit that reality is a human construct. In closing, I will quote the leading social constructionist Kenneth Gergen (2009a), who articulates his rejection of the systemic-constructivist paradigm as follows:

> Yet, while rich in practical implications, it should be noted that in most systemic thinking the units in the system are fundamentally bounded, and their relationship one of cause and effect. In the dysfunctional family, for example the parents act upon the child, who in turn acts upon the parents. For the practitioner this orientation often invites a strategic as opposed to a collaborative approach to producing change. The practitioner asks, how can I effect change in the system? (p. 378).

In conclusion, I would highlight the following points: Systemic thinking as epistemology or as an epistemological position is more or less obsolete and has been replaced by a more dynamic and relational understanding represented by social constructionism. This historical trend is even promoted by a co-founder of systemic therapy, Cecchin (1992), who himself has moved on to embrace a social constructionist position. However, the systemic methodology with its focus on circularity and its search for differences, reflection and new perspectives continues to have considerable relevance in coaching practice. Thus, a social constructionist, narrative and collaborative practitioner should consider how to adapt and develop the systemically oriented method to have it match the social constructionist epistemology. That is the ambition I will be pursuing as I present my model for coaching practice in Chap. 4 of the book.

3.4.1.4 Social Constructionism

Social constructionism can be considered the major underlying theory of several coaching approaches. The introduction of social constructionism in psychology dates back to 1973, when Kenneth Gergen published the article *Social psychology as history*. In the article, Gergen emphasizes that all knowledge is historically and

---

[11]The Danish coaching field seems to be more conservative in holding on to the term 'systemic coaching' than is the case in other countries. In 2010 a book with that exact title was published, edited by Hanne Moltke and Asbjørn Molly (2010). Several Danish consultancy firms also continue to use the term 'systemic' to describe the basis of their work – although their work is actually essentially social constructionist in nature. Several new international coaching manuals (e.g. Cox et al., 2010; Palmer & Whybrow, 2007) do not have a chapter on systemic coaching in their presentation of coaching approaches but instead include solution-focused coaching. In the German-speaking environment, where there is a long tradition for systemic work, some literature still uses the term systemic coaching (e.g. Backhausen & Thommen, 2006; Rauen, 2005).

culturally specific, and that the development of a contemporary psychology requires the inclusion and understanding of social, political and economic phenomena. The roots of social constructionism, however, go back farther in time. There are early developments, especially within sociology, that one might go back to, but I consider symbolic interactionism the most important ancestor of social constructionism. The American sociologist and social psychologist G.H. Mead (1934) described the role of the social environment in relation to the individual's development, behaviour and self-presentation: The individual's self-concept is not only framed by interactions with concrete other persons in a face-to-face dialogue but also, in a more general process of influence, by the norms, values, attitudes and positions of the social environment. Mead referred to this perspective as *the generalized others*: The individual's perception of the expectations of society and other persons influence the individual's behaviour in a given social situation. However, Berger and Luckmann's (1966) famous book *The social construction of reality* also helped pave the way for social constructionist thinking in psychology. From their anti-essentialist position the two sociologists argue that people create and maintain all social phenomena through their mutual social practices. Over the past 40 years, other, related schools have emerged within psychology, including discursive psychology (Edwards & Potter, 1992), critical psychology (Dreier, 2008, 2009; Sloan, 2000) and deconstructionism/discourse analysis (Parker, 1992).

What makes social constructionism interesting to coaching and coaching psychology? Part of the answer can be found in my earlier analysis of social change processes with the clear diversification of countless possible ways of living: There are many ways of living, many paths leading to the goal, and there are many answers to the open-ended questions. However, we no longer have figures or institutions of authority with the necessary competence and capability to offer clear-cut recommendations about how to achieve the good (working) life. This social development has sparked new trends and theories in psychology and other social sciences, which have led, among other things, to an abandonment of the traditional objectivist, truth-seeking ideals in epistemology and science. Coaching, on the other hand, can be considered an open conversation format where the coachee does not expect a simple answer but rather a worthy conversation partner for reflections on pressing issues and concerns.

The strength of social constructionism lies in its epistemology, which is connected to the post-modern tradition and its challenge to the notion of universal truths (see Kvale, 1992). In social constructionist psychology, however, the individual and his or her consciousness are assumed to expand in the relationship through processes of interaction. Thus, the position also involves a sociocentric perspective (see originally Bourdieu, 1993) and a focus on the role of relationships and communities in shaping psychological and social phenomena. Social constructionist thinking is predominantly abstract and theoretical, however. With regard to application areas such as therapy, coaching and organizational intervention, Gergen and other social constructionists often do not offer specific suggestions – apart from referring to a large number of innovative practitioners who have developed methods and conversation formats based on social constructionist theory and epistemology. Some of these applied approaches are presented later in this chapter.

In the following, I outline a number of key assumptions and basic positions that describe social constructionist thinking, mainly inspired by Kenneth Gergen's work (especially Gergen, 2009a, b; Gergen & Gergen, 2003):

1. *Context and culture form our basis for understanding our reality, and* vice versa. It is important to understand the context as the social reality that is continually created by persons in a mutual relationship. It does not exist as an independent entity. We are involved in creating the context and the culture we live in, and at the same time, the culture and context also shape our ability to create this shared reality as a common frame of reference. Gergen (2009a) mentions three main factors that contribute to the creation of this reality: "the languages through which we relate, the process of daily conversations, and the institutions in which we live" (p. 32). He continues, "Central to any ongoing relationship is the existence of shared reality" (p. 32). This is also a fundamental condition in coaching: In the individual conversation, the coach and coachee co-create a shared reality, a reality that is shaped by the way they talk to each other and the way they address the subjects and events that are the topic of their conversation. This context becomes the basis of their shared meaning-making, which is the point of departure for the developmental processes that are initiated in their conversation.

2. *'Truth' is created in a dialogue with our surroundings and through conversations and shared actions.* When we interact we create a reality that is valid for those of us who share a relationship. The social reality exists as a 'truth' for the parties who are involved in conversations and interactions. We can speak of a *local truth* that applies to the people who share a specific understanding of context and relationship. The traditional concept of truth, by contrast, is that we can use our words to paint a picture of the world as it *is*, that words can depict the world. In this understanding, truth acquires exclusive status. Social constructionists reject this notion of an absolute and universal truth. In their perception, the words that individuals use with one another only acquire their meaning through the individuals' mutual relationship. Words and speech create our reality and thus the local truths that we develop about our reality. The assumption that 'words and speech create reality' is crucial to any coaching dialogue. If words and speech create one's reality (e.g. outside the coaching conversation), it follows that the coach and coachee can also create a new and different reality together. The main challenge lies in finding ways to transform insights from the coaching conversation to the reality outside the space of the conversation.

3. *Problems in the social life occur when local versions of truth are framed as universal truths.* The social constructionist understanding of truth is not necessarily generally accepted. Even if the assumption is accepted in theory, there may be situations in life where we go against our own insights. If certain social groups or individuals view their 'local truth' as absolute, there will be consequences. On the level of society, it can lead to the marginalization of

certain groups, for example if unemployed people, immigrants or Moslems are given a label that purports to represent a universal truth; ultimately that will lead to discrimination and tension among different groups in society. 'Local truths' about what the boss *is like*, or what the staff's job effort *is like*, can cause unnecessary tension in the workplace, as certain 'truths' contribute to dominance over others. Attempts to frame local truths as universal involve the potential for conflict or an abuse of power. Let us briefly examine the possible consequences of this assumption in relation to coaching. The challenge for the coachee may be that he or she sees a particular situation, event or him/herself in a particular way that actually takes on the status of an absolute truth. In the ongoing conversation it will be the coach's responsibility to introduce or probe for other truths or positions (for example by means of circular and hypothetical questions[12]) to enable the coachee to be open to new perspectives that may form the basis of development and learning.

4. *Social constructionists are fundamentally open to many different ways of describing the world.* In a sense, this represents a form of radical pluralism and an introduction of *multi-versality* as an alternative to uni-versality, i.e. seeing the world from just one position. In the coaching conversation the goal will be to describe, name and, most importantly, appreciate certain events and persons in alternative ways. By means of the above-mentioned circular questions the coach will be able to invite the coachee to enter new and different 'universes', where events and persons are understood in a new, accepting or even appreciative manner. The social constructionists' pluralist perception has led to criticism: Some positions are simply wrong and cannot be tolerated (Nazism, apartheid, torture or 'simple' bullying)! With reference to Shotter, Kvale (1992, in the introduction) notes that it is possible to advocate *epistemic relativism while rejecting moral relativism*, i.e. that a radical pluralist, social constructionist position does not preclude a moral foundation. Gergen (2009a) clarifies this moral position by indicating a move from relativism to *relational responsibility*, a position that gives the discussion about morality a new, relational foundation. In Gergen's perception, a statement such as 'That simply cannot be tolerated!' reflects a first-order morality. This form of moral view is related to a notion of good versus evil. Not without reason, the concepts of ethics and morals from, respectively, Greek and Latin can be traced back to words like customs, practice or usage. In workplaces and organizations, one will hear people say, 'That's how we do it around here!' Following this first-order morality means hoping for the best in man, and if that moral behaviour fails to manifest itself, one has to monitor and ultimately reprimand the 'morally irresponsible'. Gergen (2009a) strives for

---

[12]Just an example: Questions that introduce shifts in position or perspective: A shift in position or perspective should promote externalization, which means that the coachee in his or her perception separates him/herself from the problem/challenge – i.e. views it from the outside, from a new position or in a different perspective. The coach might ask, for example, What would be the first thing that was different if you weren't you but your boss/manager colleague/employee? What would your challenge look like from the person's perspective?

a second-order morality, which requires a focus on the community,[13] and which he describes as follows:

> In the case of second-order morality, individual responsibility is replaced by *relational responsibility*, a collective responsibility for sustaining the potentials of coordinated action. To be responsible to relationships is, above all, to sustain the process of co-creating meaning. ... In being responsible for relationships we step outside the individualist tradition; care for the relationship becomes primary. (p. 364; italics in original)

5. *Social constructionists take a curious (wondering), open and respectful stance to other people's perceptions and traditions.* This basic stance is fundamental for giving all the participants in the conversation an opportunity for development. In systemic thinking, neutrality and irreverence were key terms. Neutrality was to be a precondition for maintaining an open mind to all points of view and convictions, while irreverence should reflect the therapist's challenging attitude in questioning the client's assumptions, positions and actions. This basic position did involve a potential for abuse of power in relation to the client (Cecchin, 1992). Social constructionism has developed a fundamentally new stance. The coach should develop a stance of curiosity – wondering, openness and respect – as his or her fundamental attitude toward the coachee. First of all, this stance makes it possible for the coach to understand the coachee's context and life world. Second, the coach's wondering attitude enables the coachee to question his or her own perceptions, convictions, values and actions. Third, the coach's wondering, openness and respect toward the coachee facilitates the responsibility for the relationship that is a condition for the open and genuine dialogue (cf. Buber, 2004) that gives the coaching conversation its special quality and depth.

6. *The main point is NOT whether our words are true or objective but rather what happens when we move into a form of understanding where reality is seen as a social construct.* As mentioned earlier, every statement, description and contribution to the dialogue reflects the way in which the person interprets his or her world and life context. Words help constitute our reality. For a practicing coach it is therefore interesting to understand and empathize with the world that the coachee describes. It is not relevant to reflect on whether the coachee's statements are 'correct'. The coachee presents him/herself and his or her world, which is created within the context that the coachee lives in. The coach's task involves appreciating the coachee's descriptions and statements and build on them. As the coach and the coachee co-create new descriptions and perceptions of the coachee's reality in their ongoing dialogue, it becomes interesting to see how this new way of addressing his or her reality affects the coachee, and how the coachee will think and act in the future.

---

[13]In this connection, Gergen (2009a) highlights two key publications, where the authors regret the inadequate focus on community that is so crucial for developing a well-functioning society: Sennet's (1992) *The fall of public man* and Putnam's (2000) *Bowling alone: The collapse and revival of American community.* In an international context, Denmark is often praised for its long-standing tradition of establishing and maintaining social communities. This is something we should safeguard.

7. *Meaning is not something that is given but something that is developed in social interactions.* Meaning is one of the key concepts in social constructionism (see Gergen, 1994). This concept has acquired a new twist, however. In classic cognitive psychology, the main focus was on the individual meaning or inner symbolization (representation, conceptualization) of the outside world. In a social constructionist framework, the focus is on how the person creates meaning with others. Meaning is viewed in a relational perspective. The coachee's individual statements in the conversation are not meaningful in themselves; they acquire meaning through the relationship and the context they are placed in. If the coach offers a comment or a statement it coordinates with the coachee's statement and thus becomes a sort of follow-up (speech) act. The coachee thus does not make meaning individually; meaning takes shape, develops and changes continually in the conversation between the coach and the coachee. Their universe of meaning is co-created in the conversation, and thus, something new will always emerge for both parties in their mutual meeting, something they could not have 'figured out' without speaking with each other.

8. *New stories can change the way we perceive the world and ourselves.* The basic assumption in social constructionism is that language helps shape the world, our reality: When we speak about our world (certain situations and events, which we find stressful or challenging) in a new way, the world too will change. This change is ultimately reflected in new ways of acting in future situations. In this developmental process, language and action should always be seen as a new entity. New stories are the result of shared meaning-making between coach and coachee. The basic idea in the coaching conversation is that the coach listens to the coachee's stories and inquires about and searches for bright spots in the story. That may be a positive exception, a re-membering of important and uplifting persons, an acknowledgement of important life values or a reinterpretation that highlights aspects that generate life and energy. This shared process of reflection and meaning-making introduces a shift in perspective that highlights bright spots and makes it possible to shape an uplifting and positive story, the ideal outcome of the coaching conversation. The conversation takes place as a process of co-creation between coach and coachee. The coach is an active, i.e. self-reflective partner as the coachee generates alternative and life-affirming stories – stories that facilitate new ways of acting for the coachee in future practice contexts that are related to the core topic of the conversation.

9. *Social constructionism is wary of such concepts as personal determination, intentionality and 'personal agency'.* Our personal drive and thus also our personal responsibility for our own actions have formed a key assumption in Western thinking, at least since the Age of Enlightenment (voluntarism: the notion of a free will). By holding people personally accountable for their actions we create a foundation for morals in our society. The Christian tradition points to *forgiveness* as God's or a fellow human being's way of relieving a person from guilt. There are, however, also positions in psychology and the social sciences (e.g. behavioural psychology) that fundamentally reject the concept of free

will and see human behaviour in a deterministic light, as governed by specific environmental conditions. Gergen (2009a) advocates a relationist perspective on agency:

> But as I have argued in the present work, both these concepts create a world of fundamental separation. The attempt in this case is to reconfigure agency in such a way that we move beyond the voluntarism/determinism debate, and bring relationship into the center of our concerns. By viewing agency as an action within relationship, we move in exactly this direction. (p. 83)

3.4.1.5 Applications and Further Developments of Social Constructionism

Social constructionism is a well-developed theory, which nevertheless has not been translated directly to practice in the form of social constructionist coaching (psychology). Social constructionism has, however, taken root in several coaching approaches, some of which I will present in the following:

- Solution-focused theory and practice
- Appreciative Inquiry theory and practice
- Narrative theory and practice
- Collaborative theory and practice.

Solution-Focused Theory and Practice

The solution-focused approach – like the systemic – has its roots in psychotherapy, especially in family therapy, and the method was originally developed by Steve de Shazer, Insoo Kim Berg and colleagues at Brief Family Therapy Center in Milwaukee, Wisconsin, USA. Historically, Solution-Focused Brief Therapy was influenced by Alfred Adler, Milton Erickson and John Weakland[14] (see O'Connell & Palmer, 2003). The solution-focused approach is not nearly as theoretically founded and elaborated as the systemic approach, but it is clearly inspired by social constructionist epistemology. I will highlight the following arguments for the influence of the solution-focused approach on various organizational and conversation practices:

- Meets growing demands for efficiency, especially with regard to duration/number of interventions.
- Moves away from the problem focus that often leads to a negative spiral in terms of finding the root cause of the problem.
- Has a clear belief that the answer to the client's challenges should be found in the client's life universe.

---

[14]Weakland was Insoo Kim Berg's supervisor at the university and has also been involved in the development of family therapy.

- Like the systemic approach, the solution-focused approach has developed a methodology with strategies and inquiry techniques that are good at initiating change processes in individuals or an organization – methods that can also be integrated in third-generation coaching.

With its forward-looking and strength-based perspective the solution-focused approach is particularly appropriate for coaching. Solution-focused coaching (SFC) has the following focal points:

1. The world is a social construct, and thus the coachee's challenges are also part of the constructed reality. In SFC, the conversation aims to create a different reality: The focus is not on examining or analyzing the problems that may be behind the challenges the coachee brings in; instead it is on identifying positions of strength and bright spots in the client's life universe and perceived world, where the solution may suddenly emerge. A problem focus might drain the coachee of energy, and an organizational development can end in chaos if the focus turns to the identification of problems and faults. SFC has a highly pragmatic perspective, which is to enhance the coachee's awareness of what he or she does well and of previous successes. The coach's role is to enhance the coachee's awareness of his or her own capacity, the things that have actually proved possible to the coachee in the past and thus support processes that lead to solutions for special challenges. In recognizing the influence of solution-focused practice on social constructionist thinking, Gergen (2009a) says,

   What if there were no problems? What if all the anguish and hopelessness that bring people into therapy had no basis? There is a sense in which constructionist thought prompts just this kind of question. It is not that we don't confront difficult problems in our lives, problems that are very real and often very painful. However, the constructionist reminds us, these realities are constructed; problems are not 'out there' as realities independent of us, but come to be what they are by virtue of the way we negotiate reality. (p. 170)

2. The coachee is essentially thought to be capable of solving his or her own problems. The coachee has the resources[15] and the personal expertise required to achieve change and positive development and is thus capable of initiating and creating a situation that contains the solutions that the coachee wants. Therefore, SFC never uses a pathologizing basic perception or negative labels about the coachee. The coach views his or her conversation partner as a person with developmental resources and strengths. In their text on solution-focused coaching Berg and Szabo (2005) makes the following assumptions about their coachees – until proven otherwise: "All clients ...

   - Are doing the best they can under very difficult circumstances
   - Are invested in ideas they generate

---

[15]Here, resources should not be understood as a personal, intrapsychological quality but as a product of a socially constructed reality. Resources develop in the individual through the relationships and social environments that the individual enters into.

- Want to … be ethical, courteous, polite, and honest and want to improve their lives
- Want to get along with others such as clients and colleagues
- Want to be accepted and belong to a group
- Want to make their lives better as well as the lives of those they love, respect, and admire
- Want to take care of important others and be taken care of by them
- Want to leave a positive legacy and make a positive difference in the world
- Want to be respected by others and to respect others" (p. 21).

3. Do what works! De Shazer and Berg (1997) clearly highlight this perspective and also describe the four characteristics of their solution-focused approach (here with an emphasis on therapy, but the same applies to SFC):

- At some point in the first interview, the therapist will ask the 'Miracle Question'.[16]
- At least once during the first interview and at subsequent ones, the client will be asked to rate something on a scale of '0–10' or '1–10'.
- At some point during the interview, the therapist will take a break.
- After this intermission, the therapist will give the client some compliments which will sometimes (frequently) be followed by a suggestion or homework task (frequently called an 'experiment') (p. 123).

They also underscore that if one of the four characteristics is missing, the practice cannot be said to be fully solution-focused.

4. The coach's role in the solution-focused process is to continually invite the coachee to explore and define him/herself on two levels: (1) What does the coachee want to change in his or her life (goal focus), and (2) what strengths and resources can the coachee use to create this different and 'new' reality? The coach appreciates and supports the coachee's goal perspectives, convictions, previous successes, strengths and resources as they appear in the dialogue (cf. Berg & De Jong, 1996).

5. Thus, the coaching process initiates a self-guided learning process for the coachee (cf. Cavanagh & Grant, 2010). The coach acts as a facilitator who seeks to facilitate what the coachee has 'forgotten', which is that the coachee actually has experienced successes and uplifting feelings in the past, that the coachee possesses strengths and resources – conditions that will strengthen the coachee's belief that he or she will be able to find a solution in relation to the current challenge.

---

[16]In Stelter (2002a, p. 240) a miracle question is described as follows: "Imagine that you go to bed at night and fall asleep, and during the night a miracle happens. The next morning, all the problems are solved! You get up, and you know nothing about these changes, because you were sleeping: How will you first notice that the miracle happened? What signs do you notice that let you know that the changes have happened? Who else will notice the changes? What do you and others do different? (see more in De Jong & Berg, 2002).

6. According to Cavanagh and Grant (2010) the solution-focused attitude occurs when the coachee moves from an inquiring or deliberative mindset to an implementational mindset. In the inquiring or deliberative mindset, the coachee explores pros and cons in relation to a particular (desirable) situation and possible goals and actions. This is also the stage where the so-called miracle question occurs. In the implementational mindset, the coachee's focus is on finding the necessary means to realize change and create development in relation to the challenges that are described.

A proposal for a conversation model for solution-focused coaching is presented by the Norwegian coaching practitioners Espedal, Svendsen, and Andersen (2006):

- *Problem, challenge.* What problem or challenge does the focus person bring in?
- *Establishing a platform.* What should the coach and the focus person talk about for the conversation to be helpful?
- *Defining a desired future.* What does the focus person want to achieve? What does the future look like once the problem has been eliminated?
- *The focus person's goals.* How can he/she tell that what he/she is hoping for is about to come true? This point is crucial in the coaching process.
- *Exploring exceptions.* When and how are there examples that the goal has already been reached?
- *Identifying resources.* What skills and resources does the focus person possess? How can these tools help the focus person achieve his or her goal? What has the focus person already done that points in the right direction?
- *Small signs of progress.* What does the focus person need to do *more of* in order to boost the progress?
- *Appreciation and feedback.* How can the coach express support and appreciation to the focus person during the process and at the conclusion of the process?

The key point is the coachee's goals, which are based on the coachee's visions of a preferred future. In the ongoing coaching process the coach seeks to focus on what the coachee has already demonstrated and done that points in the preferred direction and on the competences that the coachee actually has (perhaps without being aware of them) for creating the reality that the coachee dreams of. As the final element, solution-focused coaching seeks to move toward the preferred future by drawing the coachee's attention to the steps that he or she has already taken toward the goal and by appreciating and supporting the actions and events that already point in the preferred direction.

In conclusion, I would highlight the following points in relation to the presentation above: Although the solution-focused approach does not have a very theoretical orientation, it clearly leans on a social constructionist epistemology. The most important point is to use the epistemology as a basis of one's coaching practice. However, the solution-focused method requires the coach to develop a special capacity (and technique) for promoting a solution-oriented process in the coachee, where the developmental process revolves around the coachee's stated goals. The coach maintains a focus on the goal and the preferred future and thus acts as a form of guide that helps the coachee move forward. In this sense, there is a clear difference in position between the coach and the coachee. The coach facilitates the process and is an expert in asking the questions that move the coachee from an inquiring or deliberative mindset to an *implementational mindset*. In that sense, solution-focused coaching is a good example of second-generation coaching, and yet it is still a step removed from being a methodology and a practice that fully implements the co-creative thinking. I will attempt to make this step later by presenting coaching as a narrative collaborative practice (see Chap. 4).

Appreciative Inquiry Theory and Practice

In 1980, the then 24-year-old David Cooperrider was a Ph.D. student in a research programme on Organizational Behaviour at Case Western Reserve University in Ohio, USA: In his project he initially undertook a – completely traditional – study of interpersonal problems in an organization, in this case a hospital. He was surprised, however, with the amount of positive cooperation, innovation and egalitarian governance he was able to observe in the organization.[17] His supervisor, Suresh Srivastva, noticed Cooperrider's enthusiasm and encouraged him to pursue this track further. The chairman of the Cleveland Clinic also supported Cooperrider's project and asked him to study the factors that were present when the clinic functioned in an optimal and life-affirming manner. The term 'Appreciative Inquiry' was first mentioned in a footnote in a report to the board of the clinic. An important theoretical source of inspiration for Cooperrider's research was Ken Gergen's book *Toward Transformation of Social Knowledge*, which came out in 1982. Cooperrider viewed Gergen's 'generative theory' as a resource "to challenge the guiding assumptions of the culture, to raise fundamental questions regarding contemporary life, to foster reconsideration of that which is taken for granted, and thereby furnish new alternatives for social action.[18]" In 1986, Cooperrider submitted his dissertation, titled *Appreciative Inquiry: Toward a Methodology for Understanding and Enhancing Organizational Innovation* and thus laid the cornerstone to a strategy for organizational development that was based on a completely different set of principles than traditional approaches, which were focused on finding solutions to problems. His focus was instead on[19]

- Appreciating and valuing the best of what is
- Envisioning what might be
- Dialoging what should be.

(Cooperrider & Whitney, 2005, p. 13).

---

[17]For a historical review of the development of AI, see Watkins and Mohr (2001).

[18]The quote is taken from an article by Fitzgerald, Murrell, and Newman (2002). Retrieved 30 July 2010 at http://intranet.catie.ac.cr/intranet/posgrado/Met%20Cual%20Inv%20accion/2008/Semana%206/TheNewFrontier.pdf

[19]AI has a very comprehensive website: http://appreciativeinquiry.case.edu/

These three points, originally developed for organizational change and development, can be seen as key arguments for the importance of the appreciative approach in various organizational and conversation practices; they are also very applicable in interventions in the framework of coaching and coaching psychology. Cooperrider, Whitney, and Stavros (2008) present the following practice-oriented definition of Appreciative Inquiry (AI):

> Appreciative inquiry is the cooperative co-evolutionary search for the best in people, their organizations, and the world around them. It involves the discovery of what gives 'life' to a living system when it is most effective, alive, and constructively capable in economic, ecological, and human terms. AI involves the art and practice of asking questions that strengthen a system's capacity to apprehend, anticipate, and heighten positive potential. The inquiry is mobilized through the crafting of 'unconditional positive questions'. (p. 3)

Like AI, appreciative coaching (AC) rests on five general principles, which were originally developed by Cooperrider, and which are also used as the philosophical foundation and methodological basis for the dialogical practice in coaching (cf. Orem et al., 2007):

1. *The constructionist principle*: The relationship is considered the source of knowledge, and the way in which we speak about knowledge frames the shaping of our realities. When the coach speaks with the coachee about his or her realities in a new way, for example by highlighting and appreciating the best of what is, by envisioning what might be, and by speaking about what should be, the coachee will be able to shift some boundaries for his or her perception of realities. A 'new' reality will take shape for the coachee, which will enable him or her to act in a new way as a result of the conversation. Gergen's well-known rephrasing of Descartes' assumption also forms the basis of AC: *Cogito ergo sum* becomes *communicamus ergo sum*[20] (see also footnote 6 in this chapter).

2. *The principle of simultaneity*: Change begins the moment one inquires in an appreciative manner. Inquiring and change take place simultaneously, or, in other words, the future is shaped as a result of the Appreciative Inquiry that is taking place in the present. In the context of coaching, this means that what the coachee thinks and speaks about, what the coachee discovers and learns, and what inspires the coachee to create a new future are implicitly present in the question that the coach asks. The coach's questions create the fertile soil for what the coachee is able to think, discover and articulate. If the coach inquires about problems, the coachee is alerted to problems and thus adopts a problem perspective. If the coach instead inquires about the great accomplishments, strengths, hidden talents, exciting new ideas, possibilities, special successes, key values, traditions, special competences, uplifting stories, special insights, life wisdom or visions of a preferred and possible future, the result will basically be an appreciative perspective and fertile soil for life-affirming development.

---

[20]See e.g. Gergen, (2009a), p. 160.

3. *The principle of positivity*: Creating a basis for life-affirming development requires positive emotions and social attachment, aspects that can be promoted in the coaching dialogue by talking, for example, about hope, inspiration, enthusiasm/excitement, care, team spirit, support and joy. The more uplifting and positive a question is, the longer-lasting and the more successful the change will be. In the coaching conversation, the coach is a supportive and uplifting partner who helps initiate positive change processes in the coachee by virtue of his or her basic attitude. The positive effect of the conversation on the coachee's development can be strengthened by highlighting the situations where the coachee sees him/herself as an active co-creator.

4. *The poetic principle*: Life, even our own past, can be viewed as variable and malleable. The stories we have about ourselves, our family, our workplace and our career develop continually and may change over time. Some stories change in a positive direction, while others have a melancholy or even tragic note. However, any story may suddenly take a turn to become something else; for example, a dismissal may suddenly become liberating, or illness may become a much-needed break in a stressful working life. Linking past, present and future gives the story countless possible directions, and a forgotten event from the past may, for example, become the point of departure for a reinterpretation of subsequent events. The poetic principle makes the coach aware that the coachee's stories can be reframed and retold. The storyline changes in an active co-creative process with the coachee. The poetic principle is especially crucial in narrative coaching.

5. *The principle of anticipation*: Anticipating a dream and having positive images of a particular future may help create a special energy, which in turn affects the person's or the group's actions in a positive and life-affirming direction. The American doctor and psychologist Robert Plutchik (2002) defines anticipation as one of the basic emotions and associates it with enthusiasm and desire, emotional pleasure (at times also anxiety-provoking), where one looks forward to an expected or desirable event. Reference should also be made to studies about the Pygmalion effect, which can be described as a form of self-fulfilling prophecy. In that connection, Rosenthal and Jacobson (1992) have done studies on teachers' expectations of students and found that when the teachers expected high performances from certain children (as a result of a positive reputation), these children in fact showed unusual progress in their learning. Thus, reality can be affected by our expectations.

The five general AI principles were reshaped into a methodology, a change and dialogue practice, the so-called 4D-model, which can be broken down into four stages: Discovery, Dream, Design and Deliver. Orem et al. (2007) use the same stages in their process model for the coaching conversation. In the following, I present the expanded Danish 5D-version (cf. Storch & Søholm, 2005) and describe the individual stages in reference to an appreciative coaching approach (see Fig. 3.3):

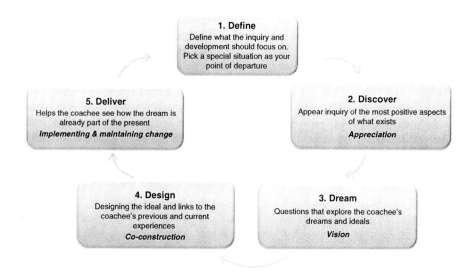

Fig. 3.3 5D-model (cf. Storch & Søholm, 2005; orginally based on Cooperrider and Srivastvas (1987) 4 D-model

The individual stages in the model will now be given concrete form and exemplified in questions for a coaching conversation with a case-person I will call Carl:

Stage 1 – Define:
The coachee presents his or her case. The coach facilitates the conversation by *enhancing the focus on a concrete area or topic* that the coachee wishes to develop, for example to improve his or her situation in the workplace, to develop certain competences, to achieve change in a particular field. In our case, Carl wants new challenges, possibly by finding a new job.

Stage 2 – Discover:
The coach begins by exploring *the most positive aspects* of the coachee's present situation. As a coach I adopt a wondering and non-judging position and ask about particularly successful episodes in Carl's working life, about where he is most effective: Can you describe tasks and situations, where you really enjoy your job or where you are really good at your job? Describe an experience where everything went exactly as you wanted! What do you actually do when things work out for you? How does it feel? In this phase there is a shift in perspective in the coachee's basic experience where there is room to talk about what works and what succeeds, and where the focus moves away from problems and shortcomings.

Stage 3 – Dream:
Based on the strength-based perspective (established in Stage 2) our focus now turns to the future and *the coachee's desires, dreams and ideals.* The coach's intention is to challenge the coachee's customary thoughts and notions by supporting him in developing and playing with future scenarios: Carl, how do you envision your

working life 1/5/10 years from now? What do you work with? What are you most engaged in then? What special competences have you developed? If you had three wishes, what would they be? What do you notice about yourself as you talk about your future?

Stage 4 – Design:
Now the emphasis is on outlining and shaping the coachee's dreams and ideals by *heightening his or her awareness of certain future scenarios* and possible paths for getting there. The coach seeks to link the specific visions of the future ideal practice (articulated in Stage 3) with the coachee's current best practice and the small successes that have already been achieved (articulated in Stage 2): The coach might ask Carl: Which aspects of your dream or vision create life and excitement for you? What are some central and non-negotiable priorities and values that you have discovered by imagining this future? What have you already done, and what could you do again to move toward this future dream? What might support you on your journey? What seeds have you already shown that might sprout and grow large? What new actions could you identify that point toward your new future? If you were already acting the way you are in your future scenario, what would you appreciate, and how would it make you happy? What makes you proud already now?

Stage 5 – Deliver:
In the final stage, the coach supports the coachee in *developing confidence and belief* in the feasibility of the outlined ideal visions and the described future as a concrete possibility. For the coachee, the key objective in this phase is to perceive and experience the dream in the present. The coach heightens the focus on what already exists and on what is important in the potential new future in the form of a specific future scenario, for example focusing on the coachee's special skills, previously achieved successes, obvious possibilities or specific individuals who could support the coachee's dream. As a coach I might ask, in what ways are you already living your dream now? Think about where we started, and where you are now! What are you already doing now that points in the directions of your dream? What could you be even more aware of doing (differently)? What new demands and commitments are you establishing for yourself? Who might support you on your way? Whom might you thank for their support? What do you most feel like initiating in the near future?

By including the basic social constructionist ideas the appreciative coach aims for a fundamental shift in a perspective or a perspective transformation. The traditional focus on shortcomings and problems is replaced with a conversation about possible positive changes that are initiated through a focus on the coachee's strengths and competences and on the possibilities offered by the environment. Gergen (2009a) expresses it as follows: "Importantly, AI locates the roots of the future within the grounds of the past; the participants are not indulging in mere pipe dreams, but drawing from their multiple potentials to generate realistic possibilities for the future" (pp. 329–330).

3.4.1.6 Narrative Theory and Practice

The narrative approach, which is clearly a further development of social constructionism, has its origins in anthropology, where narrative research has a long-standing
tradition, and from where it has spread during the past quarter of a century to the
social sciences and psychology. In a social science research perspective, narrative
studies are used as an in-depth and relevant means of portraying human experiences,
often collected by means of qualitative interviews.[21] In the post-modern world,
where the grand narratives have lost their power of identification or their legitimacy,
other people's specific experiences and stories can provide support for tackling
one's own life situation. Narrative research is often used in contexts where research
subjects face special challenges (for example health issues, unemployment, life
crises, stress, therapy). Often, there are attempts to bring the various parties in
a research process closer to a shared understanding: the researcher, the research
participants and the research recipients. The growing importance of narrative
research is related to the fact that the objectivist scientific ideal is proving less
and less useful. In this perspective, it is no longer relevant to search for universal
truths. Instead, *local truths* specific to certain groups or challenges have become
increasingly valuable for understanding and changing social reality. Today, research
with and about people is much more interested in the utility value in relation to
specific contexts where the acquired knowledge can contribute to inspiration and
reflection in relation to one's own life situation.

It is the same basic idea that is pursued when the narrative approach is
applied in practice in psychotherapy, coaching and other counselling disciplines
and dialogue forms: We can learn about ourselves through others and their
stories and narratives; for example the coach or other co-coaches can allow
themselves to be touched by the coachee's story in relation to their own life
situation. One narrative method is called *witnessing*. This is a particularly effective way of sharing experiences and social realities with each other, an effect that is especially pronounced when the narrative approach is used in a
group context, for example in narrative group coaching (see e.g. Stelter, 2010a;
Stelter, Nielsen, & Wikman, 2011 and Chap. 5). With regard to the overall
meaning of the narrative approach in organizational and conversation practices
I would point to the following arguments:

- Counteracts tendencies to social isolation and thus meets a growing demand for
  community spirit and sharing. In relation to special target groups, the narrative
  practice can also facilitate 'empowerment' and the development of social capital
  (see e.g. Stelter et al., 2011).
- Focuses on what creates meaning and identity in the person's life.

---

[21] I have myself conducted a narrative study of participants' experiences with mindfulness
meditation (Stelter, 2009a). Also later in the book I use the narrative method to present qualitative
findings from interviews with participants (Chap. 5) and expert coaches (Chap. 7). Readers who
would like insight into the narrative research are referred to e.g. Riessman (2008).

- Interweaves events that the narrator previously saw as isolated incidents.
- Helps create new stories by linking experiences and events together in a new way that is equally meaningful yet more uplifting.
- Has developed a methodology with strategies and inquiry techniques that are good at initiating change processes in individuals or an organization – methods that promote third-generation coaching in particular.

What Is a Story?

A story ties specific plots and events together to form a coherent storyline. The acknowledged narrative psychologist Theodore R. Sarbin (1911–2005) defines story as follows:

> symbolized account of actions of human beings that has a temporal dimension. The story has a beginning, middle, and an ending. The story is held together by recognizable patterns of events called plots. Central to the plot structure are human predicaments and attempted resolutions. (1986, p. 3)

Storytelling[22] is a fundamental part of being human: "Lives are told in being lived and lived in being told," says philosopher David Carr (1986, s. 61). The story has both an individual and a socio-cultural perspective:

1. *For the individual, telling something about oneself helps develop one's identity*: In interaction with others – i.e. conversation partners who respond to the story – the story makes sense of a course of events and the person him/herself. The story is a means of addressing events from the past and linking them to the present and the future. Furthermore, the story also has a performative function: It lets the person test a specific reality on the listener and thus tentatively present him/herself in a certain way to the other. In this case, the story becomes part of the person's self-presentation. The story helps invite the reactions of others, inviting them to relate to the story. The others may feel excited, touched or provoked.
2. *The story also has a socio-cultural meaning. Stories are involved in shaping culture.* That applies to all levels of culture: Stories can shape the nation, society, an organization, a working team, an association or an individual family. Individual stories can affect the general cultural stories (especially in manageable contexts like the workplace and the family). Individuals can contribute or even provide direction for some of the stories that influence the workplace. And conversely: Stories that shape our culture (for example in the workplace) influence the individual's stories (e.g. the shocking story about the boss that one's husband or wife tells after work). Bruner (2006) describes the fundamental role of the story by highlighting the link between individual and culture:

> ... *the* principal way in which our minds, our 'realities', get shaped to the patterns of daily cultural life is through the stories we tell, listen to, and read – true or fictional. We 'become'

---

[22]In this context I treat *story* and *narratives* as synonyms (cf. The New Oxford Dictionary of English, 1999).

active participants in our culture mainly through the narratives we share in order to 'make sense' of what is happening around us, what has happened, what may happen. We pattern our realities on these narratives and come to live in a world fashioned by them. (p. 14; italics in original)

In the coaching dialogue, the coach influences the coachee's story by asking story-generating questions (a process that is facilitated by involving the factors mentioned below). Shaping a story in the coaching dialogue is cumbersome at times and initially incoherent, as the story takes shape gradually during the conversation and is not necessarily clear from the outset. The coachee brings up certain events and experiences, but it is the coach who guides the coachee by means of questions, for example by creating attention points or by inquiring about specific individual or being having an interest in understanding certain connections between people and events. For both parties, the purpose of the narrative process is to create a coherent structure that is meaningful for them both. In order to tie events together and thus form a coherent story, the narrative has to contain certain factors that help give the story shape (Gergen, 1994; Gergen & Gergen, 2006; McAdams, 1993; Polkinghorne, 1988):

- The story should take place within a *well-defined context*: It is the coach's responsibility to help the coachee clarify the situation and context.
- The actors of the story are characterized by certain character features and a stable *identity*: A well-shaped story contains persons as well as objects that maintain the same identity throughout the story. Once the persons or the plot has been defined in the story they maintain their identity throughout the rest of the story. There may be exceptions to this, which will have a significant impact on the story as a whole. Furthermore, the identities of certain individuals may also be portrayed in the framework of a developmental process.
- In many cases, the story begins with an *initial event* that provides a certain dynamic in the story: On Monday morning I came in to work and started the day with a very important conversation with employee Y.
- The story often progresses in a way where certain individuals express a striving for a specific goal. In the coaching dialogue, the coachee expresses a *specific intent* in relation to the ongoing developmental process. Intent is based on certain convictions and values that are important to bring out as part of the coachee's stories. But it is also important for the coachee to have an opportunity to examine the intent of other actors. Intents that may deviate from the narrator's own, and which thus constitute a conflict potential or a source of tension between the parties.
- The story develops a dynamic by highlighting certain *consequences and reactions*, as they play out among the actors.
- Normally, a story has a climax, as the whole story approaches a high point. In the coaching dialogue it is important to highlight this climax as a potential point of departure for a change process.
- The interaction among the various actions and events are the basis for defining the *plot* of the story. The plot is designed to create a certain meaning by describing

the actors' experiences and actions in relation to each other and by structuring
the events in a certain way. The narrator strives to present the plot and thus the
whole story with a particular intent. Hence, stories seen from another actor's
perspective will sometimes follow a fundamentally different progression.

Gergen (1994) distinguishes between three basic types of narrative forms: (1) *The
stability narrative*, which links events so that the individual's trajectory remains
largely unchanged in relation to goal or outcomes, (2) *the progressive narrative*,
where events are linked together in such a way that the movement over time is
rising, i.e. the story becomes increasingly positive, and (3) *the regressive narrative*,
where the events are linked in such a way that the movement over time is descending
and increasingly negative. The narrative coach strives to add new elements to the
coachee's story to enable a shift in dynamic during the coaching process, from a
regressive to a more progressive trajectory.

In his book *The stories we live by* (1993), McAdams notes a difference between
two types of narratives: *story* and *myth*. He defines myth as the type of narrative
that conveys a form of truth about a person, a group or a culture. A personal
myth, for example, becomes a truth for the individual that forms the basis of his
or her identity. Often, the individual is only likely to contact a psychologist or a
coach once the personal myth becomes a burden and makes life difficult for him
or her. Myths are a source of continuity, and this continuity is essential for the
development of one's personal identity; thus, the myth remains valuable as long as it
does not cause problems. Myths should be deconstructed in coaching when they are
a source of grief or problems, or when the coachee wishes to break free from them.
This is where the *story* comes in as an alternative narrative format. A *story* has
a more dynamic character. The narrative coach works from the basic assumption
that narratives can be transformed and developed – a position that clearly lies in
extension of social constructionist epistemology. It is therefore never too late to
create an uplifting narrative (story) about oneself in relation to specific events and
periods. The progression of the narrative intervention is from myth to story, which
in turn may become a new myth – for as long as it lasts.

Key Assumptions in the Narrative Approach

In my view, the narrative approach expands on social constructionist epistemology
and also reintroduces dimensions that have otherwise been banned from social
constructionist thinking. For example, I am seeing a clearer acknowledgement of
intentionality as important for human actions. In the following, I will highlight three
key assumptions:

1. *Agency* describes the human capacity to choose among possibilities, make
   choices, mobilize energy and take deliberate action based on personal considerations and plans. In this view, the individual is seen to take a proactive relationship
   to his or her world: People are capable of taking initiatives and of taking life into
   their own hands. Individuals can act on the basis of their intentions, which spring

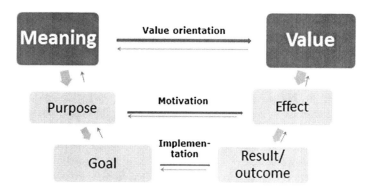

Fig. 3.4 Levels of intentional orientation: meanings and values as central in the concept of intentionality (see also Nitsch, 1986; Stelter, 2009a)

from their active interaction with their social and material environment, and not only on the basis of outside impulses or 'fate'. When an individual speaks about his or her actions, the narrative takes its point of departure in certain events, which are linked and structured around a plot, so that the story makes sense to the actor/narrator. Narrative thinking uses the metaphor of the *'landscape of action'*, a concept that was originally developed by the literature theorists Greismas and Courtès, which Bruner transferred to psychology, and White applied in narrative therapy (Bruner, 1990a; Greismas & Courtes, 1976; White, 2007).

2. *Intentionality* describes the actor's continual intent in relation to the world as expressed in the person's intentions in relation to specific 'others', tasks or situations. The person always relates to his or her social and physical environment. Generally, intentionality is reflected in the person's values and unfolds in meaningful action. In coaching conversations it is reflected, for example, in the coachee's aspirations and striving in relation to specific work tasks or a possible future. Intentionality can be represented hierarchically (see Fig. 3.4):

Narrative coaching operates especially on the top level, where the value perspective is included with a focus on the meanings of actions. This marks a clear difference from first-generation coaching (e.g. the GROW model), which is mostly concerned about the goal. In narrative practice one encounters the metaphor of the *landscape of identity*[23] (or *landscape of consciousness*), which the authors mentioned above use as their second dimension, and which should always be viewed in interaction with the landscape of action described above. The metaphor of the landscape of identity focuses on the actor's thoughts, feelings, convictions or beliefs (Bruner, 1986) and thus on the coachee's self-concept and

---

[23]I use the same term as other narratively based authors (e.g. Nielsen, 2010), although one might with equal right speak of the landscape of intentionality. However, I find White's (2007) term 'landscape of consciousness' less apt than my chosen term.

self-perceived identity. Unlike the social constructionist position, this view treats identity as something that also reflects the individual's special convictions and values. Narrative coaching conversations aim in particular to explore the mutual exchange between the *landscape of action* and the *landscape of identity* in order to create a depth in the conversation that will enable the coachee to understand him/herself and his or her actions.

3. *Deconstruction* expresses the potential for change and additional possible interpretations and was originally a counter-reaction to idealist philosophy and structuralist literature theory. Deconstructionists (e.g. Derrida, 1978) oppose structuralist text reduction, which appears as an attempt to eliminate the internal contradictions in text or speech. In the deconstructionist perspective, by contrast, there is an assumption that the story may hold multiple possible interpretations and thus multiple realities. In the narrative coaching conversation, the coach and coachee seek to reinterpret certain dominant and potentially difficult stories about the coachee's reality, myths that 'are due' for reinterpretation and reframing. According to White (2004), deconstruction deals with procedures that undermine the taken-for-granted understanding of life and identity. With reference to Bourdieu (1988), White aims to 'exoticise the familiar', i.e. to break with one's original intimate relationship with certain ways of living and thinking and go on a journey of discovery in one's own life, which will eventually lead to a new plot in selected stories.

In the following chapter (Chap. 4) I will return to the narrative approach, presenting my own understanding of it and its translation into a practice that is also supplemented with considerations from what is described in the following: collaborative practice.

3.4.1.7 Collaborative Theory and Practice

Collaborative theory and practice places renewed focus on interpersonal relationships and communities as sources of knowledge and the generation of meaning (see e.g. Anderson & Gehart, 2007). As a dialogue form, the collaborative practice is less structured than the narrative approach. The coach will be more likely to follow his or her own inner 'compass' and co-reflect on what the coachee brings up. The collaborative approach is a refreshing response to the growing social isolation and thus a counter-balance to the growing trend toward individualization in society, which leaves it up to the individual to find the answers to his or her own challenges and existential issues. Collaborative theory helps produce a practical concretization of social constructionist thinking. In the collaborative practice, people are seen as existing in mutual relationships, and the parties receive support to find answers to individually meaningful questions from one or several listening and co-reflective 'others'. The traditional way of learning from someone else has been to be *persuaded* and thus convinced that the other, by virtue of his or her professional authority or life experience, could reasonably be assumed to 'be right'. But in a time when persons of (professional) authority find it increasingly difficult to offer firm and clear-cut answers to complicated work and life issues it is becoming increasingly important to *provide a space for conversation and dialogue*, where the parties can share their challenges and experiences. Here it is essential to have a dialogue partner who is able to listen rather than offer recommendations or advice, which in many cases is not quite right for the specific situation and challenges the other is facing. In this sense, collaborative theory and practice follow the main premise of social constructionism: We create meaning in relationships, not individually. The individual does not control the outcome of the conversation, the relationship or the situation; it is the parties' collaborative meaning-making (see Sect. 3.1.2) that ensures quality and progress in the conversation, the relationship or the situation (McNamee, 2004). The first-order change perspective, which has worked in the past, and which now is encountering limitations due to the (hyper-) complexity of the world, is supplemented with a *second-order change perspective*, which relies on a living exchange between the conversation parties and their positions, and which, ideally, can help initiate a change process for all the parties in the contexts where they work and live. The 'best' or 'right' way to provide information – a requirement of good counselling or leadership in the age of modernity – is replaced by *spaces for collaborative conversations and development*, which are better suited to facilitating personal, social or organization transformation processes in the current late- or post-modern age. To quote McNamee (p. 18):

> Our focus is centered on the participants engaged in the immediate moment and the wide array of both common and diverse voices, relations, communities, and experiences that each brings to the current context.

In the following, I describe some of the basic conditions of collaborative practice:

1. *Responsiveness*: A key condition of the collaborative dialogue form is the mutual responsiveness of all the participants. The collaborative practice thus facilitates an entirely new conversation culture, where one listens to the other and in turn strives to inspire the other with one's own thoughts and reflections on a particular story or description that one of the participants presented. Wittgenstein (1953, p. 122) speaks of a new form of understanding: "that kind of understanding which consists in 'seeing connections'." In this sense, listening is more than simply understanding what was said. Listening is not just about absorbing information but involves making meaning for oneself as a listener and inviting the other into the reflections it gives rise to. The original speaker then listens to other person's reflections and considers them. The complexity increases, the more times the process is repeated, and the more people are involved. The contours of a new landscape of meaning emerge as a result of the participants' way of being with each other. Katz and Shotter (2004) describe this interaction as follows: "To think we are in only a mechanical cause-and-effect relation to events in our surroundings is to ignore the crucial role of our spontaneous, living bodily responsiveness to the other and the otherness around us" (p. 73).

2. *Relational attunement*: The previous quote leads us to the special conditions that need to be in place in the collaborative, responsiveness-oriented dialogue

form. The participants have to demonstrate a willingness to be involved in each other and to show sympathy, in contrast to a conversation culture where the goal is to prove oneself right. Instead, the goal is to develop a presence and an attunement where the participants are constantly trying to tune in to each other. When listening to someone's story, one should pay attention to oneself and the, initially often implicit, sensations the story produces, and then reflect on the effect that the story has on oneself. In this way, the conversation partner's story or challenge becomes one's own. With inspiration from the Danish theologian and philosopher Løgstrup, the Danish educational researcher Kirsten Fink-Jensen (1998) speaks of *attunement* as an articulation where one gives shape to something by using a variety of expressions, and where this 'something' may be a bodily sensation, a sensory impression or a particular personally theme. To further elaborate on these thoughts, I would describe relational attunement as a *shared or co-created articulation*, where a sensation, a sensory impression or a theme is addressed collectively, and where the participants achieve a meeting. People become each other's sounding boards. Relational attunement generates new knowledge that can only take shape in a relationship characterized by mutual responsiveness. The process may resemble a dance, where the partners find a common rhythm and reach out to each other through mutual understanding and shared meaning-making – with respect for the other and themselves, with the knowledge that there will always be differences, and with the acceptance that everybody goes their separate ways after the final dialogue.

3. *Withness-thinking, knowing-with or the art of being with the other*: Relational attunement is achieved by means of a special form of co-thinking, which Shotter (2006) calls withness-thinking (I briefly mentioned this concept in Chap. 2, in the section on coaching and learning as a social and collaborative practice; see Sect. 2.3.2.). From the listener's position the goal is to develop a special form of sensory sympathy with the other, not necessarily as an attempt at feeling and thinking like the other but as a sense of the other's position from one's own life perspective and position. This does not quite match the typical understanding of empathy, defined as *having understanding for someone else's feelings and being able to put oneself in the other person's place*. It is in fact closer to *empátheia*, Greek for passion or compassion. It is a passion to immerse oneself in the narrator's situation, allowing oneself to be gripped by it and linking the narrator's story to one's own life and experiences or thoughts while listening. Shotter (p. 600) describes withness-thinking as a way of being with a strong element of body sensation and embodiment.

> *Withness (dialogic)-talk/thinking* occurs in those reflective interactions that involve our coming into living, interactive contact with an other's living being, with their utterances, with their bodily expressions, with their words, their 'works'. It is a meeting of outsides, of surfaces, of two kinds of 'flesh' (Merleau-Ponty, 1968), such that they come into 'touch' or 'contact' with each other. ... In the interplay of living moments intertwining with each other, new possibilities of relation are engendered, new interconnections are made, new 'shapes' of experience can emerge.

The point is thus not to interpret what one hears or to attempt to reach a 'correct' understanding of the story. It is not a *representation* or a depiction of what the other person 'really' means and thinks. This makes it clear that we cannot actually hear and see what is going on in the other person and in his or her world. The best we can do is to influence the way we think and act, based on what we hear and see. What the other person says may cause the listener to think and to find new ways of understanding the world and acting in the world. We can share these reflections with the speaker who inspired them in us. *Withness-thinking* becomes a shared process of knowledge production between the dialogue partners. In a mutual process of withness-thinking and presence, the conversation becomes a dynamic dialogue between both parties or – if it takes place in a group – among the dialogue partners. Dialogue is understood here in its original Greek meaning: Dia-log = through (διά/dia) speech or discourse (λόγος/logos). The participants develop in a mutual relationship *through speech and discourse*. The dialogue becomes the art of conversation, where one is simultaneously with the other and with oneself.

4. *Conversation ethics*: In a coaching relationship, the coach's inquiry is aimed especially at the coachee's experiential world. In the coaching dialogue, development happens on the basis of the coach's withness-thinking and a sympathetic position. In this process, both/all participants[24] move forward and develop. Questions are initially primarily aimed at the coach's need to engage in withness-thinking in relation to the coachee's life context and to develop a sense of what is happening. Unlike a strictly narrative inquiry strategy, which follows a particular structure (Lowe, 2005), Shotter and Katz (1996) speak about '*striking moments*'. These are the moments when one or both participants experience challenge, concern, confusion or movement in a new direction, where a new perspective emerges, and where the dialogue is pushed toward transformation and development. It is the sense of being present and allowing oneself to be moved by the other's thoughts and reflections. A special conversation or discourse ethics is beginning to take shape as the basis of the special qualities that characterize this dialogue. One is present for the other and for oneself. One creates meaning with each other and finds ways of creating development for oneself and for the other (Anderson, 2007a). One listens to the other and attempts to understand the dialogue partner on his or her own terms, and one engages in withness-thinking and responds. And here, one's reflections on one's own position help generate the developmental potential of the dialogue. The *normatively ethical position* is that the other may learn and develop by engaging with me in my role as a dialogue partner who looks only at myself, my own life world and my understanding of it. The dialogue is the concrete expression and

---

[24] In group coaching, hopefully everybody moves forward – albeit each in their own way.

application of the *normatively ethical position*. Here it also becomes crucial for the coach to inquire whether and how the coachee perceives the relationship as supportive (see also de Haan, 2008).

Collaborative practice can be applied across a variety of conversation contexts, for example in meetings, team development or creative developmental processes. In these contexts all the participants perceive themselves as equal partners from the outset. Power and status issues must be minimized. In coaching or other consultancy conversations, the situation is slightly different. Here, the coachee assumes that the coach manages the dialogue, and that the focus is on the coachee. Collaborative practice is assumed to be the dialogue form that most clearly abandons the use of a more or less specific set of questions and inquiry structure for the coach. By engaging in collaborative practice the coach attempts – as much as it is possible in the coaching context – to establish a *symmetrical relationship* with the coachee. However, this striving for symmetry should be considered an ideal, which also defines the aspiration of the protreptic dialogue[25] (Kirkeby, 2009), but which may at times be unattainable, for example because of the coachee's special developmental aspirations.

How to integrate collaborative theory and practice into coaching is discussed in Chap. 4, which seeks to merge this approach with other approaches, especially the narrative approach.

3.5 Additional Theories

As is clear from the selection of theories presented here, I operate predominantly in the universe of social constructionist theory. But, as I have already discussed in connection with considerations on identity and learning theory, I also consider it essential to be open to other theoretical approaches that involve perspectives from experiential psychology and emotional psychology. I do this cautiously, to avoid creating an arbitrary eclectic theoretical position. The prerequisite of successful coaching processes and other helping conversations is that the coach or psychologist is aware of his or her theoretical framework and applies it consistently and with care (see Grencavage & Norcross, 1990).

In the following, I will look at three approaches:

- Positive psychology
- Experience- and emotion-focused approaches
- Mentalization

---

[25]Protreptics or philosophical (management) coaching aims to direct the coachee (e.g. the executive, the mid-level manager and the employee) and, ultimately, the company toward what is essential for the individual and for the community. In this form of coaching, the coach and the coachee together focus on reflecting on the fundamental values that guide the individual's actions.

3.5.1 Positive Psychology

Traditionally, psychological science and practice has focused on mental dysfunction, human psychological disorders such as psychotic symptoms (e.g. schizophrenia, dementia, mania), affective disorders (e.g. depression), anxiety and stress-related conditions, eating disorders, personality disorders and substance abuse. With then President of the American Psychological Association Martin Seligman as one of the initiators, a psychology was developed that aims to study the emergence, form and effect of positive emotions as well as human strength, happiness and well-being (Seligman, 2002; Seligman & Czikszentmihalyi, 2000). This new focus in psychology appears a perfect match for the basic developmental intention that is pursued by coaches and coaching psychologists. Considering that most coaching clients are not essentially suffering from any psychological disorders but are instead interested in focusing on learning, growth and more constructive ways of handling certain challenges, it seems relevant to include positive psychology in coaching (see e.g. Biswas-Diener, 2010).

There is, however, a risk associated with positive psychology, which is easily associated with an ideology of 'positive thinking' – and indeed, the boundary is blurred, at least to a psychological layperson. The consequences of positive thinking are addressed critically by Ehrenreich (2009). She illustrates how this antirational ideology of positive thinking has virtually entered into a symbiosis with the speculative venture capitalism that has been so pervasive in recent decades. Various forms of 'pop-psychology' have made a flourishing trade in lectures, workshops, CDs, self-help literature etc. claiming that people can overcome illness and other existential problems by altering their basic attitude and working positively with themselves. Positive thinking may become one of the sophisticated self-control strategies that already dominate our society, and which have so many negative consequences (for example in the form of eating disorders). These self-control strategies make the individual fully and solely responsibility for his or her personal development and well-being. As such it places a heavy psychological burden on those who fail to succeed in life. Hence, coaches, psychologists and others in the helping professions should carefully consider how they go about including strategies from positive psychology in their work with their clients.

With this critical note in mind, I will now focus on the basic convictions and research presented by positive psychology. The main focus of the research has been directed at phenomena such as positive emotions, resilience, strength, optimism, hope, meaning and flow. Psychopathology and a focus on psychological disorders are replaced with a focus on *flourishing*. Fredrickson (2004) developed the so-called *broaden-and-build* theory, which describes the influence of positive emotions on the individual's personal, physical, intellectual, social and psychological resources. Researchers speak of a positive spiral, where emotions and actions mutually condition each other in a positive direction. Based on this research, Fredrickson and Losada (2005) have calculated the optimal ratio of 3:1 between experiences of positive and negative emotions (see www.positivityratio.com). This ratio underscores that it is not desirable to neglect or avoid negative emotions; in fact, a certain amount of negative experiences helps strengthen our psychological resilience. Fredrickson (2009) describes ten forms of positivity: joy, gratitude, serenity, interest, hope, pride, amusement, inspiration, awe and love.

With a view to developing resilience, the researchers point to a particular underlying psychological attitude (Seligman, 2002; Reivich & Shatte, 2002): The key condition for developing psychological resilience is the presence of *optimistic explanation or attribution styles*, that is, the effort to avoid certain unhelpful explanation patterns such as jumping to conclusions, tunnel vision, magnifying the negative and minimizing the positive, personalizing, externalizing guilt, over-generalizing, irrational mind-reading or emotional reasoning (worst-case scenario thinking).

The Values-In-Action inventory of strengths (VIA) (www.viacharacter.org) is a well-known inventory of positive psychology. The assessment is based on 24 character strengths grouped into six basic values: wisdom and knowledge, courage, humanity, justice, temperance and transcendence (Peterson & Seligman, 2004). Research has found that taking a strength-based approach to work, parenting or relationship promotes resilience, confidence, vitality, life perspective and optimism (see e.g. Park & Peterson, 2006; Peterson, Park, & Seligman, 2006; Peterson, Ruch, Beermann, Park, & Seligman, 2007).

How this strength-orientation and an underlying positive perspective can be in-tegrated in practice, and how positive psychology can be linked with the previously presented approaches will be addressed with the use of some concrete examples, which are also relevant for and applicable in coaching:

- *Three good things*: In all simplicity, this exercise involves writing down three good events from the day before going to bed, for a period of time. Studies (Seligman, Steen, Park, & Peterson, 2005) have found that this exercise increases the feeling of happiness and reduces depression. The basic principle of the exercise can be applied in a variety of ways, for example via the following coaching question: When were you really pleased with yourself today? or, Which particular success could you mention in relation to your work/your relationship with X in the past week? In this type of exercise or question, the link to narrative-social constructionist thinking is obvious. Here, the exercise would be used to deconstruct a particular dominant reality or story/myth that one has constructed about oneself. The intention with tasks or questions about strengths is to help the coachee create a new and alternative self-narrative.
- *Gratitude exercise*: This exercise involves thinking of someone that one feels profound gratitude toward. The task involves drafting a letter to this person, telling the person what he/she has done for one, how much one appreciates this, and how it has affected one's life and development. To take the exercise a step further, one might arrange to meet with the person, in part to read this letter aloud. This exercise has clear links to narrative practice. In a coaching context, the coach would attempt to inquire about particular persons that the coachee may

have forgotten about,[26] who may be found to have played a special role, and to whom the coachee is grateful for the impact the person has had on his or her life. In a collaborative group coaching process one may show gratitude toward a fellow coachee, who has enabled new insights and understanding by witnessing and reflecting.

- *Savouring*: This exercise is about developing a special sense and taste for a particular life situation and its special meaning for oneself and one's development (see more in Bryant & Veroff, 2007). The coach may try to direct the coachee's attention to the specifically valuable quality of the situation, for example by acting on behalf of the coachee to verbalize the potential meaning of the situation for the coachee. The coach may enhance the coachee's ability to savour the situation by asking especially attention-focusing questions. Essentially, this type of dialogue is no different from other appreciative processes or appreciative inquiry.
- *The potential uplifting future*: This involves inquiring about a potential future, for example once the person 'succeeds', when a particular conflict has been resolved, when a difficult employee or co-worker has changed considerably and might even be a pleasure to work with. The goal is to envision oneself (and others) in the situation as vividly as possible. This may take the form of a miracle question (see Sect. 3.4.1.5) or a homework assignment where a scenario is described in a longer narrative.
- *Use your strength in a new way*: This involves imagining how one might use an already acknowledged strength in a new way. A small example: In a group coaching intervention with young Team Danmark sport talents[27] who had just begun the first year of their upper secondary education, it became clear that the participants experienced their school day as overwhelming and very stressful. We focused on how good they were at structuring their time in relation to their athletic career, and how they were able to juggle long training hours, transportation and preparing for and participating in competitions. I made them aware that they were actually really, really good at structuring their time. They were rather surprised to find that they possessed this strength. Then I asked them, 'How can you transfer this strength to the new challenges you are facing in school?' From a narrative perspective the intervention could be interpreted as follows: Their experience of 'lacking the skills to manage the challenges of studying' was *deconstructed* with an emphasis on their capacity for structuring

---

[26]White (2007) speaks about "the absent but implicit". In any story we select certain events and repress or forget others that might have some importance for the creation of a potentially more uplifting story. In the coaching process it is important to highlight and articulate the positive, the successes or important persons that were left out of the original story. That creates a basis for reauthoring the original story.

[27]This intervention was part of a research project in the Team Danmark line at the upper secondary school *Falkonergårdens Gymnasium*. The project is described in Stelter et al. (2011), among other sources. More on that in Chap. 5.

their time in relation to their sport. I highlighted their *agency* and thus created the condition for them to develop a new story about their capacity and ability to create a good everyday life at school.

These examples highlight the inclusion of positive psychology in other forms of coaching. In the social constructionist universe, for example at the TAOS Institute (www.taosinstitute.net), there is debating about how positive psychology might be integrated with Appreciative Inquiry (AI) and other social constructionist practices. The examples presented here suggest the potential.

3.5.2 *Experiential and Emotion-Focused Approaches*

The narrative-social constructionist tradition sparks an interest (in me) to turn to the person him/herself, just temporarily, with a few questions and a specific focus on the person's subjective experiences, perceptions and emotions. This interest is shared by several theorists within the narrative-social constructionist framework who have turned their gaze in the same direction.

From an epistemological perspective, *narrative psychology* may be considered an expansion of the social constructionist position that reintroduces experiential, bodily and emotion-focused dimensions (Crossley, 2000; Polkinghorne, 1988; Stam, 2001; Stelter, 2008a), which are the subject of interest in the phenomenological and the humanist-existentialist tradition, among others (see also the section on identity theory in Chap. 2). From a platform of narrative psychology, Crossley (2003) expresses a need for a different form of psychology that shows restraint with regard to exclusively defining the self in linguistic and relational discourses instead of considering and examining the individual's subjectivity by focusing on experiences, embodiment and the individual's affective/emotional orientation to the world. In particular, Shotter and Lannaman (2002), Stam (1998) and Sampson (1996) have been interested in combining phenomenological and social constructionist thinking, without proposing a naturalist position where the person is viewed in the light of certain stable character features but instead in a perspective that includes experience, perceptions and emotions as the basis of the individual's creation of a self-narrative. This inclusion of perception and experience is not similarly evident in narrative therapy and coaching. How this experiential tradition can be incorporated productively in narrative coaching will be demonstrated in the presentation of my own approach in Chap. 4.

In the following, I present two theoretical positions, both with a focus on subjective experiences and emotions and their impact on the development of individuals and relationships: First I will focus on *first-person experiences* and their impact on the development of the aesthetic-sensory dimension of coaching and other helping conversations. Next, I present *emotion-focused therapy*, which may serve as a source of inspiration for addressing the subjective aspect in the coaching conversation. In closing, I briefly outline a *mentalization-based approach* that aims to focus on our awareness of our own mental state.

3.5.2.1 First-Person Experiences as the Basis of Aesthetic-Sensory Processes in Coaching

In the following I outline a theoretical foundation for sensory focusing – a focus that aims to strengthen the individual's direct involvement and action potential in specific contexts. I view aesthetic experiences as a special cognition process that is based on bodily-sensory involvement from a *first-person perspective*, a pre-reflexive approach to the world that does not directly provide access to reflexive and verbalized cognition. According to Varela and Shear (1999), first-person events are "lived *experience* associated with cognitive and mental events" (p. 1; italics in original). As an expansion on the traditional understanding, the cognitive aspect in Varela and Shear's understanding thus also includes embodied and experiential components. Below, I describe the special character of the first-person perspective, which also serves as a basis for understanding aesthetic-sensory perception and experience:

1. The first-person approach is a bodily-sensory and *embodied perspective*. This means that cognition is situative, concrete and based in the body. This understanding is also gaining ground in cognitive science – as a move away from the notion that our cognition and thinking function more or less like a computer and toward an understanding that rests on sensory-motor coordination and integration. Varela, Thompson, and Rosch (1993) speaks of cognition as *enaction*, writing

   We propose as a name the term *enactive* to emphasize the growing conviction that cognition is not the representation of a pre-given world by a pre-given mind but is rather the enactment of a world and a mind on the basis of a history of the variety of actions that a being in the world performs. (p. 9)

2. Via *the immediate, sensory experience and orientation* that an embodied first-person perspective can provide, the individual gains access to an understanding of him/herself and the world that goes deeper than a reflected and language-based understanding. The aesthetic-sensory understanding is achieved by means of an analogue (i.e. holistic) form of information processing, where the world is understood as a whole, not in fragments.

3. The first-person perspective provides access to *pre-reflexive and implicit knowledge*, but because of its lack of linguistic explicitness, it is a challenge to generate dialogue about this knowledge. Some approaches and strategies have attempted to bridge the gap between sensory and linguistic communication (Gendlin, 1997; Stelter, 2010a; Stevens, 2000; Varela et al., 1993).

4. The sensory-aesthetic and first-person perspective is based on the individual's direct relationship with the specific situation that is rooted through *concrete* or *imagined actions* (e.g. visualization). According to Varela et al. (1993), the *first-person approach* is constituted via actions that are sensorily guided and situated. The body incorporates the situation, and the self is anchored in the context. This sensory awareness forms the basis for a meaning-making understanding of the situation.

5. The first-person approach generates *personal meanings* based on the person's perception, interpretation and understanding of the situation. The person senses his or her environment and creates his or her own realities through meaning-making interactions with the current context. Meaning emerges via the person's *actions* in the situation with *the lived body*[28] as the central point of reference (Merleau-Ponty, 2012). By incorporating the environment, the person experiences the situation as meaningful.

6. The first-person approach is oriented toward *knowing-how* (Ryle, 1949), i.e. I am involved in the situation; I am sensorily guided by my immediate involvement and actions in the situation; I am in the situation via my pre-reflexive intentionality, which is rooted in practice; I am not concerned about rules for my actions; things happen as I act. My actions are based on spontaneous and non-verbal knowledge. I know how to proceed. My actions are part of my sensory-motor habits.

This first-person approach may be viewed as a sensory and experiential foundation of the self, where the development of the self is driven by the interaction between person and environment in the field of concrete actions. The roots of the self stem from the individual's embodied presence in the world. In this connection, Merleau-Ponty (2012) uses the term *body schema*, a term that characterizes the body's experiential and dynamic behaviour in specific environment situations. In the body schema, the body's habits and implicit knowledge manifest themselves. Sensory-aesthetic experiences in the first-person perspective are associated with the pre-reflexive and tacit knowledge that the person develops and applies in context: I know how to act in this situation, but I find it difficult to put this knowledge into words. My dialogue with my environment is often pre-verbal. My sensory relationship is given, as my body is anchored in the situation. Person and environment form a whole, and words often simply get 'in the way'. A verbalization of sensory-aesthetic experiences requires a *transformation* (Stelter, 2010a): Felt sense (Gendlin, 1997) is transformed in a symbolization process to form a verbal expression. How this verbalization can be initiated by a coach will be addressed in Chap. 4.

3.5.2.2 Emotion-Focused Approach/Therapy (EMT)

Emotion-focused approach/therapy (EMT) is a recent development in the humanist and experiential therapy forms that emerged after World War 2 as the so-called third wave in psychotherapy (Greenberg, 2002). Like behaviourism and cognitive therapy in the second wave, they emerged as a challenge to the prevailing psychoanalytical position. The experiential approaches focus on the meaning of life and on

---

[28]In the English-language phenomenological literature, the term would be *the lived body*, in German the term would be *Leib*. The essence is the sensing body, which acts as the person's anchor in the world.

helping clients achieve a meaningful existence (Wampold, 2010a). In a theoretical sense, these approaches are based on humanist-existentialist philosophers such as Kierkegaard, Husserl and Heidegger.

EMT is presented here as part of a therapy universe, but certain key ideas also apply to coaching. The key aspect of the approach is *an emphasis on emotions* as the target and basis of change, the importance of relationships and a *new perception of the self* (oneself) as the basis of change. The role of the therapist or coach is to act as a sort of process consultant.

Wampold (2010a) mentions certain additional shared characteristics of therapy and other helping conversations: (1) a phenomenological perspective, which means that therapy should develop an understanding of the client's life perspective, (2) the assumption that human beings strive for growth and self-actualization, (3) a belief that human beings are autonomous, and (4) respect for all individuals, regardless of their roles or actions.

Greenberg, who is a professor of psychology in Toronto, Canada, and the head of The Emotion-Focused Therapy Clinic, is both a practitioner and a researcher who has studied and written extensively on change processes in psychotherapy. In cooperation with others, Greenberg (Elliott & Greenberg, 2007) has developed Emotion-Focused Therapy (EFT) with inspiration from two of the most influential experiential therapy forms: Carl Rogers' person-centred therapy (Rogers, 1942, 1951) and gestalt therapy (Perls, Goodman, & Hefferline, 1951). EFT[29] was developed on the basis of a 25-year research programme on psychotherapy, and Elliott and Greenberg (2007), who were involved in developing the programme, characterize it as an evidence-based therapy method. EFT work is framed by an understanding that considers emotion an essential source of human growth and meaning-making processes. There are five conditions (Elliott & Greenberg) that any therapist has to meet to work within the EFT framework: (1) recognition of (neo-)humanistic values, (2) knowledge of process-experiential emotion theory, (3) a person-centred but process-guiding relational stance, (4) an empathic and exploratory response style and (5) a marker-guided and evidence-based task strategy. These five conditions will be explained in the following:

Neo-Humanistic Values

EFT considers *emotional experience* a dynamic process that is crucial for all human functioning. With an *emotionally present and genuine* approach, the therapist promotes the human attachment process and thus enables new client experiences. *Agency* and *self-determination* are considered fundamental, adaptively developed

---

[29] Initially (late 1980s/early 1990s) the therapy form was called 'process-experiential therapy', while the term 'emotion-focused therapy' referred to a related form of couples therapy, but since the late 1990s, the term emotion-focused therapy has been used about both couples and individual therapy.

human motivations, and *growth*, according to EFT, results from innate curiosity and adaptive emotional processes, thus leading differentiation and adaptive flexibility.

Emotion Theory

According to process-experiential emotion theory, emotion gives people the capacity to process or 'digest' complex and situationally relevant information quickly and automatically in order to be able to act to meet important organismic needs, i.e. to live in accordance with the sense of perception a person has of him/herself in his or her own experience (Rogers, 1959). Emotion is seen as crucial to human well-being, functioning and change, and our *emotional schemas* – implicit, idiosyncratic structures of human experience – form the basis of self-organizing processes such as consciousness, action and identity. The therapist or coach has to help the client understand and transform his or her emotional schemas by means of *empathic listening* and *expressive interventions*. By reflecting on and reassessing his or her emotional schemas the client ideally learns to develop more adaptive emotional responses and is thus able to meet specific challenges more capably.

A Person-Centred Yet Process-Guiding Relational Stance

This requirement is about a certain way of communicating with the clients, which is described as a mix of *following* and *guiding*: Essentially, the therapist or coach should follow the client by appreciating the client's initiative and acknowledging the client as a genuine and active agent who is seeking to make meaning in his or her life. At the same time, the therapist or coach also acts as a sort of experience guide for the client. The therapist or coach guides the process by actively guiding the client *toward something*.

The optimal therapy/coaching situation is described as an active collaboration between the client and the therapist/coach, where following and guiding are integrated in creative tension. Importantly, the therapist/coach should remain focused on the client's experience and present his or her interventions as options rather than expert statements or claims of truth.

Empathic and Exploratory Response Style

Empathic exploration as a special therapeutic response pattern employs *exploratory reflections*, where the goal is to convey empathy and to facilitate the client's reflection process. Another important part of this process is *exploratory questions* such as, What are you experiencing right now? or, Where in your body is that feeling located?

This therapeutic response form is described as engaged and expressive but also as empathic and gently probing. The goal is to promote the client's self-exploration of his or her own *present felt sense* (see also Gendlin, 1997).

A Marker-Guided and Evidence-Based Task Strategy

EFT has developed evidence-based descriptions of therapeutic markers and tasks in conversation sessions. Markers are client behaviours in sessions that signal the client's readiness to address a particular problem, topic or task. An example is a *self-critical split marker*, where part of the client criticizes another part of him/herself.

The task of the therapist/coach is to bring current objectives into the session, for example resolving the conflict that may arise in connection with the experience of a self-critical split. Briefly put, the therapist/coach first listens for possible task markers and then offers appropriate interventions; i.e. the therapist/coach first follows the client and the task the client presents through the markers and then guides the client in a productive process of addressing these tasks.

In addition to these main features, EFT includes six treatment principles: EFT is based on an empathic relationship, where the therapist/coach is emotionally present, respectful and very aware of the client's experience. The relationship should create a safe and focused atmosphere that enables the client to express and explore his or her personal problems and emotional suffering.

The first and main principle therefore is *empathic attunement*. This implies, among other things, that the therapist/coach has to give up pre-conceived notions about the client; further, that the therapist/coach actively engages with the client's experiential world, capturing which emotions and meanings are most crucial and important to the client at any given time. In addition, the therapist/coach should strive to develop *a strong therapeutic* or *dialogical bond* by showing empathy, care and emotional presence and by *collaborating* about the goals and tasks of the conversation process. The therapist/coach is actively involved in the conversation process by accepting the goals and tasks that the client brings in and by providing information about the conversation process, which promotes the client's understanding of the therapy or coaching efforts.

In addition to these three relational principles, which make up a model for optimal client-therapist/coach relations in EFT, there are *three additional treatment principles, which are more task-oriented.* The therapist/coach should seek to help the client resolve personal, inner, emotional problems by working with personal objectives, challenges or tasks.

The first of these principles is *experiential processing*. The key here is that the therapist/coach should pay close attention to the client's current state. Thus, the therapist/coach should help the client process what is most relevant at any given time and in the manner that is most relevant for the client. EFT calls these forms of engagement micro-processes. Micro-processes are understood as productive ways of processing one's inner experiences, as they unfold minute by minute. This means that the client actively explores and expresses his or her inner experience and dares reveal his or her inner experiential world to another person, in this case the therapist/coach. Furthermore it is about self-reflection, as the client gains understanding of his or her own experience, thus creating new meaning. Finally, it is about planning actions, i.e. different ways of acting, thinking or feeling in the future.

Focusing on the completion of key tasks in the dialogue is the next task-related principle. This is about discovering the main objectives of the therapy/coaching and key tasks in cooperation with the client and helping the client keep them in focus throughout the course of the conversation. The idea here is that although the client is the one who knows when he or she is ready, for example, to move on with a task, the therapist/coach should actively support this movement by engaging in attentive listening for any signs (markers) of this readiness.

The final task-related principle is *self-development*. EFT aims to support the client's potential and motivation for self-determination and growth. This is pursued by listening for and helping the client explore where in his or her experience there is a potential for personal growth and development. Essentially, Elliott and Greenberg (2007) state that EFT aims for a constructive balance between emotional experience ('heart') and self-reflection ('mind').

3.5.3 Mentalization-Based Approach

Mentalization was developed by, among others, Peter Fonagy, who originally had a psychodynamic focus, and Eia Asen, a systemically oriented family therapist, and is not considered a new intervention or therapy form but rather an approach that can be integrated into a wide range of conversation approaches and methods. The capacity for mentalization can be considered one of the most essential factors in any form of conversation-based intervention and the basis of understanding oneself and others. Asen and Fonagy (2011) describe mentalization as "seeing ourselves from outside and seeing others from inside" (p. 1). Mentalization describes a person's capacity for insight into his or her own and others' mental states and their connection to emotions, thoughts and actions. Many of the authors mentioned above use concepts that refer indirectly to mentalization. From a systemic platform, Cecchin (1987) spoke of curiosity, which I – with reference to Peter Lang – rephrased to *wondering*. Shotter (2006) speaks of *witness-thinking*, which may be understood as mentalizing other people's universe of emotions, thoughts and actions, where conversation partners meet in the "interplay of living moments intertwining with each other" (p. 600). Mentalization is a foundation of mutual understanding and thus improved attachment. Essentially, one may assume that improved self-understanding also improves one's capacity for grasping other people's perspectives, which in turn may be helpful for one's own self-concept and self-reflection. Mental states – the object of mentalization – are essentially *intentional*, i.e. they are directed at something, and they are about something (Allan, Fonagy, & Bateman, 2008). Thus, mentalization-based conversations provide access to one's own and others' life universes. Examples of mentalization in coaching might include:

- Making sure the coachee feels safe during the conversation session
- Promoting insight in the coachee with regard to how a third party might be so angry or so outraged
- Describing to the coachee how the coach would experience and perceive the event in question
- Helping the coachee understand the signs of progress that emerge during the conversation

Thus, the quality of mentalization affects the coaching conversation in two important ways: An effective and developmental coaching process relies first of all on the coach's capacity for mentalization and secondly on the same capacity in the coachee (Allen et al., 2008). With reference to Asen and Fonagy (2011), I offer a description of various possibilities for strengthening mentalization by including a systemic-social constructionist perspective of inquiry:

1. *Openness and wondering*: The coach should show genuine interest in the coachee's perspective. By exploring the coachee's life, the coach challenges the coachee to examine his or her own emotions and thoughts. The coach's wondering position challenges the coachee to take a fresh look on him/herself and his or her interactions with others by encouraging the coachee to reassess certain assumptions in his or her perception of the outside world.
2. *Shifts in perspective and circular questions*: The special inquiry technique of the systemic approach is a good example of mentalization-focused questions. By effecting shifts in perspective and domain, by adopting another person's perspective or by adopting a meta-perspective these questions help expand one's own horizon of understanding and develop a better grasp of other people's perceptions of the situation – without, however, being able to know for sure what the other really feels and thinks. In itself, the willingness to engage someone else's perspective can make a crucial difference.
3. *Construction of a personal and social reality*: When the coachee feels fixated, it is important for the coach to clarify the key epistemological position of social constructionist and narrative theory: that the individual is involved in creating his or her own personal and social reality. Certain basic positions can be changed and elaborated. By involving other people's understandings of specific events the coaching conversation can form a basis for further developing the coachee's perception of reality and the stories that the coachee has about him/herself or specific events. The capacity for mentalizing by seeing others from inside can help create these new realities for the coachee.
4. *Impact awareness*: An important dimension of the coachee's capacity for developing mentalization skills lies in understanding how one's own emotions, thoughts and actions might affect others, and how they contribute to creating a reality for others. The capacity to see the other from inside with regard to this impact can generate crucial change in the coachee.

5. *Humility* is a key condition for understanding another person. This requires a willingness to be surprised and to learn from others. This perspective applies to both parties in the coaching dialogue.
6. *Humour*: To not always take oneself too seriously and to be able to laugh at situations that one has brought upon oneself or others are important conditions for seeing oneself from outside in a new and sometimes liberating way. The coach's professional challenge lies in creating opportunities where the coachee can see him/herself from this humorous angle.
7. *Reflective contemplation* can be viewed as a particularly mentalizing stance, which is characterized by a situationally adapted and relaxed attitude in the coach and coachee in relation to the topic and each other.
8. *Relational attunement* is the possible result of reflective contemplation and is – as earlier described – a state where the coach is attuned to the coachee, and where both parties achieve an understanding of the topics that promote mentalization in them both.

The art of mentalizing rests on the coach's sensitivity in relation to noting the lack of contact that the coachee has to him/herself and to others' perspectives. Furthermore, as an important point, the coach should be aware of his or her own way of mentalizing and thus his or her capacity for achieving intensity in the relationship with the coachee.

3.6   Closing Remarks

The reader has now been given a basic orientation about a theoretical universe that can be applied to second- and third-generation coaching. The theories presented here can all be included in the coaching dialogue without necessarily clashing in the concrete practice. However, one should of course remain aware how these theories are applied, and how they may be at odds with each other with regard to their basic epistemological position. From an epistemological point of view, a systemic or a social constructionist perspective may not be fully compatible with a phenomenological-existentialist, an experiential or an emotion-focused perspective. Furthermore, one should be aware that some theories and approaches are more appropriate for a given case than another. That concern renders *case-conceptualization*, i.e. the decision about which approaches to include in a specific case, essential (Stevens & Morris, 1995). These theories and the choice of theory in regard to the case should enable coaching practitioners to develop and reflect on their practice in a nuanced manner. Certain theories, for example the systemic, are no longer used in coaching in their original form, but in a modified form they are incorporated into newer, relational theories, which are based on social constructionist theory. However, social constructionism too has its limitations, as the theory does not readily facilitate an investigation of the unique subjective dimension and the individual's/coachee's relationship with him/herself and his or her life world. This is where, phenomenological-existentialist theory, with its focus on experiential aspects and one's relationship with oneself, really proves its worth. This dual perspective on relational and existential aspects is highlighted in a comparable way by the Danish philosophically oriented coaching researchers Frølund and Ziethen (2011). The authors speak of a *complementarity perspective*, where the coach is encouraged to focus – via the relational perspective – on the coachee's organizational challenges on the one hand and – via the existentialist perspective – on the coachee's self-relationship on the other. How the various theories can be used to form a framework for a trans-theoretical approach to coaching will be discussed in the following chapter.

Chapter 4
Narrative Collaborative Coaching: Theory and Practice

In this chapter I will discuss the dimensions that I consider essential in third-generation coaching practice. With these dimensions I aim to develop a coaching format that matches some of the key changes and developmental and learning-related challenges that we are facing as a society, and which can thus be considered crucial for establishing third-generation coaching (cf. Chap. 2):

- The coaching process is focused less on goals and quick fixes, because the coachee needs room for self-reflection in order to be able to take an action-oriented approach in his or her practice as a manager, employee, job-seeker, stress-sufferer, career-maker etc. The basic idea is that the in-depth, meaning-making and value-oriented dialogue between coach and coachee should ulti-mately enable the coachee to link his or her personal and professional identities with concrete action perspectives.
- Coaching is a reflective process that considers both an existential-experiential and a relational perspective. The reflective aspect is also expressed in the special position of the coach. The coach is not merely a facilitator but, in certain stages of the dialogue, an equal *self-reflective fellow human being* and a *generous listener*, who is able to reason over the challenges that the coachee is facing, and which the coach relates to in his or her life perspective. By involving him/herself in the dialogue, the relationship between coach and coachee is at times symmetrical.
- The coaching conversation is based on a close link between person (i.e. coachee) and context. This inclusion of the context and the specific situation promotes meaning-making in the dialogue. The coachee thus becomes more aware of how certain actions impact his or her identity and self-concept, and how these actions are involved in representing certain life values and convictions.
- The coaching conversation facilitates a new narrative in relation to the challenge that currently concerns the coachee. This narrative is a product of the collabo-rative dialogue practice as it unfolds between the coach and coachee and also reflects the developmental process of the dialogue. The art of coaching is about changing the person's past history collaboratively by incorporating new events

R. Stelter, *A Guide to Third Generation Coaching: Narrative-Collaborative Theory and Practice*, DOI 10.1007/978-94-007-7186-4_4,
© Springer Science+Business Media Dordrecht 2014

and persons and by challenging and recreating the story's plot. Earlier – often troubling – narratives are always treated with respect and may form the basis of new narratives that emerge in the dialogue between coach and coachee.

4.1 Why Coaching as a Narrative Collaborative Practice?

The following highlights the special impact of social complexity and societal changes on the ideal format of coaching (for an in-depth discussion and review of the background of coaching, see Chap. 2). The four aspects in the following sections are basic dimensions of a coaching dialogue that is influenced by the coach's and the coachee's striving for insight through (self-) reflective processes.

4.1.1 Coaching as a Reflective Space

The English sociologist Anthony Giddens (1991) emphasizes the importance of self-reflexivity as a key condition for our ability to manage our lives as members of late-modern society. Our existence is determined by the post-traditional order, where firm social ties and traditions are abandoned, and where the question of 'How should I live?' must be answered in relation to a range of everyday challenges. The intention is to accomplish certain ambitions concerning the current expression of one's self-identity. Giddens considers self-identity a continual and strong individual development project. In that connection, coaching can be seen as a means of self-reflection that may contribute to the successful maintenance and development of one's self-identity; thus, coaching helps the coachee understand him/herself better and position his or her actions in the world on a value-based foundation. Coaching shifts the reflection process between the coach and the coachee(s) and thus operates in a shared space.

4.1.2 Coaching and Meaning-Making

In order to render their actions meaningful in specific situations, individuals continually seek to anchor their actions in the various contexts and social structures in their work or private life (Bruner, 1990a) – an anchoring that is no longer given by a generally accepted frame of reference (e.g. based on religious values or widely accepted moral standards). Bruner (1991) argues that the mind structures our sense of reality by means of mediation through "cultural products, like language and other symbolic systems" (p. 3). He specifically emphasizes the notion of narratives as one of these cultural products. In a coaching context, I claim that coaching is a method that helps people create new, alternative and more uplifting narratives about their lives in various social contexts. These narratives are shaped in a self-reflective process and help individuals or groups of people co-create coherence and meaning as a reflection of their relationships with specific others and specific contexts (Stelter, 2007). Coaching has the capacity to strengthen meaning-making processes by introducing metaphors about the coachee's culture (see e.g. Myerhoff, 1982; Turner, 1967; more on this in the presentation of Case 1 in Sect. 5.1.1).

4.1.3 Coaching as a Post-Modern Space of Learning and Development

Learning and continual (professional) development are crucial in today's world. But the nature of learning has changed since the 1970s and especially since the advent of electronic information in our everyday lives (see also Sect. 2.3). The key difference is that important authority figures in our society (e.g. school teachers, managers, mentors, doctors and clerics) have lost their knowledge monopoly. In our late- or post-modern society, knowledge is generated in specific contexts and in local communities of practice (a work team, a classroom, etc.) (Wenger, 1998). Learning is situated and shaped in specific organizations (e.g. a company, a school or a hospital), framed by social discourses, actions and specific (working) relationships. Learning is thus a process of *co-creating* knowledge (Pearce, 1994). Based on this new concept of learning, the emergence and growing popularity of coaching can be seen as a logical consequence of these new societal conditions. Thus, coaching can be considered an essential framework for focused learning and developmental processes.

4.1.4 Coaching Promotes Dialogical and Reflective Leadership

In relation to coaching in a work-related context, we have to consider certain new and special challenges facing management and leadership today (Schein, 1992). Only a few decades ago, a person in an executive position automatically commanded authority and received unconditional respect (see Helth, 2009a). However, the growing degree of autonomy in many job areas and employees' growing (knowledge-based) expertise in many industries, organizations and professions is leading to increased complexity, as mentioned earlier. This means that managers have to rely more on shaping their leadership position together with their employees and other stakeholders (Ferdig, 2007; Walji, 2009). That requires a new management and leadership approach. Managers have to shape their own leadership style. Leadership becomes a reflective and dialogical project, co-created in interaction with the staff. As a result of these challenges, managers often seek assistance by cooperating with colleagues (e.g. through mentoring or training programmes), or they hire a coach to support them in their self-reflective process in relation to their leadership style. To further promote the development of leadership practices, the focus is often on values (Kirkeby, 2000). The manager's value-based decision-making may be a focus area in reflective coaching dialogue, where specific events are addressed through specific value reflections.

4.2   Epistemological Basis: Bridging the Gap Between Phenomenology and Social Constructionism

The following section presents a theoretical framework for coaching as a narrative collaborative intervention. I seek to strike a balance between an individual experiential, embodied perspective on the one hand and a social, cultural and community-oriented perspective on the other. In this way, theoretical roots from phenomenology are combined with social constructionism. Phenomenology looks to present-moment and embodied experiences with the aim of enabling the individual to focus on specific situations that he or she is involved in. Within the framework of social constructionism, the focus is on discourses between individuals, the importance of social relationships and the relational and cultural construction of reality. Although the two theoretical approaches are different in many ways, the gap between them can be bridged, which makes it possible to use them in an integrated coaching model. The bridge-building aspects are related to:

1. The construction of reality
2. The concept of meaning

The integration of these two aspects is key to understanding the theoretical framework where phenomenology and social constructionism meet and are able to merge in an integrated coaching model that, by incorporating both experiential and co-creative aspects, matches my understanding of coaching as a narrative collaborative practice. In the following two sections, the discussion turns first to (1) the construction of reality and next to (2) the concept of meaning.

4.2.1   The Construction of Reality

Neither phenomenology nor social constructionism views reality as definite and final. Reality is either constructed in the present experiential moment and subject to change from one situation to another (phenomenology), or it is constructed socially in a relationship with others (social constructionism). I present these two approaches in more detail in the following with the purpose of describing their respective perceptions of reality and their mutual differences.

Phenomenology has become a true 'experiential science' and philosophy with a main focus on how individuals perceive and attribute meaning to the world in which they are themselves an integrated part. Phenomenology may be considered a method for exploring oneself and others in the framework of existential philosophy. Husserl (1985), the founder of phenomenology, speaks of a 'descriptive psychology', where the point of departure for psychological examinations is the subject's perception of a phenomenon (Ihde, 1977). The phenomenologists have developed an empirical method, *epoché*, which allows for an open approach to the phenomenon, and which involves bracketing one's immediate judgment and interpretation of a situation. That is a requirement if one wants to examine something in a phenomenological framework, as we are embedded in the world and therefore incapable of observing the world from the outside. In coaching, the coachee may use epoché to learn to understand him/herself in his or her subjectivity. Here, one may speak of an *individual experiential construction* of reality. There are a number of specific strategies or investigative methods that put the individual in touch with his or her lived experiences or give others access to one's own life world (see Depraz, Varela, & Vermersch, 2003; Stelter, 2007, 2008a). The crucial feature of this process is to focus on the individual's immediate bodily-sensory *intentional relationship* with a specific environmental situation that shapes the subjective reality, which is completely unique – precisely because of the person's specific intentionality in relation to the environment. This subjective reality is not a universal, objective reflection of a possible given reality but rather a reality that gives the individual access to him/herself and his or her world, a world that others do not have any direct access to.[1] Merleau-Ponty (2012) describes man as a subject that uniquely constructs and constitutes him/herself (and the world):

> But how could there be several absolutes? How could I in the first place ever recognize other Myselves? If the subject's only experience is the one I obtain by coinciding with it, if the mind, by definition, eludes the 'outside spectator' and can only be recognized inwardly, then my *Cogito* is, in principle, unique – no one else could 'participate' in it. Might one respond by saying that it is rather 'transferable' to others? (p. 391; italics in original).

Because individuals differ in their access to and perceptions of themselves and a given environmental situation it is fundamental for us as fellow human beings to respect each other's different perceptions of the outside world and practice sharing each other's realities. That is where I find the social constructionist perspective especially essential.

How do *social constructionists* view the concept of 'reality'? In social constructionism, the focus is on the role of relationships in shaping the individual and the specific social contexts that the individual enters into. Social constructionists are interested in how we create our reality within the framework of social relations and specific communities – or how our reality is shaped in the framework of the relationship(s) we enter into. The relational perspective also views 'personality features' and the emergence of emotions and thoughts as *social* constructs rather

---

[1] Phenomenologists draw a sharp distinction between phenomenology versus rational and empirical traditions in philosophy and psychology, for example represented through introspection as a means of 'looking in on' one's own mind, a reflexive form of self-observation, by examining the state of one's own thoughts, emotions and sensations.

than something that is inherent to or shaped inside the individual. To the social constructionists, reality is created through social discourses and interactions among people, for example in a workplace, a family or a team. Reality is thus created in the relationships that we are part of (Gergen, 2009a). What appears as 'reality' is a social construct. Originally, the social constructionists Berger and Luckman (1966) described the nature of reality from a sociological perspective: "The sociology of knowledge understands human reality as socially constructed" (p. 211). This understanding has later spread to psychology and to certain psychological and conversation-based intervention forms: There is no longer any attempt at examining or 'changing' anything about the person; instead the focus is on how the person is constructed through the relationships that he or she is part of. The goal becomes to examine, interpret and discuss these relationships and the person's role in a new and more life-affirming way.

The epistemological assumption outlined above makes it 'possible' to decon-struct and reconstruct a specific social reality by means of conversation or some form of psychological intervention (e.g. in a class, a sports team, a work team or an organization), for example by influencing human interactions. To quote Gergen (1997):

> The degree to which a given account of world or self is sustained across time is not dependent on the objective validity of the account but on the vicissitudes of social processes (p. 51).

A social constructionist-inspired intervention strategy such as Appreciative In-quiry (AI) (Cooperrider, Whitney, & Stavros, 2008) has taken on special importance in relation to developing more uplifting discourses and narratives. The AI process is constructed in the community between or among partners (e.g. between coach and coachee, in a team or in an organization), who are capable of co-creating a new, shared social reality through interaction. By basing their dialogue on *positive*, life-affirming and strength-based topics, by discovering and imagining possibilities and by pursuing their dreams, the participants can create a reality that promotes their development, both personally and as a group or a team. AI is easily integrated into the coaching process, as it is often more helpful to focus on the participants' possibilities and strengths than it is to dig into the specific problems and causes that might hinder progress.

4.2.2 The Concept of Meaning

Traditional objectivist theories have an underlying assumption about the perception and understanding of reality as something *out there* in the world; we perceive the world while creating an *image* of it. Here, the world is understood by means of concepts that focus on internal representations of an external reality. This traditional perception is replaced by a definition of reality as something that is constructed in the framework of the individual's interaction with his or her concrete environment.

From a *phenomenological perspective* Husserl (1950) speaks of *constitution*, which he views as a function that precedes meaning. As part of a transcendental intersubjectivity that focuses on intentionality in relation to the environment, *constitution* offers the individual a set of prefabricated meanings that are embedded in culture through language. In our world we incorporate meanings, which we receive through our culture, as part of a transcendental intersubjectivity. Meaning is shaped by experiences, perceptions and (implicit) knowledge that the individual shapes in various social contexts. This process is constitutional: The individual develops *meaning* by acting in a specific socio-cultural context. That is how the 'external' world becomes real: through the individual's situated reflections and interpretations. From a phenomenological point of view, meaning is shaped in an interaction between one's experience and one's perception of the experience (Gendlin, 1997). Meaning is often expressed in a verbal and metaphorical form, but it can be expressed in a variety of ways including drawing, physical expressions, dance or text. By highlighting and making room for perceptual and experiential meaning the coach supports the coachee in developing a better existential understanding of him/herself as a person and of the cultural and social context that the coachee lives in; an understanding that primarily has a bodily-sensory basis.

In *social constructionism*, meaning is negotiated among the participants in a specific social framework or community of practice (a working group, a class, a department or a sports team). Gergen (1997) writes,

> There is an alternative way of approaching the problem of social meaning: removing the individual as the starting point opens a range of promising possibilities. Rather than commence with individual subjectivity and work deductively toward an account of human understanding through language we may begin our analysis at the level of the *human relationship* as it generates both language and relationship (p. 263; italics in original).

Ideally, the participants in the social context realize that their position[2] and attitude only define one of many possible perceptions of the world. Thus, an open-minded and unprejudiced interest in examining whether others see the world differently, or how they perceive a particular task or challenge, is a very useful basis for good dialogues and social negotiation situations. Encountering someone else's point of view can inspire conversation partners to personal or professional growth. It can offer all the members of a social group or organization a chance to grow and mature in their perception of the world, and ideally it can lead to a better understanding, a form of consensus or an appreciation of differences.

In a community of practice (a work team, a sports team, a group of co-workers), all the participants take part in a process of meaning-making. Here the conversation or social negotiations often unfold through personal accounts and narratives. Narratives are linked to certain events, concrete contexts and actions

---

[2]In this context, it is important to maintain that position is not the same as role. Position is a highly dynamic concept, while the role concept is more stabilizing and restrictive despite the possibility of the role-bearer to create his or her role (Mead, 1934, speaks about the difference between *role-taking* and *role-making*).

that the person either is or has been involved in, and which are often related to others (friends, colleagues, team mates, etc.). A story is structured around a specific 'plot' that creates a coherent narrative with regard to action and meaning. The plot also gives the narrative a basic orientation (Polkinghorne, 1988). The plot presents a certain meaning, which is created by describing the various actors' experiences and actions in relation to each other and by structuring the events in a certain way. An encouraging and uplifting plot, which can be elicited by certain appreciative questions, can help generate narratives about good cooperation in a practice community. For example: On the one hand an uplifting narrative in a team can be shaped around experiences of good interactions and about enjoying each other's company despite recent setbacks. On the other hand, myths (which are also a form of narratives[3]) are created around certain members in a group or in relation to external relations or special events. For example, a myth can arise in a sports team when an individual player's error in a specific situation is viewed as the reason why the team lost. In this way, narratives can create a form of reality that emerges through the involved parties' social discourse. Furthermore, one should also be aware of power structures and restrictions and of specific conditions that might affect people's possibility for participating freely in dialogues (Foucault, 1972). In some organizations and social contexts it may be impossible to negotiate on equal terms due to the dominance of powerful actors. Coaching is generally based on a *collaborative* and *democratic* relationship (Grant & Stober, 2006). With this basic condition in mind it may be impossible to have a constructive dialogue if the dialogue is controlled by a dominating party who is not willing to negotiate or reflect on his or her own position (read more about coaching as a special dialogue form in Sect. 3.1).

After clarifying the fundamental epistemological foundation of narrative collaborative coaching I will present a practice model where deep reflection processes are the guiding element.

4.3   Narrative Collaborative Practice in Coaching

Coaching as a narrative collaborative practice should be understood as a third-generation approach that combines elements from experiential, social constructionist-collaborative and protreptic/philosophical/ontological approaches to coaching. The ambition is to develop second-generation coaching, where systemic-social constructionist coaching formats are especially dominant. In third-generation coaching, the coach's ambition of remaining neutral is toned down, and the main focus is on collaborative and co-creative dialogues. The coach and the coachee (or group of coachees) are dialogue partners and have a mutual relationship as reflective fellow human beings in a relationship that is characterized by varying degrees of

---

[3]See Sect. 3.4.1.6.

symmetry over time. In the coaching dialogue, the coach and the coachee often talk about values and meaning-making, about motivation/passion and the important things in life, as both enter a reflective space that looks beyond the mundane challenges of everyday life. Thus, ontological and existential[4] questions come up in the dialogue. The coach and the coachee become *philosophers* in relation to 'the big questions in life'; questions that have a strong impact on their identity and self-concept and on their way of thinking and functioning in concrete life and work contexts. This dialogue form reduces the traditional asymmetry between coach and coachee. Both adopt a more wondering basic stance, where they explore key human issues and search for new perspectives on existence. This mindset ultimately also produces specific answers to specific, down-to-earth challenges or questions in relation to, for example, work, career or family life. Reflecting on and discovering one's basic values and key aspirations can make it easier to provide direction for one's work, career and life.

The following three aspects are often integrated features of highly successful coaching sessions. They serve to open up the reflective space that the coach invites the coachee into. The aspects should be understood as ingredients of third-generation coaching:

- *Providing possibilities for meaning-making*: Meaning-making is considered one of the main objectives of the coaching dialogue. Meaning is fundamental, because we attribute particular values to our experiences, actions, interactions with others, lives and work. Things become meaningful when we understand the way we sense, think and act by telling certain stories about ourselves and the world we live in. Meaning is a far cry from 'information'.[5] Meaning-making is based on previous experiences and expectations for the future and integrates past and present experiences as well as ideas about what the future might bring in a holistic way. Meaning develops in the interplay of sensations, reflection, speech and action.

- *Talking about values*: In our society, which is characterized by growing diversity in social and organizational values, we should encourage coachees to reflect on values as guiding markers that can help them organize their private and professional lives. Values are not necessarily eternal and universal but are often rooted in practices and events in local communities. Surely, freedom, love or justice can be described as eternal values, but in our everyday life, interactions and cooperation with others there will be additional values that are highly contextualized. The ultimate goal is to facilitate and improve leadership, communication and cooperation by reflecting on key values as a fundamental

---

[4]The ontological approach to coaching is especially interested in examining human nature (see Sieler, 2010). One prominent representative of existential coaching is Spinelli (2010). Here the main focus is on supporting the coachee in understanding and handling special challenges seen from the person's life world and general positions, convictions, values etc.

[5]See Sect. 3.4.1.1 about Bateson.

condition and quality in human endeavours and behaviour that will continue to provide a sense of direction in relation to specific goals.

- *Providing a space for unfolding narratives*: Sharing stories with someone else and developing and exchanging narratives and accounts, either in the relationship between coach and coachee or in a group context, are crucial activities in the process of social meaning-making. The individual's anchoring in a cultural context is always based on specific values and meanings. Narratives serve to structure events and tie them together in a timeline. The storyline makes narratives – the source of meaning-making – coherent, and as a result they make life meaningful. Narratives establish a consistent storyline and shape our ability to see and perceive events, actions, other people and ourselves as reasonable and meaningful. The plot in any narrative provides the basis for developing an internal structure and dramaturgy. Telling and listening to stories enables us to perceive and interpret our lives as meaningful.

In the following I present an intervention theory that incorporates the aspects that are mentioned above. The systematic approach that is presented here forms the basis of the narrative collaborative coaching practice for individuals as well as groups. I base my description on individual coaching but also point out that the intervention theory is equally relevant, perhaps even more relevant, for group coaching. The goal of any coaching conversation is to create meaning based on the personal experiences and collaboration that will be described in detail here.

4.3.1 Coaching Between Personal Experience and Collaboration

As a consequence of the epistemological basis described above, coaching as a narrative collaborative practice will be based on two key dimensions of meaning-making:

1. Meaning is created through the current experiences and (implicit) knowledge that the individual acquires in various life contexts. The concept of experiential meaning-making can be related to the theory of experiential and sensory-aesthetic learning (as described in Sect. 2.3.1).
2. Meaning is shaped in a collaborative process through social negotiation and narratives that describe the person's life practice. Meaning is created in an interaction between coach and coachee and can be viewed as learning through social and collaborative practice (as described in Sect. 2.3.2).

These two dimensions frame the understanding of complexity throughout the coaching process and should be seen as integrated and fused in the dialogue itself. In this presentation, the two dimensions are treated separately for analytical reasons in order to provide a clear overview of the complexity of the coaching conversation.

4.3.1.1   Meaning-Making Through Personal and Sensory Experience

One of the key dimensions of the coaching intervention is the coachee's *individual experience* and *personal meaning-making*. This is where the phenomenological perspective unfolds in practice. Together with the coach the coachee seeks to understand his or her subjective reality or the subjective perceptions and experiences of the culture and context that he or she lives in. The focus is on the implicit and often sensory-bodily dimensions of certain situations, behaviours or persons. It is a perspective that sheds light on essential and existentially meaningful experiences and values in what one remembers from before – especially uplifting moments – and in what feels right and important to oneself. The coach strives to bring out a link to practice, habits and routines that are embedded in the flow of the story. An immersion in the practice itself, a sensory reliving of it, will often be a source of new awareness for the coachee, an awareness of the things that one 'just does' without really thinking about it, but which carry an underlying meaning that we strive to put into words.[6] In the conversation, the coach initiates a process that gives the coachee an opportunity to develop a sensory experience of a very specific situation or event. Only when it is put into words is the experience shaped into an *event* and thus imbued with meaning for the person. In phenomenologically inspired literature, the *felt sense* of a given situation is described as a possible way of approaching the experience through language (Gendlin, 1978, 1996, 1997; Stelter, 2010a). The method is called focusing (see www.focusing.org). A detailed exploration and verbal description of certain bodily and situationally specific perceptions provides a more profound insight into the coachee's thoughts, emotions and action patterns. Gendlin (1978) defines the felt sense as a form of inner aura or physical sensation in relation to a specific situation, event or person. However, the felt sense is often pre-reflexive, pre-conscious and nonverbal. The coach's sensitive inquiry helps the coachee get in touch with these implicit, sensory-bodily and pre-reflexive dimensions. This form of perceptual and experiential examination is a challenge, because it is difficult to put something into words that is essentially implicit, sensory-bodily and pre-reflexive. Stevens (2000) mentions that the usefulness of the method depends on how articulate and expressive people are in terms of describing their experiences. Stevens sees a further challenge in the fact that the words that are used are often related to a vague network of semantic units, both for the speaker and the listener, which means that the speaker and the listener have to create their universe of meanings together. In relation to this point I refer again to the concept of withness-thinking (Shotter, 2006), a dialogue form that strives for relational attunement, which creates and maintains the intense interaction between dialogue partners, where the sensory dimension plays such a significant role (see also Sect. 3.4.1.7 on collaborative theory and practice).

---

[6]To Merleau-Ponty (1993) it is crucial that speech and language are closely linked to the experience itself; he says, "Because meaning is the total movement of speech, our thought crawls along in language" (s. 43).

How to Contact One's Sensory-Aesthetic Experiences?

The coach's understanding and application of sensory-aesthetic reflection processes and questions enable the coachee to gain access to additional dimensions of his or her subjective reality and the meaning that is associated with certain situations, actions and persons (see also Chap. 2, Sect. 2.3.1). Sensory-aesthetic experiences emerge in a special cognition process based on bodily-sensory involvement from a first-person perspective (see more in Chap. 3, Sect. 3.5.2, Experiential and emotion-focused approaches). In the following, I present some basic principles and methods that describe sensory-aesthetic learning processes in the coaching conversation.

The Present Moment

The first basic principle that enables sensory-aesthetic experiences is the individual's orientation to the *here-and-now of the situation*. In the *present moment* the focus is on the immediate experiences associated with the situation. Stern (2004) describes this moment as "a subjective, psychological process unit of which one is aware" (p. 25). He highlights several characteristics that define the present moment more specifically, and as one key aspect, Stern mentions, "The present moment is not the verbal account of an experience" (p. 32). The present moment is experienced for example in the concrete *practice situation*: I am aware of what I am doing, and things develop in the flow of the action. The ancient Greeks described this perspective with the term *kairos*, which means 'the opportune moment' or the moment when things happen. *Kairos* is related to action – an action that emerges but which one is far from able to describe in words. *Kairos* is related to *knowing how*. With reference to Aristotle and Dewey, Depraz et al. (2003) describe the way artisans or doctors are rooted in practice:

> The know-how of each of them belongs to a skilful and prudent management of the contingency of particular circumstance, a certain art of seizing, in situation, the opportune moment (the *kairos*) – what materials are employed for such a structure, how to respond to the demands of a patient? – independent of all possible predetermination in terms of the project. Clearly, the truth of action is measured here by its utility and by its efficacy, which merges purely and simply with its good and its virtue. … Only *praxis* corresponds to an immanent activity which contains in itself its own end (p. 160).

Practice contains an inherent 'logic', and this logic takes shape in the present moment, which also contains *kairos*. The quality of this moment lies in the individual's awareness orientation to the flow of action itself and the factors associated with the environment, task and person that are involved in defining the action. The individual's alertness and sensory awareness in the situation produces an orientation that prepares the person to arrive at new perspectives. This inner readiness is also an important element for the psychological understanding that Stern (2004) strives for with his concept of present moments in psychotherapy and everyday life.

Epoché

This awareness and alertness to the here-and-now of the situation springs from *epoché*, a Greek word that describes a basic stance where an individual avoids and suspends all assessment and judgment of the situation or him/herself. The founder of phenomenology, Edmund Husserl (1931), describes his understanding of *epoché* as a way of enhancing consciousness and gaining access to one's own personal reality. The non-judging stance that is so essential in epoché is also the fundamental stance in the coach's relationship with the client. Depraz and Varela (2000) present three phases that describe epoché as the person's special relationship with his or her own experiences:

(A) A phase of *suspension* of habitual thinking and judgement. This is a basic precondition for any possibility of change in the attention which the subject gives to his own experience and which represents a break with a 'natural' or non-examined attitude.
(B) A phase of *conversion* or *redirection* of attention from 'the exterior' to 'the interior'.
(C) A phase of *letting-go* or of receptivity towards the experience (p. 123; italics in original).

Depraz and Varela view these three phases as interlinked, as B and C always appear as a consequence of A while also initiating A anew; thus it is not really possible to speak of a beginning or an end for this process.

Epoché involves a change in awareness and judgment in relation to the actual act, a change that springs from the present moment of the situation. In this sense it can be viewed as a *meditative state*, where the individual lives and experiences the *here-and-now* of the situation – a perspective that bears many resemblances to mindfulness.

Mindfulness

Mindfulness can be defined as a specific intentional orientation that involves maintaining a certain form of deliberate, non-judging and purposeful awareness. The focus is on cultivating mindful awareness and alertness from one moment to the next with an open, curious and accepting attitude (Germer, 2005; Kabat-Zinn, 1994). Germer (2005) describes the content of 'mindful moments' and the basis of mindfulness: Mindfulness is *non-conceptual* and involves no thinking or imagining. Mindfulness is an *experience of the present* and occurs in a *present moment*. Mindfulness is *non-judging*. Emotional presence becomes impossible once one begins to judge what is happening and reflect on what it means. Mindfulness is *intentional* and is always based on an orientation toward and an immediate awareness of something concrete (e.g. one's breathing or a certain inner image). Once thoughts begin to intrude, and one drifts away from immediate awareness, it is always this return to the intentionally oriented alertness in the present moment that creates continuity in the mindfulness experience. Mindfulness is *nonverbal*.

The experience is thus not immediately accessible to language. With certain inquiry techniques, based, for example, on *focusing*, one can help transform the experiences to language – keeping in mind that something is lost in this process. Mindfulness is about *exploring*. The person attempts to explore deeper-lying levels in his or her sensations and experiences. This requires openness and curiosity in a process that has no other purpose than alertness, emotional presence and awareness and everything that follows from the experience. Mindfulness can feel *liberating* in the sense that targeted training of mindfulness can help the person develop a sense of 'breathing space' in relation to overwhelming or emotionally troubling aspects such as worries, suffering, pain, anxiety and grief.

Today, mindfulness is often associated with a cognitive-behavioural approach (e.g. Segal, Williams, & Teasdale, 2002), for example as a training approach aimed at depression or stress. However, mindfulness might just as well be associated with a phenomenological-experiential tradition. Passmore and Marianetti (2007) use mindfulness as a method for lowering the tempo in the coaching conversation in coaching. Spence (2008) uses mindfulness as a training method aimed at achieving behavioural changes. In my coaching I use mindfulness to prepare a reflection process and enhance the conversation in order to improve the *coachee's awareness focus* – a perspective that places the coachee's non-judging, present moment centre stage. Siegel (2007) speaks of mindfulness as a means of achieving a higher degree of empathy and attunement in relation to oneself and others.

Descriptive Inquiry

When the coachee approaches a state of epoché and mindfulness, the coach's descriptive inquiry has a particularly beneficial effect on the process of reflection. The coachee is helped to offer "pure" descriptions of his or her sensations concerning a specific situation. The focus is on the aesthetic-sensory dimension of thoughts and emotions. The main point is that the coachee should remain on a concrete descriptive level by abstaining completely from explanations or judgments. With his focusing method, Gendlin (1978) seeks to capture the *felt sense* of the situation through a *handle* or *keyword*, a concept or a headline that the coachee has a chance to *resonate* on in the ongoing inquiry process, i.e. to reflect on whether the handle adequately describes the sense that the coachee seeks to capture through language. Descriptive inquiry invites the coachee to engage in an explorative, embodied and sensory perception of personal experiences.

Horizontalization

This method can be seen as a supplement to Gendlin's focusing and is directly inspired by Spinelli (2010), who proposes horizontalization in order "to avoid placing any unsubstantiated hierarchies of significance or importance on the client's statements of experience, and instead to treat each statement as having initially equal value" (p. 102). This phenomenological method helps the coach keep the coachee on a descriptive, explorative and experiential level, where everything that comes up appears new to both parties (Ihde, 1977).

Intentional Perspective

The individual's intentional and fundamental embodied relationship with his or her world is an important cornerstone for understanding the individual's sensory-aesthetic involvement in the situation. Merleau-Ponty introduced and established an understanding of the body as a 'perceiving organ', a body that relates to the specific environmental situation via perception and action (Merleau-Ponty, 2012). His concept of the intentional orientation and basis of perception/sensation is key to understanding pre-reflective knowledge as something that is given and immediately available in the situation. The mind 'reaches out' to its environment and thus always relates to it. In this sense, human beings are always in (a relationship with) their environment via an operative intentionality (cf. Freemann, 1994).[7]

The Meaning-Making Process

Sensory-aesthetic learning is a meaning-making process. Traditional perception theories are based on a concept of the world as an objectively existing 'reality': In the perception process, an inner representation emerges as a sort of depiction of the outside world. New theoretical approaches take a different perspective: Here, reality is constructed on the basis of the individual's dialogue with the concrete environment. In this process, *meaning* is created in the actual action context. The world thus has no pre-determined form, pre-established content or stable reality but takes shape only in the interplay between perception and action in the context. Generally, the meaning-making process can be described as a dynamic, situative and dialogical concept. Meaning should always be understood as contextualized and is framed by 'situated action', as Bruner (1990a) puts it. The meaning-making process integrates *past* (i.e. previous experience), *present* (i.e. current experiences) and *future* (i.e. expectations and anticipated outcomes). Meaning is developed further in an *interaction between experiencing and something that functions as a symbol* (Gendlin, 1997, p. 8). This symbolization may occur in verbal form or through other forms of expression (dance, drama, visual arts, writing, thinking etc.). Here, the aesthetic process finds its symbolic expression, as the person enables others to relate

---

[7]The ideas presented here about intentionality are supplement by ecological psychology (Gibson, 1966, 1979). Gibson speaks about *affordance*, a concept that is not found in any standard dictionary, but which can be defined as *an offer from the environment of a certain sensory experience*. A specific environmental constellation *suggests a certain act*, where the interaction between person and environment enables the individual to manage environmental challenges appropriately. Unlike the presented phenomenological notion of intentionality, Gibson (1979, p. 238) emphasizes the 'information' per se that the environment contains, and which appears in the form of *affordances*. Although phenomenology and ecological psychology are not fully compatible, they do complement each other in their understanding of the interaction between person and environment. In his or her conversation with the coachee, the coach may direct the coachee's attention to the specific possibilities that a certain environmental context invites, and which the coachee has failed to notice.

to his or her personal meaning-making process, which gives rise to a dialogue with the other-person perspective in the social context, for example in coach-coachee relationship or in a practice community.

The Absent But Implicit

From a narrative perspective, White (2007) speaks of rediscovering or re-membering the absent but implicit in order to highlight the importance of previous events, situations and persons that the person (in this case, the coachee) has forgotten but which have a special importance for meaning-making in one's life. The key is to relate to forgotten experiences and incidents and to associate them with an existing narrative in order to integrate uplifting and valuable elements from one's past into the narrative. This might include a teacher or a former supervisor who had a special impact on one's approach to tasks. Re-membering the importance of this teacher or supervisor gives the coachee an opportunity to retell and enrich his or her story and becoming more aware of his or her cultural background, certain life values or aspirations. That offers the coachee a chance to alter the plot of the story and tie events together in new ways. This re-membering thus helps build a larger whole and meaning in relation to one's actions. Creating the link to forgotten events from the past gives the coach an important role as a co-creator of the coachee's meaning-making and uplifting narrative process.

Metaphors and Verbal Images

A metaphor is a figure of speech where the speaker uses words in a figurative sense to describe an object, a situation, a person or an event in order to spark new images, narratives or sensory descriptions. The use of metaphors and figures of speech is the best way to put a *felt sense*, a perception or an embodied experience into words. Lakoff (1987) sees metaphors as a point of departure and a source of capturing embodied experiences, and in their linguistic research Lakoff and Johnson (1980) describe how our language and our everyday life is permeated by metaphors. Therapists or coaches, according to Cox and Theilgaard (1987), should move on "perceptive 'tip-toe', trying to detect what is on the brink of being called into existence for the first time" (p. 23). In order to bring that out which has not existed before, the two therapists propose an active use of metaphors in the conversation process. Through the metaphor, the coach invites his or her dialogue partner(s) into an experiential universe, where the parties have the best opportunity to delve into each other's worlds, and where it becomes possible to experience a sort of *relational attunement* (see Chap. 3, Sect. 3.4.1.7.). The dialogue partners develop a sense and an impression of what is going on in the other person. Thus, both parties are encouraged to use metaphors. Coach-generated metaphors can be distinguished from coachee-generated metaphors. Coach-generated metaphors may relate, for example, to the metaphorical interpretation of certain statements by the coachee and the use of a metaphorical narrative. Coachee-generated metaphors aim especially at verbalizing specific experience and felt senses and serve as a way to reframe previous and originally hidden memories into metaphorical images and narratives. The use of metaphors in the coaching dialogue is thus an essential means of expressing personal meanings that lie hidden in certain experiences. In the ongoing coaching conversation, however, metaphors are used in the collaborative dialogue between coach and coachee to initiate a transformation process that ultimately aims to generate new insights and action possibilities for the coachee. The use of metaphors also reveals how personal and collaborative meaning processes are interwoven: Metaphors are sensory-aesthetic, and they serve to connect conversation partners, as metaphors become a shared medium of mutual meaning-making and understanding.

In an example from the case 'Tangoing with the boss', which is presented below, I describe how a single metaphor, presented by the coachee, helped initiate a change process (see Chap. 5, Sect. 5.1.1).

4.3.1.2   Meaning Through Co-creative and Collaborative Practices

The second essential and important dimension in narrative collaborative coaching is how meaning is created in a co-creative and collaborative process between coach and coachee (see also Paré & Larner, 2004). The coachee comes in with a certain understanding of his or her reality, which was created in the life outside the coaching room, framed by the relationships that the coachee is part of in his or her workplace, family, spare time and other life contexts. The coach may offer a single new voice among the actors that the coachee interacts with. The coach can become a crucial voice because the coaching conversation is a unique and actively chosen context, where the coachee seeks new perceptual impulses. The task of the coach is to help the coachee reflect on the cultural roots and social relationships that determine how the coachee perceives him/herself and his or her social reality. In the following I explain how the coach can take part in the shared meaning-making process, a process that incorporates individual perceptions and experiences and focuses on the reality, the relationships, the culture and the contexts that the coachee is part of.

If we zoom in on the coaching dialogue itself, social meaning-making as a minimum involves the dyad between coach and coachee, but coaching may benefit from being carried out in a group or team under the leadership of a coach. Coaching as a narrative collaborative practice relies on the art of cooperation. It has the capacity to become a dialogue that creates something truly new for everyone involved (coach and coachee/coachee group). The process and the outcome of the dialogue may be planned and structured in general terms. In the following overview I present some assumptions and guidelines to offer the reader an impression of narrative collaborative coaching for individuals and groups in practice (see also Anderson, 2007a).

Assumptions and Guidelines for Coaching as Narrative Collaborative Practice:

• Both coach and coachee(s) are conversation partners with their respective
  expertise and conceptual framework. Both/all the participants in the dialogue
  contribute to shared meaning-making and knowledge production with their
  respective perspectives on the topic.
• Both/all participants do their best to be open-minded, flexible and willing to
  change in order to facilitate their own and mutual development and a basis for
  reframing perspectives and positions.
• The participants show attention to themselves and others and notice and appreciate differences that may prove fruitful with regard to their development and
  learning.
• The participants appreciate each other's contributions to the dialogue and the
  knowledge that is unfolded in the community; at the same time it is also important
  to accept potential and lasting differences.
• Generous listening is essential to the process of (mutual) exploration, where an
  interested or wondering stance helps create a fruitful and developmentally intense
  dialogue.
• A flexible stance makes it easier to reframe one's own and others' positions; it
  shows an open-minded approach to one's own development and helps to facilitate
  learning through others.
• The coach reframes certain comments or reflections offered by the coachee,
  sometimes interpreting or reframing them on the basis of his or her own
  conditions. The coach (and in group coaching, also the other participants) also
  offers associative comments in relation to the coachee's reflections ('When you
  say that, it makes me think of …').
• The coach uses questions that invite the coachee(s) to move forward and to
  embrace a shift in perspective. Here, various types of circular questions[8] from
  systemic coaching can be very helpful (see also "circular versus linear questions"
  in Sect. 3.4.1.2.).
• Both coach and coachee are encouraged to use metaphors and figures of speech.
  Metaphors help unfold sensory reflection, expand one's understanding of certain
  acts and observations and promote mutual understanding.
• The coach is encouraged to link the landscape of action (a focus on the
  intentionality, purpose and goal of the act) with a landscape of identity (a focus
  on personal values, convictions, aspirations, dreams and hopes, all of which form

---

[8]Circular questions are questions that invite the coachee to adopt a meta-position, i.e. a position
where the coachee stands next to the challenge he or she is facing. This position lets the coachee
view the challenge from the outside. Placing oneself mentally or physically next to the challenge
introduces a separation between the person and the challenge. This separation makes it possible to
explore the relationship between the coachee and the challenge. Circular questions are helpful in
exploring relationships, connections, hopes, dreams and visions of the future (cf. De Jong & Berg,
2002).

the basis of the coachee's understanding of him/herself and his or her identity) on an ongoing basis – and vice versa (see also "Key assumptions in the narrative approach" in Sect. 3.4.1.6.).

- The coach should seek to associate certain values and aspirations with persons and events that have held special meaning for the coachee. In this process, the narrative is expanded and enriched and may therefore develop in a new direction with an altered plot and storyline. This expanded understanding and its associated narrative serve to strengthen the coachee's sense of identity.
- The conversation with the coachee and the unfolding storyline are structured around certain ways of scaffolding in order to help the coachee develop and expand his or her understanding in an appropriate pace.
- Both coach and coachee may create (narrative) documents. The coach may for example send an e-mail after the session to offer additional reflections on the coaching conversation. The coachee is encouraged to write things for him/herself and others (e.g. poems, short essays, specific reflections or new interpretations related to certain events, persons etc.).
- Outsider witnessing: Here, others from the coaching group, perhaps invited guests, offer their reflections and serve as a sounding board for what the coachee said. The witnesses are asked to reflect on their own thoughts upon hearing the coachee's story, sharing their thoughts on the narrator's aspirations (wishes or dreams) and identity, and describing how the story affects them and their aspirations in relation to life, work, relationships etc.

I consider these general dimensions and basic principles fundamental to narrative collaborative aspects in the coaching process. Here I would like to remind the reader of the social constructionist-inspired theories and practice approaches that were presented in Chap. 3 and their various potential contributions to narrative collaborative processes in coaching. Of course, all of these approaches are capable of functioning on their own, and there are coaching interventions that rely exclusively on just one approach (e.g. solution-focused coaching). My overall purpose in including the various social constructionist approaches is to enrich the conversation with specific inquiry strategies, all of which follow a deconstructionist trajectory[9] and facilitate the co-creation of new understandings and thus new narratives for the coachee. These narratives should be developed in such a way that they are viable in specific life and work contexts and increase the coachee's general psychological well-being.

In the following I present four dimensions that focus on meaning by means of collaboration between coach and coachee:

- Appreciating and focusing on strengths and opportunities
- Reflecting on values, aspirations, hopes and dreams

---

[9]In Chap. 3 I mentioned *deconstruction* as one of the key aspects of the narrative approach. In this sense, my presentation is to some degree eclectic, but I do follow a stringent line with a persistent focus on the narrative collaborative quality of the dialogue process.

- Externalizing conversations, re-authoring and alternative stories
- Witnessing (see Sect. 4.3.1.3.)

Appreciating and Focusing on Strengths and Opportunities

The coach works from the following basic assumption: The coachee has come in because of some challenges, which I need to take seriously, but in the coaching conversation, I focus mainly on the uplifting aspects and on where the coachee is successful. I take this approach in order to initiate a change and developmental process. The specific intervention practice may combine various social constructionist-inspired approaches in the narrative collaborative process (see a more detailed description of the various approaches in Chap. 3).

From a *solution-focused perspective*, the coachee may be invited to outline a preferred future scenario, thus focusing on certain resources that the coachee actually possesses, and which have come into evidence on previous occasions. Specifically, the coach and coachee may work toward an understanding that paves the way for a new narrative, which lets the coachee begin to see opportunities for realizing the preferred future scenario (see more in Berg & Szabó, 2005; Cavanagh & Grant, 2010; Espedal, Svendsen, & Andersen, 2006).

From an *appreciative perspective* one would look, for example, at the following three essential aspects of the work and life contexts that the coachee highlights: appreciating and valuing the best of what is, imagining what might be and engaging in a dialogue about what should be. In a narrative collaborative perspective these three elements are considered to form three different plots that provide a basis for working toward a more uplifting narrative about a specific topic. An example: A female coachee presents a situation in her workplace where she experiences significant frustration related to recent cut-backs and a growing workload. As a first step, the coach should provide a space for the coachee to speak about the situation as it is perceived. Providing a space for this first story is important, for several reasons: First, the coachee needs to be able to 'unload' and tell the *whole* story. Second, the coach's open-minded interest helps the coachee develop a fundamental sense of acceptance and trust in relation to the coach. And third, it gives the coach an opportunity to listen to a story that forms the basis of the ongoing dialogue and developmental process with the coachee. From an appreciative perspective, the coach may then choose to focus on the best of what is in the coachee's workplace. Ideally, the coachee will then discover that there are enough positive qualities, for example in the collegial relations, that the current challenges can be seen in a more positive light. The coachee may, for example, discover that there are plenty resources among her co-workers that make it possible to handle the cut-backs in a creative and innovative way (see more about AI-coaching in Orem, Binkert, and Clancy 2007).

Certain perspectives from *positive psychology* can easily be integrated into the underlying deconstructionist pattern that characterizes coaching as a narrative collaborative practice. Here I am thinking especially of the support that the coach offers to the development of the coachee's optimistic explanation and attribution styles, which may be considered essential in developing psychological resilience. These attribution styles may begin to play a larger role in the coaching dialogue if the coachee chooses to look at her strengths instead of the problematic aspects of her interactions with the environment. Questions such as 'Could you mention three things where you have really excelled in handling this difficult situation?' or 'If you imagine that you were the boss, what would be your first positive initiative in your team?' offer ways of strengthening new ways of dealing with challenges, and they counteract a focus on problem-oriented explanation patterns (see more on positive psychology coaching in Biswas-Diener, 2010).

Reflecting on Values, Aspirations, Hopes and Dreams

One of the crucial perspectives in narrative work is to link the coachee's action perspective with the factors that drive the coachee to act in a specific way and to anchor this motivation in the coachee's value and culture-based foundation as well as his or her identity and self-concept, which are based on this foundation. As mentioned earlier (see Chap. 3), *agency* is one of the key basic assumptions that define the narrative approach. The individual is considered to have a proactive stance in relation to his or her environment: The coachee is capable of taking initiatives, taking life in his or her own hands and acting in pursuit of intentions, which are always framed by the coachee's active interaction with his or her social and material environment. The act and its intentions are always meaningful to the coachee and essentially anchored in values and convictions that are the source of the coachee's aspirations, hopes or dreams. Often, the coachee is not fully aware of the values that are such an essential guide for his or her actions. They lie dormant under the surface of action. The coach's questions about the value base of an act may serve to wake them up, activating them and initiating a process of reflection and development. This gives the act a deliberate identity-related link to values and convictions, which will feel very satisfying to the coachee, as the purpose and goals of the concrete tasks are reflected and anchored in the coachee's identity and long-term aspirations, hopes and dreams. The conversation often reveals that certain values and convictions date far back in time to certain persons and to situations and cultural contexts that the coachee was a part of, and which carried great importance for the coachee. This link to the past in combination with placing the values in perspective in relation to future actions constitutes an essential working perspective in narrative coaching. Specific contemporary events and acts are associated more clearly with previous life contexts and events as well as with aspirations and possible action in the future. This enriches the coachee's story about a particular topic and makes it more important and valuable. This expanded life perspective gives the coachee a better basis for understanding him/herself and his or her actions.

How can this *focus on values* and their *influence on action* (and vice versa) be initiated in the coaching dialogue? In a one-on-one conversation, the coach acts as a reflective dialogue partner (a witness), for example by appreciating the value base that the coach sees in the coachee's actions. The coach focuses on the possible *effect* or *consequence* of a certain event on the coachee. The coach might make the following statement:

> *I noticed that [event Y] is very significant for you and the way you think and act. Could you tell me a little more about that, and how it affects the way you act in the context we were just talking about?*

In the subsequent conversation the goal is to link to concrete *experiences*, i.e. to examine how these consequences are reflected in specific experiences and other events involving the coachee. In the ongoing dialogue the dialogue partners seek to examine possible general values and their roots in the coachee's past. In this process, the key is to thicken the story's plot and to *thicken the narrative* in an uplifting direction in order to add new dimensions to the narrative. The coach asks the coachee to try to link the presented values with specific persons or contexts in the past:

> *Can you think of someone from the past, perhaps someone from your family, a former colleague, a boss, a teacher etc., who represents some of the values that you were just talking about, and who may have influenced the way you think and act today?*

Eventually, these values can be included in a conversation that seeks to clarify possible future action. The coach might ask – for example by involving this person from the past:

> *What do you think this person would propose with regard to the decision you're facing?*

Externalizing Conversations, Re-authoring and Alternative Stories

The key quality of each narrative process depends on the collaborative practice. And in this narrative collaborative process, the *externalizing conversation* and *re-authoring* are important methods to help the coachee scaffold his or her learning by experiencing certain social and cultural contexts and the importance of these experiences to him or her on a personal level. Scaffolding is required to move into the "proximal zone of development" (Vygotsky, 1962). The purpose of the scaffolding process is to help the coachee move from an other-regulated problem-solving strategy to the development of a self-regulating action strategy in relation to a given issue (see Nielsen, 2008). In the narrative process, scaffolding is based on meaning-making that focuses especially on values, aspirations and self-identity.

In an externalizing conversation, the coachee is invited to tell his or her story. In many cases it is clear that the coachee has internalized the problem, as if it stems from the person's own personality features or aspects. In narrative coaching, however, the conversation is based on a different basic stance: the problem is not the coachee as a person. The problem is the *problem*, which is external to the person. In this sense, externalization offers the coachee a new perspective by providing an alternative way of viewing and talking about the problem (White, 2004).

In re-authoring, the coachee's story is treated as a manuscript that is written by the coachee – in collaboration with the coach. This implies that the coachee is free and able to re-author his or her life story. In this context, re-authoring can be seen as a different form of externalization, where the coachee adopts an externalized position as author by viewing his or her life story from a different vantage point. In narrative coaching, re-authoring techniques are integrated with the externalizing conversation process.

4.3.1.3 The Narrative Collaborative Coaching Process

The narrative collaborative coaching process can be divided into two parts, which are presented in the following. *Part 1* consists of two stages: description and relation mapping. *Part 2* consists of three stages: evaluation-re-evaluation, motivation-anchoring and conclusion-recommendation. There is a certain overlap with the basic steps in narrative therapy. Allowing for the fact that the course of a given conversation will always reflect concrete situations and personal conditions, the course of a narrative collaborative coaching conversation may be outlined in the following ideal-typical format:

Part 1:

Stage 1: Description The coach invites the coachee to tell his or her story about life in general or a specific challenge, for example a work-related issue, general work-life balance etc. The story may involve multiple themes or plots. While the coach listens to the coachee's story, he or she attempts to identify *internalized problems* with a particular impact on the coachee's self-concept and identity. The coach encourages the coachee to externalize the problem, for example by naming the problem and talking about it in the *third person*.

Stage 2: Mapping In the conversation with the coachee the coach attempts to identify hopes, values, and dreams in the coachee's story. The coachee begins to develop – or map – a sense of the meaning and purpose of his or her actions, which are brought closer to the preferred self-identity. However, the story that is told is often underdeveloped in relation to what the coachee wants to be or stand for. To borrow from Geertz' (1973) anthropological theory, a key concept in narrative theory and practice is the *'thin' descriptions* that certain uplifting stories or narratives are framed by, and which are overshadowed by the prominent and often problem-laden story in the form of *'thick' descriptions*. In the narrative collaborative coaching process, efforts are made to thicken the thin descriptions by adding events that the coachee may have forgotten, or which have been repressed and not allowed to unfold. The coach seeks to identify any *unique outcome* or to examine the coachee's *initiatives* and/or events that the coachee may have forgotten,[10] repressed or neglected. These unique outcomes or neglected events (which are simply waiting to be brought out into the light) may help the coach and coachee establish alternative tracks in stories together. The coachee may offer many examples of failure (= the current thick descriptions) that support a negative story track. The coach may ask the coachee try to think of specific exceptions or unique events that are part of the previous experiences, uplifting exceptions and events that only now, in the current conversation, come up to the surface and thus help create a form of counter-plot to the dominant existing story. The counter-plot provides access to a *transformation* (*a rite of passage*[11]), the alternative story that may enable the coachee to see new opportunities. The mapping of the coachee's positive self-identity to the negative description of the coachee's actions in the unfolding sequence of events (thin versus thick descriptions) enables the coach to identify certain learning gaps in the coachee's learning. The revision of the previously dominant story and the reframing of alternative narratives take place in a collaborative process between coach and coachee, ideally within the coachee's *proximal zone of development* (Vygotsky, 1962), i.e. on a level where the coachee can keep up and help effect the change that is a condition for overcoming certain perceptions and productively re-authoring parts of his or her life through a new and more uplifting story.

Part 2:

Stage 3: Evaluation, Re-evaluation, Re-authoring Conversations In order to bridge the learning gaps that were identified in stage 2, the coach continues to thicken the thin story tracks by looking for cracks where the coachee's story can be imbued with new life, uplifting events and unique outcomes in order to strengthen the coachee's sense of identity. The alternative story is further supported through plot adjustments. In this stage, the coach seeks to include new lived experiences and events in order to provide scaffolding[12] to

---

[10]Here, strategies for *re-membering* are used with the purpose of integrating certain events or meaningful persons in the coachee's life that have been forgotten or only exist in thin descriptions. Re-membering can be considered a way of thickening descriptions.

[11]In its original sense, *rite of passage* is defined as a ritual or ceremony marking the transition from one level of development to the next (e.g. Christian confirmation as a transition from youth to adulthood). In the narrative practice, rite of passage is viewed as a sort of turning point, after which the story can unfold in a new, transformative direction.

[12]The scaffolding concept comes originally from Vygotsky (1962), who argues that cognitive development is associated with the child's language development and the child's participation in social interactions, for example with a supportive other. In the narrative practice, the term is used as a means of adjusting the coachee's learning and development in relation to his or her level of readiness. The coach's questions should match the coachee's proximal zone of development, i.e.: Is the coachee ready and able to incorporate, e.g., certain unique events and to see them as potential ways of enriching the current re-authoring process? Sometimes, some of the coach's questions may be too distant to the coachee's current self-concept. Hence, scaffolding – the appropriate question in relation to the coachee's development level – is a crucial task for the coach.

bridge the coachee's learning gap. The coach asks the coachee to re-evaluate the effect of his or her actions on his or her own sense of self-identity, values and beliefs by expanding the coachee's imagination and focusing on meaning-making resources (e.g. by incorporating relevant persons and events from the past). The coachee is also encouraged to map his or her aspirations, values and self-identity based on new action perspectives and freshly emerged possibilities that may be appearing on the life horizon. This stage is often viewed as a turning point, where the coachee begins to discover new possibilities and actions instead of repeating old story tracks.

Stage 4: Motivation and Anchoring The coach helps thicken the plot of the story and consolidate the coachee's desire for change. Narrative coaching aims to develop and shape a thick description of an alternative story that is embedded in relevant meaning-making processes, and which creates a connection to the coachee's additional stories by anchoring this alternative story in the coachee's values, convictions, goals, hopes and obligations. At this stage, the coachee seeks to motivate and anchor the re-authoring that was mentioned above based on his or her aspirations, convictions, values, self-identity and strengths.

Stage 5: Conclusion and Recommendation The coach co-creates conclusions with the coachee by focusing on appreciative statements about the coachee's identity and by highlighting special convictions, values, hopes and dreams that are crucial for the coachee in certain contexts. The coach may ask the coachee to write the statements down, either as words on a piece of paper or in the form of a letter. Finally, the coach invites the coachee to commit to action by describing a possible action plan for change and by focusing on how the coachee's *bridging tasks* can convert hopes and dreams to reality in order to help the coachee hold on to hopes and any commitments to change.

Witnessing

Witnessing is a method that is generally based on including others in the coachee's reflection process. White (2004) also speaks of *defining ceremonies*. The participants take turns to be audience and speaking actor. Someone witnesses what the coachee just said by reflecting on the coachee's statements in light of his or her own world view, values and everyday challenges. Witnessing serves as an element in the *deconstruction* of the coachee's existing reality, a reality that may be perceived as stressful, unsatisfactory or challenging. Witnessing by others aims to facilitate the coachee's re-construction of his or her reality, in part by means of thickened narratives that break with thin conclusions about the person's life, identity and relationships (see Case 3, Sect. 5.1.3). This is in keeping with the post-structuralist tradition, which considers identity a social construct, a public emergence. This emergence takes place in narrative collaborative coaching through witnessing processes and defining ceremonies. Identity is changeable and is shaped in the framework of the contexts and relations that the person is a part of. Thus, any narrative collaborative coaching conversation essentially has a deconstructive perspective via the relationship between the coach and coachee(s) and via the development of new thickened stories about the coachee's life and contexts and relationships that the person is part of.

In a one-on-one coaching context the coach may serve as a witness by reflecting on what the coachee said in light of his or her own value and life perspective. Here, the asymmetry between coach and coachee is suspended, as the coach abandons the neutrality that was previously considered a special characteristic of the coaching dialogue (cf. Hede, 2010; Stelter, 2002a). In this function, the coach can be described as a *fellow human being*. This gives coaching a new character, where the dialogue between coach and coachee in certain stages and situations develops into a genuine conversation between two people, freely sharing their respective life perspectives with each other (see also Sect. 3.4.1.7) – a true feature of third-generation coaching.

The optimal use of witnessing processes, however, is in the group context. In narrative collaborative group coaching one coachee can take centre stage as the narrator, while the other group members serve as *witnesses*. After the coachee has told his or her story, the coach asks the other witnesses/group members to describe how the coachee's story resonates with their own experience and to describe the insights the coachee's story generated for them. In this format, the coach, coachee and witnesses form a community of practise (Wenger, 1998), where everybody assumes a non-central position but acts as supports for each other with the purpose of reflecting together and providing appreciation and additional strength in the development of new stories about their life and identity. After the coachee has presented a certain event, situation or challenge to the group, the coach can develop a conversation with the group around the following questions:

1. *What stood out for you in the coachee's story? – What expression, what phrase caught your attention as a witness?*
2. *What image does that give you of the coachee's life, identity and world in general? What does this expression/phrase tell you about the person's intentions, values, convictions, hopes and ambitions?*
3. *What does this expression/phrase tell you if you relate it to your own life?*
4. *How does the story move you? Where has your experience with the story taken you?*

In the first question it is essential to capture what one heard in a word, expression or phrase. This gives the story a headline or a name in relation to what is central to the person who listened to the story. In the next question, the witnesses (the 'audience') are encouraged to consider how this story might connect with their ideas about the coachee's intentions, values and aspirations. Here, the coachee can access new insights by hearing how he or she is perceived by others. The other person's reflections can often be the first step toward an expanded self-concept. Others can often see much more in us than we can see, allow ourselves to see or hope to see in ourselves. The third question may be even more important. Here the witness talks about how the story and its key dimensions help spark a thought process, and, finally, how it affects the witness' own way of thinking and acting. In this way, stories affect others. We can mutually inspire each other to move in new and hopefully more life-affirming directions. In narrative collaborative dialogues we speak about how we are mutually affected by each other through certain words, concepts and events that we listen to and reflect on, and which can produce entirely new meanings in the listener. These differences in meaning can serve as a force of renewal in both individual and community-based developmental processes.

4.4 Closing Remarks

In this chapter I have endeavoured to provide an overview of my own third-generation coaching approach which is based on an integration of various theories and practices that are both existentialist-experiential and constructionist-collaborative. Meaning and reality are created both as a result of individual and embodied experiences on the one hand and social relationships on the other. Meaning and reality are created in a close relationship between what we do (action) and what we stand for (values, convictions, aspirations and dreams). Third-generation coaching as a narrative collaborative practice helps us verbalize what we are thinking, and the way we want to be – and act. Words and concepts are given added nuance by the participation of the coach and perhaps others in the coaching conversation. Meaning is described, weighed, adjusted and anchored in a new way in one's mind.

A higher degree of symmetry between coach and coachee(s) helps to develop a new dialogue form that aims to create depth in the conversation, where the aim is to savour each other's stories and create a sensory relationship between the other person's story and one's own life and meaning universe. Here we can find inspiration from protreptics. I will quote Ole Fogh Kirkeby (2008), a Danish professor of management philosophy, who has initiated a revival of this ancient Greek conversation culture:

> Protreptics is about achieving the highest degree of awareness of one's own statements. And this does *not* primarily refer to an understanding of one's own motives, projections etc. but of the meaning of the word in relation to values, criteria and ontological conditions and consequences (p. 502; italics in original; translated for this edition).

And he continues:

> The purpose [of protreptics] is a *why*, and its precondition is that any *why* can be reconstructed in the form of value. Protreptics is propaedeutics[13] for the creation and preservation of this reflexivity (p. 511; italics in original; translated for this edition).

But in contrast to protreptics, my narrative collaborative approach places a greater emphasis on the narrative and thus the autobiographical element. However,

---

[13] Introduction, preparation.

the individual autobiographical element should not stand alone but should be expanded through the narrative collaborative quality as the *shared* basic intention of the dialogue partners. The other's story may serve as a catalyst for a reflection on one's own life challenges[14] and initiate developmental processes that mobilize hidden values and a renewed understanding of the self and the opportunities that may appear (this is especially apparent in Case 3 from a group coaching session that is presented in Sect. 5.1.3; in a one-on-one coaching the coach may serve as the reflective partner in the dialogue). Thinking and reflecting through the other's story affects one's own life and may lead to a new understanding of one's own life. Here, a *why* plays a key role in relation to developing one's own self-concept and agency. Here, the narrative can unfold its quality: Stories frame the individual's lived experiences and offer an image of how the individual manages and lives with his or her life challenges, challenges that we all confront in our late- or post-modern age, which is characterized by diversity, differences and the possibility of living and acting in a wide variety of ways. Narrative collaborative coaching offers dialogue processes that help ensure empowerment and a social foundation for the coachee's self-identity. Narrative collaborative group coaching in particular can help develop social capital,[15] which is one of the pillars of the development of social networks in civilian life and in practice communities in working life and organizations (see also Stelter, Nielsen, & Wikmann, 2011), and which enables a viable developmental process.[16]

The narrative approach is applied in a growing number of areas. Bruner (1990a, 2006) was the pioneer. He was dissatisfied with the development that cognition research had taken and found it necessary to develop a new and more holistic understanding of human thinking and action. Meaning in action became a focal point of his understanding, and that paved the way for the role of narratives in meaning-making. The narrative understanding is used increasingly in *qualitative research* (Bochner, 2001) to give the reader an adequate impression of research participants' thinking and actions. Later in the present book, I use this narrative presentation form myself when I present a number of cases in a narrative form. It makes it easier for the reader to relate to someone else's story and thus grasp its meaning in relation to his or her own situation. The narrative approach is also becoming increasingly widespread in interpretations and practice in the field of organizational theory (Cooren, 2004; Ford, 1999). Organizational contexts are examined from a narrative perspective, which enables new ways of initiating change

---

[14]I use the term life challenges here. This includes any type of challenge concerning all the contexts of life (work, career, interpersonal relationships, crises, stress, transitions etc.).

[15]Social capital describes the sense of coherence that develops in societies, organizations, families and other social communities. Social capital is a resource that goes beyond the individual and helps generate a positive influence in the social spaces where it is developed (see Bourdieu, 1983; Putnam, 1995).

[16]The follow-up study that I did together with my coaching and research team found that the coaching group intervention had a positive effect on the participants, also 5 months after the completion of the process. Read more about this in the next chapter.

processes. What I found most surprising was the application of the narrative approach in medical treatment (Charon, 2006, 2011; Greenhalgh & Hurwitz, 1999). Doctors are becoming aware of the holistic perceptual perspective of narratives and their healing power. Finally, I refer to the most recent concepts in neurological research (Gazzaniga, 2005), where the left brain hemisphere is viewed as the 'interpreter' that generates certain explanations and interpretations about internal and external events.

With these examples from other contexts, I hope to encourage the reader to engage in working with narratives as one of the basic patterns and a dynamic approach to coaching and other types of dialogical processes.

Chapter 5
Case Studies and Effect Studies of Coaching as a Narrative Collaborative Practice

In this chapter I present findings demonstrating the potential effect of coaching as a narrative collaborative practice. The presentation falls into three parts, focusing on different perspectives on the effect. In my scientific understanding, I consider the combination of different research and study approaches and thus different types of effect evaluations essential.

First, I describe individual cases from my own coaching practice, viewed from my perspective as a reflective practitioner. Next, I present stories from participants in a research project on narrative collaborative group coaching. These stories paint a nuanced picture of the benefits for the participants in taking part in collaborative processes, viewed from a perspective that focuses especially on the participants' life worlds and personal experiences. Finally, I present results from a randomized, controlled study that used a variety of psychological scales to measure effect. The research involved both an intervention group and a control group. This type of empirical data makes it possible to present findings from a quantitative perspective that can be generalized statistically. By employing this variety of research approaches I aim to offer a nuanced picture of coaching and its effect and impact from the participants' point of view.

5.1 Case Studies of My Own Practice

In the following, I present a number of case studies from my own practice as a coaching psychologist (see also Etherington & Bridges, 2011). The case presentations include selected situations and processes. In the subsequent reflection they will be used to shed light on theoretical aspects that are described in the theoretical sections of the book. The three cases describe a variety of situations taking place in different formats:

R. Stelter, *A Guide to Third Generation Coaching: Narrative-Collaborative Theory and Practice*, DOI 10.1007/978-94-007-7186-4_5,

The first case revisits a key conversation sequence from a single session with a HR director. The focus here is on what happens, virtually from moment to moment. The second case tells the story of a full five-session coaching process with another director. Here, my focus is mainly on examining the overall dynamics of the process. How do change and development unfold over time, in this case a 4-month period? In the third case I present a key episode from a group coaching session with young sports talents, a process that was part of a large-scale research project. The case presentations aim to clarify connections in the coaching process and thus provide a form of practice-based evidence for my approach (cf. Barkham, Hardy, & Mellor-Clark, 2010).[1]

With regard to these case studies it should be noted that I am presenting my own perspective on the conversations, my story as a reflective practitioner.[2] I seek to relive the experiences that I recall having in the situation. All the descriptions of conversations are based first of all on notes that I made while coaching (I do that consistently). Next, shortly after the conversation I wrote down the stories that were presented in order to preserve as many details as possible. The persons involved in the cases gave their consent for the material to be used in this publication.

The case descriptions that are presented here are viewed from my perspective. In addition to illustrating my practice, the descriptions might also serve as inspiration for the reader's own professional development. The presented format may serve as a resource in the reader's own work as a coach, consultant or similar capacity. It is a key aspect of ongoing professional development to use one's own experiences in a deliberate and reflective manner and to reflect on session events after the fact.

In the second phase of the case study, I interpret the presented cases based on the intervention theory that was presented in Chaps. 3 and 4, supplemented with theory that I consider relevant for analyzing and interpreting the specific dimensions of the individual case. Relating theory to case descriptions and case analyses is characterized as 'analytical generalization'. Obviously, case studies cannot be subjected to statistical generalization. However, the findings can be generalized in other ways, by means of analytical generalization, which, as Yin describes (1994), aims to enable the researcher or, in this case, the practitioner-researcher, to expand and generalize relevant theories in relation to the examined cases. Thus, the findings of the presented case studies are subjected to a careful assessment.

In the following, the three cases are presented with subsequent reflections and analytical generalization.

---

[1] Read about various research approaches concerning evidence in American Psychological Association (2006).

[2] Schön (1983) describes the reflective practitioner as a professional who is able to reflect both *in* and *on* his or her practice. More about this point in Chap. 6.

5.1.1 Case 1: Tangoing with the Boss. Developing a New Working Relationship

The first case involves a coaching session with Bente,[3] a HR manager in a government organization. Recently, a former colleague of hers was promoted to be the new director of the organization. Bente did not apply for the position as director, and she emphasizes that she is very happy with her current position.

In our conversation, the coachee points out that she has great respect for her new director's professional competence, but that she would like to see her boss act as a more visible and proactive leader. In her conversation with me (R), Bente, the coachee (C), describes her relationship with her new boss as follows:

C: I would like to have a more nuanced relationship with my boss.
R: What would be your optimal perception of your boss?
C: That I could rely on him.

To me, this reply suggests that Bente does feel a significant distance to her boss and a certain degree of uncertainty about where he stands in relation to her. I express my curiosity about this and inquire about Bente's relationship with her boss, now that they no longer occupy equivalent positions. The conversation produces a very descriptive image where Bente suddenly, almost to her own astonishment, presents this telling characterization:

C: We are dancing around each other!

As a coach I am fascinated with this description, and I cannot suppress a little smile. I also notice how well the statement seems to reflect Bente's experience: She nods once more. She seems to sense the image very clearly, probably as a body sensation, and she expresses how pleased she is with the aptness of the description. In my next step, I am almost surprised at how quickly I proceed. But in the moment it seems right. Spontaneously, I address the metaphor but modify the image, turning it on its head. With a smile, I ask:

R: How would it look if you were to dance together?

Bente answers my metaphorical question immediately and with similar spontaneity by going into the image and expanding on it:

C: It would be either modern waltz or the tango!

As a coach I am really pleased to see Bente coming along so spontaneously, and I clearly sense how the conversation takes on a new dynamic, and how Bente and I develop a closer rapport (relational attunement). We both begin to enjoy the conversation. I continue:

---

[3]The name is anonymized.

R: Which do you prefer?

"The tango," says Bente spontaneously, and then she laughs, almost taken aback by her own spontaneity and audacity. She is clearly excited about what she blurted out. She is beginning to be amused with herself and her own statements, and to me, the conversation feels light and fun. It clearly has undertones that go beyond the normal social conventions of the workplace – undertones that lend the conversation a refreshing vitality. We are both enjoying this, and the vitality adds a degree of intensity to the conversation that feels special to me. So I continue to play with the image and address the unusual aspect it contains by asking and noting:

R: What does tango mean to you as a dance? – He'll be doing the leading, that's
*   for sure!*
C: Yes. I think I would surrender to him! That might be fun to try.

To me, her answer seems like a release. In my perception, 'surrendering to him' implies a sort of enjoyable submission, although she is not abandoning herself in the relationship. Bente also seems to feel an inner sense of relief. After a moment's silence, I ask – also bearing in mind that she will be seeing her boss again the following morning:

R: If you think about the situation now, how does it feel, how will it be for you?

Bente's reaction is spontaneous and immediate, as she exhales:

C: I think I'm going to be much more relaxed!

A more serious look returns to her face, she seems relieved. At this point, I almost have the sense that Bente has felt much more tension about the situation than I initially thought. For a moment, she reflects on what just happened. After a few seconds she says,

C: Well, that's an entirely new perspective for me!

And the levity seems to return. We exchange smiles, sharing our delight over the great meeting we just had, and how much fun it has been to talk like this. Bente rounds off the conversation for herself by concluding,

C: Wow, thank you. That's an entirely new dimension for me. I'm just making things
*   difficult for myself. I love this new perspective.*

Weeks later, Bente tells me how much our conversation has affected her. She explains that she draws on the image of tangoing with her boss as her own 'little secret'. Over the past few weeks, she has often wanted to smile in situations where she was together with her boss. The image has helped her. She has a much clearer sense of her own role and of the position that she attributes her boss, and which she expects him to assume.

5.1.1.1   Reflection on the Case

By virtue of their mutual connections, several elements in this conversation can be taken as indication that the conversation was successful. The conversation contains certain ideal-typical aspects that can be generalized theoretically and thus serve as inspiration for a narrative collaborative coaching practice. (In this section, certain key theoretical concepts are highlighted in italics). I have chosen to share this particular sequence with the reader in order to present something that is exemplary and generalizable in relation to a successful coaching dialogue, a dialogue that has the capacity to spark transformation and form the basis of a new narrative about a challenging and inflexible job situation. The underlying situation is familiar. The client presents the coach with a story of a conflict-ridden event, offering his or her perspective on it, and the coachee has difficulty modifying his or her perceptions and understanding. The relationship appears inflexible – often doubly so, as both parties have difficulty rising above their perceptions. At the beginning of the conversation, the coach simply tries to understand what is going on. The coach attempts to form an understanding that is shaped by the coachee's story. The coach strives to expand his understanding by expressing that he is *curious*, a curiosity that also becomes important for the coachee. New facets, new angles and new individuals are involved, and that creates a thicker narrative. This is where the coach creates a new sense of *alertness* and *attention* in the coachee. The coach's *curiosity* 'rubs off' on the coachee. Through an unreserved sense of curiosity, the coach facilitates the coachee's *mindful-reflective presence*. The coachee dives into her world in a new way. At the same time, the coach's attention and interest encourage the coachee to reflect in-depth. The addition of new details and the discovery of new dimensions create an expanded narrative. By actively thinking along with the coachee (*withness-thinking*) the coach facilitates mutual *relational attunement*, which is beginning to bear fruit (see more about collaborative theory and practice in Chap. 3). The coachee's subjective experience begins to unfold, and *new connections* (Wittgenstein, 1953) and thus *new meanings* begin to appear to the coachee during the conversation.

Let us now turn to the actual dialogue: My interpretation of the case is based on the notion that this *relational attunement* helps prepare Bente to embrace the metaphor that she presents: "We are dancing around each other!" Precisely because this expression is a *metaphor*, where Bente uses the word dance in a figurative sense, it vitalizes her understanding of her relationship with her boss. Furthermore, the metaphor also anchors the relationship in a bodily sensation in the coachee's perception. I perceive the presentation of this metaphor as a clear invitation – an invitation that is probably not deliberately initiated by the coachee. But the image really speaks to me. And here I seize (or bet on) the opportunity. I *play* with the metaphor – in a move that, in a sense, is almost as surprising and spontaneous as when the coachee described her relationship with her boss as the two of them dancing 'around' each other. I turn the metaphor on its head and thus radically transform or shift the perspective (read about shifts in perspectives in Sect. 3.3.1.).

By moving so spontaneously and quickly, I am running a risk, because I cannot be sure that this shift in perspective lies within the coachee's *zone of proximal development* (Vygotsky, 1962). Thus, there is a risk that the coachee may not be able to use the question as *scaffolding* that helps her develop her understanding of her relationship with her boss.

At the same time, in a wider sense, the question, "How would it look if you were to dance together?" can be viewed as a form of *externalization* (White, 2007), where, as a coach, I offer the coachee an opportunity to distance herself from the problem. Furthermore, the story takes on an uplifting twist with the new term, 'tango', which invites the coachee to embrace an entirely new narrative about her interactions with her boss. But there is more to my question:

My initiative hits the bull's eye for the coachee – perhaps as a result of the relational attunement that we have achieved in the first phase of the conversation. By turning the metaphor around, creating the opposite image, my question, "How would it look if you were to dance together?" becomes a *striking moment*, the moment of change that Shotter and Katz (1996) speak about. This triggers a de- velopment for the coachee that has far-reaching implications for her understanding of the challenge that she initially saw in relation to her boss. Suddenly, something happens – also in a *bodily-sensory* dimension. The image begins to take root right away, as she envisions a particular form of dancing – waltz or tango. The coachee accepts my invitation and plays along. According to the Dutch philosopher Huizinga (1950), play is influenced by awareness from a different reality. Huizinga emphazises that play always remains distinct from all the other forms of thought in which we express the structure of mental and social life. The coachee's metaphor and my reshaping of it appear as a new form of thought that facilitates a new understanding of the coachee's reality. In the dialogue, play continues as role- playing or *pretend play* (Buytendijk, 1933),[4] where the coachee adopts a new role or a different social position by 'surrendering' to her boss, as she puts it. In the framework of developmental psychology, this form of play lets the child test behaviour patterns in relation to significant others (playing house, etc.). In this case, the coachee *plays* with a new position in relation to her boss. This play behaviour has a clearly *explorative* character as it examines different potential realities. This explorative character is especially clear in the coachee's choice of a specific form of dance: the tango. Tango unfolds in a framework of special agreements and forms of expression that influence the relationship between the (dance) partners. It is this explorative and playful element that helps bring so much life, dynamics and new insights to the coaching dialogue in this phase. This playful exploration transforms the coachee's perception of reality. From a structuralist-constructionist perspective, Piaget (1962) speaks about *accommodation*, a modification of the assimilation plan in relation to new and unknown situative conditions, which can be achieved through

---

[4]In 1919, Buytendijk was appointed professor of general biology at The Free University in Amsterdam. In 1946 he was appointed professor of general psychology at the University of Utrecht. He had a crucial impact on the phenomenological theory of play.

explorative play, among other means. In a narrative post-structuralist perspective (White, 2004) this play behaviour is viewed as another possible interpretation of reality. A reshaping of the metaphor in the coaching conversation *redefines the plot*, as *dancing around each other* becomes *tangoing together*. This new plot enables a narrative that lays the seed for one possible reinterpretation of reality. This reinterpretation provides the coachee with a new set of possible actions and, in the specific situation, a sense that the relationship has the quality that she was hoping for. Something that began as playful exploration makes it possible for her to act differently in her specific working relationship with the new boss.

5.1.2 Case 2: A Little More Skanderborg in My Life

The following case presents the story of a full five-session coaching process with Curt,[5] a director with specific administrative and economic responsibilities in an international corporation. Curt has a wife and two young children. The story is based on my notes from our conversations. The descriptions of Curt's situation and experiences emerged through my dialogue with him and represent my interpretation of what I heard him say during our conversations. It is not a stringently chronological representation; this gives me the freedom to create a coherent storyline that remains true to the actual process and the overall outcome:

Curt steps into my office, slightly hectic and out of breath. He apologizes because he is a few minutes late, but I smile and tell him not to worry about it. Curt seems a little tense. I ask him what brings him here. He lists a whole range of issues that he would like to discuss: his career – now and in the future; determining what he wants; his family – especially having more time with his children; his interactions with co-workers and family; his temper and 'bleak outlook', where just about everything is beginning to seem wrong. It seems that Curt has really looked forward to speaking with me. The words are pouring out of him. To me it seems that he has decided to trust me from the outset. We have a good rapport straight away.

He begins by outlining his educational background and his career. He describes himself as ambitious and acknowledges his urge to compare himself with others, especially colleagues but also former fellow students via the online network LinkedIn. "Some of them have pulled ahead, and I have to admit it's hard to be the

---

[5]The name is anonymized. Certain details in the story are not fully unfolded or have deliberately been left vague in order to ensure the coachee's anonymity. The person in the case story wrote the following to approve my use of the case story here: "Dear Reinhard, Thanks for your message. Yes, thank you, I am generally doing well, although I still sometimes lose sight of what is important and then I feel like that I am going down the drain, but then it's really great to be reminded of what it's all about, by reading your chapter about Curt for your book. It was fun to relive, and fun to see how some of the thoughts I have today actually began – especially the point about trying to socialize more with others in my working life instead of hiding behind my computer screen. You're most welcome to use the description in your book. I think it's well written and interesting to read."

best all the time. A colleague was made manager before me. He was a salesman, and I was the geek – that's how others create results," is his assessment of the successful rival. "I feel really bad when someone below me in rank pulls ahead in their career. The last time it happened I just couldn't cope. That was in my previous job. I had to quit. I was angry and bawled out my boss. I felt completely powerless and acted like a petulant child."

We talk a little more about the qualities that his successful rivals might have. Based on that, he adds that a particular colleague may have developed a better relationship with the person in charge of promotions. In the course of the conversation I further inquire about how these colleagues differ from Curt, and whether there is something he might learn from their approach and behaviour.

I also ask Curt what it means to be the best, and he replies, "It's a quest for higher pay and prestige." He describes himself as a consummate perfectionist. When I ask him about the costs associated with striving to be the best, he says that it takes up a lot of time, and that it has a negative impact in relation to his family and children and other activities. "I spend far too much time on my work. I often sit down at the computer again as soon as we are done with dinner. I am not involved enough with my family, and I find it difficult to relate to my children. Often, all we do is watch the cartoons together on TV," he admits. "I would love to spend more time with my kids." But something gets in his way: Curt explains how he is constantly hearing two voices inside his head that make him feel guilty about relaxing. The first voice says, "There are just a few little things you need to sort out, then you can relax and enjoy life for a while." And the second voice says, "There's always going to be something. At this rate, you won't have time until you're retired – or dead."

He also is not happy in his current job. Due to the economic downturn, there have been budget cuts, for example with regard to extra equipment in his new company car and with regard to business trips, which Curt considers an important feature that makes his working life a little more enjoyable. He is frustrated with the way things are at work right now, and his job satisfaction is suffering. He wonders how so many of his colleagues can remain unconcerned about the situation or even seem to thrive at work. "I almost find it hard to believe that they really feel that way," he says.

What keeps him going right now is volunteering in a community project that he is wholeheartedly involved in. "It's something that is really meaningful. And I would love to spend more time on it – also generally in the community and in local politics," he says.

I gradually form an impression of Curt: He is very focused on comparing himself to others, being the best and not wasting time by socializing with colleagues. He is making things hard for himself. He wants to be the best at his job, but he forgets that there is such a thing as interpersonal relations, a form of socializing that he experiences to some extent in his volunteer work.

My reflections lead to a particular question, and together with our subsequent work and ongoing reflections, the answer has a crucial impact on the remainder of the coaching process. I ask him, *"Could you mention and describe a situation in your everyday life that you experience as meaningful, which you enjoy, and where you really appreciate social interactions with others?"*

Curt immediately thinks of a situation: "Yes, every year when I go to the Skanderborg Festival [a well-known Danish annual music festival] with some of my old friends." I sense his energy as he explains: "You know, there's the anticipation, the excitement you have before you actually go. And once you're there: good music, flirting with girls without wanting it to lead to anything. Well, and the guy talk, the easy way we have of communicating. It makes me feel young. It's so relaxing. You forget about tomorrow. I catch myself thinking, I don't want this to ever end!" I share his excitement and ask what he finds most valuable about the situation. Curt answers without hesitation: "It's the community, it's the depth. All of that feels meaningful." He sees the Skanderborg Festival as a stark contrast to his working life. "At work, I'm always monitoring my performance and striving to avoid mistakes." I ask him how good relationships and forming a community might affect his working life – not least with regard to the possibility of promotion.

That leads to the introduction of 'Skanderborg Light' as the basis of a fundamental reorientation and a plot to help Curt create a new narrative about both his working life and his personal life.

In the next session Curt again opens the conversation by mentioning situations where he is dissatisfied, but he also begins to mention specific bright moments. For example, he mentions a good meeting in the owners' association of his housing area: "That was fun," he says with pleasure and adds, "I miss going out and spending time with others!" We agree that for our next meeting he should focus on the things he is good at, and which give him satisfaction. "Make a little scrapbook," I advise him.

Curt opens the next session by saying that he has become more carefree. I play with the words: "Carefree, ahh: Caring. Free!" Curt smiles and goes on to describe how he has been since we last met. "I appreciate situations with good collegial interactions," he says and tells me that he received acknowledgement from his boss and his colleagues who appreciate his contributions. Curt is happy about noticing things that he suddenly finds easy, and he attributes this to his own previous efforts. "I appear to be harvesting the fruits of my past efforts." He also describes having a much better relationship with his children: "Now, I often just stand in the kitchen, talking to my wife and kids, and I also sit down with my kids more often, where we do things together – it's really nice," he says. He still fears the situations where he 'falls into the black hole'. "Fortunately, it happens quite rarely now," he says with a tone of relief.

"What has happened in your life that has made you feel better now?" I ask. Again he mentions the word 'carefree' and says that his work is less prominent in his mind now. "I have also learned to say 'never mind'. I enjoy life a little more than before, but at the same time I'm not sure if that's really okay." Here he thinks especially of his future career potential, and whether his new approach might hold him back. "What would it take for you to be more than just carefree?" I ask. He reflects on his career and on how he might create a better work-life balance. And suddenly he begins to talk about specific new possibilities. That it might be a good idea to look for a job in the centre of town instead of working in the suburb where he is now. "It would be nice to be around other people, to watch them, to go shopping on the way home from work – that's quality of life for me," he says in a happy tone. We go on to talk about key values that he has begun to appreciate more in his life: sharing his life with his family, travelling more, enjoying the small pleasures in life. "I have definitely learned to relax and *come to terms* with who I am," he says in conclusion to our talk.

In our final conversation we focus mostly on the positive changes that have occurred in the process. Curt says that the family has initiated a little renovation project in their flat, which has given his wife and him lots of new energy and a sense of sharing. In relation to his work he notes with satisfaction, "I get a little less worked up about my work, I work less in the evenings, but it's definitely not because of any lack of commitment. I just have more energy, and things make more sense to me."

When I ask him, "What's the main thing you have learned after you started coaching?" Curt summarizes, "I am better at saying 'never mind', I get less worked up; I'm just more confident, and I no longer feel like a petulant child, as I did that time with my former boss."

5.1.2.1   Reflection on the Case

Toward the end of the process, the coachee seems to feel much better about himself and his life and work situation, and he has a realistic assessment of himself and what he can deliver. Coaching has helped him improve his self-esteem and develop an uplifting narrative in relation to his work and family life. Furthermore, his change is rooted in a specific new strategy, which is to be able to say 'never mind' and thus get less worked up about things. What happened in the coaching process to enable this transformation?

The coaching narrative that is presented here has a clear structure and storyline. The coachee presents the coach with a relatively large number of non-specific challenges in regard to both work and family life. In addition to these issues, he complains about a 'bleak outlook', where his world appears to collapse, and where he experiences fundamental existential doubt. By means of shared reflection and the coachee's in-depth description, as a coach I form an impression of his situation, which leads to the crucial question in the coaching process. This question focuses on a unique event that will help deconstruct the coachee's existing narrative. The question aims to focus on an uplifting exception within an appreciative framework: 'Could you mention and describe a situation in your everyday life that you experience as meaningful, which you enjoy, and where you really appreciate social interactions with others?' The question can be considered the climax and *turning point* of the narrative, where the coachee begins to be prepared to change his current personal *myth*, that is, his currently dominating and identity-shaping narrative about himself, by focusing on events and situations where he finds the relationships with his boss, colleagues and family more uplifting and meaningful. With this, the storyline begins to change from a downward trend to a clearly upward trend.

The case has a storyline with ideal-typical features and is therefore particularly well suited for clear theoretical reflection. Certain events in the process and selected coaching interventions should be theoretically generalized in order to provide inspiration for the reader's own narrative collaborative coaching practice. (In this section, certain theoretical concepts are highlighted in italics). In the following, I will expand on this storyline and – including certain theory elements, especially from narrative theory – describe what I see happening with Curt as well as my own reflections both during the process and today from my current position as a reflective practitioner-researcher:

In the initial stages of the process, Curt needs to present his experiences of past and current life situations and events. This is where he presents his *personal myth*, to borrow McAdams' (1993) term for a type of narrative that conveys a form of truth for Curt with regard to his person, and which thus plays an identity-founding role (see also Sect. 3.4.1.6). Here, the myth is the dominant narrative with the currently unfolded 'thick' descriptions. Ultimately, it is this myth that is causing him problems, and which he wants to change – in cooperation with me as his coach. In a narrative coaching process, I might have chosen to work with *externalization* (cf. Sect. 4.3.1.2) by naming the myth and speaking about it in an approach where the coachee takes a small step out of the story and relates to it from an outside perspective. As I experienced the coaching situation, however, other aspects appeared more salient. First of all, Curt clearly needed to present his story in the way that was most familiar to him, and secondly, I needed to understand his personal myth and integrate the many events from his past and present into a coherent storyline. In narrative collaborative practice, it will always be an open question – and a continuous balancing act to determine – just how much space to give the existing myth. In a sense, there is no reason to thicken it unnecessarily; on the other hand, in some situations the coach may need to develop a more in-depth understanding in order to spot possible cracks that might shed light on events that have the capacity to drive alternative narratives. In hindsight, I see that I was searching for certain hypotheses to facilitate my understanding of Curt's life. In Curt's presentations I sense a certain dismissal and denigration of social interactions with co-workers and superiors, which he characterizes as a waste of time. Fundamentally, however – based on what I hear between the lines – these interactions do seem to carry great importance in the working relations in Curt's workplace, not least in light of his hopes of continued advancement. I also begin to sense Curt's *articulation of values that are crucially important* to him, including interpersonal socialization and the meaningful quality of certain work tasks, something he currently only finds in his volunteer involvement in his local community. So far, these values have not thickened in other descriptions in his stories about himself. But the *learning gap* appears to be closing (cf. Sect. 4.3.1.3), and I sense a growing readiness in Curt (cf. Vygotsky's concept of the zone of proximal development) for a question where I, as his coach, can ask about a *unique event* or *outcome* in connection with an incident that had a significant uplifting character, and which is based on the aforementioned key values concerning interpersonal socialization and meaningfulness.

Based on my question about this unique event, Curt brings up his participation in the annual Skanderborg Festival with old friends. This event has precisely the uplifting character that he lacks in his everyday life; in addition, it is infused with some of the life values that he considers essential. My challenge as a coach now lies in discovering how this special event can be integrated into his everyday life, and how it can be used to thicken uplifting stories about Curt's everyday life and working life.

I introduce the concept of 'Skanderborg Light' as the title of a new and more uplifting story. In the subsequent session, Curt begins to talk about uplifting events from his working life. This is the first time that he initiates a shift in focus. Thus he begins to take the first steps toward deconstructing his personal myth and thicken descriptions into an alternative story. I support his effort to link these *events* with underlying *meanings and values*, where he talks about the benefit of socializing with others and enjoying their recognition. The learning gap, which had previously prevented a change process, has become noticeably narrower. He is beginning to be able to see cracks that make room for shedding light on the uplifting qualities. He expresses an entirely new intention when he says, "I miss going out and spending time with others!" In cooperation with me as his coach he begins to alter the plot in his life story. The remainder of the coaching process is shaped by a *re-authoring* conversation where Curt puts his new vision into words. Initially, this vision simply revolves around being 'carefree'. I play with the word – in the hope of providing appropriate scaffolding – by saying 'caring, free'. The re-authoring process is supported by certain *bridging tasks*. Curt emphasizes the importance of other people as crucial for his quality of life. A *conversation about key values*, which he is appreciating more and more in his life, begins to take on more gravity in his life stories. He articulates the outcome when he says, "I have definitely learned to relax and *come to terms* with who I am." This statement expresses a greater satisfaction with his self-perception. His former personal myth begins to crumble, and a new and more uplifting and life-affirming story begins to take shape with the involvement of several small and *uplifting events and reflections*.

5.1.3 Case 3: About Believing in Oneself

As the final case I present an excerpt from a narrative collaborative group coaching session. The participants are six young sports talents who represent one of the coaching groups involved in a research project at the Team Danmark line at the upper secondary school *Falkonergårdens Gymnasium*.[6] Young elite athletes have to

---

[6]Team Danmark is an elite sport organisation supporting athletes in regard to their sport and their educational or professional development. Falkonergaardens Gymnasium is a high school (upper secondary school) with a department for young athletes where the educational programme is extended by 1 year.

address three key challenges: (1) establishing a career in elite sports, (2) developing an identity as a young person growing up in a complex world that is generally characterized by individualization trends and self-presentation requirements and (3) balancing their sports career, education and personal life. The group coaching intervention applied in the research project aimed to stimulate the available resources in a process of mutual competence development and community-based reflection, where the young people share their joys (and sorrows?) and successes, learn from each other and develop their understanding and action strategies in relation to the challenges posed by their everyday life and athletic career.

The selected excerpt is from a conversation between Maria and Patrick, where the role of the other four participants in the sequence is to listen. The conversation turns out to be one of the most important events in the process for several of the participants, especially for Maria. Here is my description of the experience:

I perceive 16-year-old Maria as an incredibly target-oriented and ambitious student and elite athlete. She is clearly aiming for an international career and has already taken part in several European championships in her age group. In a later coaching session, her class mates say with a smile that the previous year, their first year, she could sometimes be a little 'too much'; almost desperate in her desire to be one of the best – at school and in her sport. At times she was unapproachable. She confirms this assessment now, as the others describe their impressions in a group conversation. During this period in the first year, she had a stress-related breakdown, and the school's Team Danmark coordinator was very supportive of her for a while. As a result of the breakdown, Maria has in fact begun to tone down her ambitions as a student. But she is still uncompromising in her sport. At one point during that day's session, Maria articulates her expectations of her sports coach: *"It's really important for me that my coach considers me a talent. If I'm not told that I am a talent, I'll quit!"*

Patrick, a very reflective, talkative and outspoken canoeist, responds immediately to Maria's intense statement. He thinks that she is being too defeatist: "No, you have to believe in yourself," he says. "I don't understand why you make yourself so dependent on what your sports coach thinks and says. The main thing is that you think you can make it!"

At first, though, Maria sticks to her expectations of her sports coach: "No, it's just important to me. I need to have the sense that things are working for me, and that my coach can see that I'm doing well, and that I'll be able to compete."

Patrick insists and becomes increasingly engaged: "But you know it better than anyone. You just have to believe in yourself! No one can tell how things are going to develop . . . "

As a coach, I notice Patrick's engagement, which goes beyond merely reasoning about what was said. He almost seems to want to convince Maria to embrace his own conviction. In order to take the conversation in a new direction I say to him, "Patrick, I can tell that you're very involved in Maria's story. What does that involvement say about you and who you are?"

Patrick picks up the ball and runs with it; he starts with a detailed and gripping story about his school days, when he was in the 4th grade of primary school, a story that is very open and honest, although this is only the third time we meet. I am surprised at this frank revelation and impressed that he dares be so open with his classmates:

> *"When I was in the 4th grade, I had a stammer, couldn't read properly, and I was overweight and didn't look too good," is how he begins his story. "Not many people believed that I could ever become the person I am today. I didn't really have any support from home, my mother in particular had had a rough childhood, and at a young age I learned to look after myself. I didn't want to trouble her with my problems. For example, if I locked my bike at training and found that I had left the key at home, I would simply carry the bike home. I kept my reading difficulties to myself. I just couldn't bear to burden my parents with it. The same with the stammer: Fortunately, there was this speech therapist who said that she could help me with all that. These experiences and the fact that I was able to handle my problems convinced me that I could fend for myself. I came to trust that things would work out for me. I learned that I could rely on myself, so now I think that I can make it if I want to."*

There is a moment's silence after this story, which seems to grip everybody in the room. Patrick has impressed me. He seems unafraid that this story might have negative consequences for him and his reputation. Paul, Patrick's best friend, who is sitting right next to him, is the first to break the silence; with admiration in his voice he says, "And I thought I knew you, Patrick. That's pretty intense! It's hard to imagine that you're the same person now as you were then."

Maria is fairly astonished by Patrick's story. She is sitting across from him, thinking. The story clearly makes an impression on her. After a while she says, astonished, "I can't believe that it was my remark that started all this." She adds, to Patrick, "You make me think. It's amazing that you were able to keep believing in yourself."

Later, it becomes evident that this event had a profound effect on Maria's relationship with her sports coach, herself and her approach to her training. She actually revisits Patrick's story in the final sessions. Everybody says that their perception of training has changed. In this connection, Maria says, "I have a different approach to discipline now. I used to do things because I had to, because the sports coaches told me to. Now it's *self*-discipline. I want to do it. When I fail to see the point with something – what the individual training elements are good for – then I ask my coach. Something has happened to me – to us, actually."

5.1.3.1   Reflection on the Case

This case is a gripping example of what can happen in narrative collaborative witnessing processes. The situation becomes an enriching and developing experience for everyone, not only for the two people directly involved in the exchange. Generally, witnessing can be understood as a conversation with a particular, rule-bound structure. As a coach I guide the process by means of questions where the focus shifts between the presentation of a certain event or statement and the subsequent reflection on the meaning and value of the statement for the witness or witnesses (in this case Patrick), or the witness' reflection on possible meanings and consequences of the event or statement for the original storyteller. Witnessing varies back and forth in focus between *action landscape* and *identity landscape*. (A particular ideal structure is briefly presented in a section on witnessing in Chap. 4). This ideal structure is not always possible, as it is not appropriate or ideal for all settings. Indeed, in my work with the young sports talents I have repeatedly chosen not to explain exactly how the witnessing process should ideally have proceeded (a meta conversation about the process), but all participants have been quick to acknowledge and appreciate the opportunity to respond to and reason about other participants' contributions and receive the other participants' comments and reflections on their own contributions. Thus, the witnessing process sometimes takes on a looser structure than that described in Sect. 4.3.1.3.

How should we interpret what happened in the conversation between Maria and Patrick? Maria opens with an honest and open but also rather direct and uncompromising statement. Her statement appears to have a strong spontaneous effect on Patrick, who has proved an engaged and active participant in the process, also in the two previous coaching sessions. Patrick's statement, however, can be perceived as equally direct and straightforward. Essentially, this clash of two positions may pose problems for a witnessing process, which has a very different purpose from a discussion. In a discussion, each party wants to present their best arguments, use their rhetorical skills to persuade the counterpart and other discussion participants to embrace their point of view. Group coaching and witnessing, on the other hand, have *nothing* to do with a discussion. Witnessing is an invitation to reflect on what is said, based on one's *own values* and the *meaning* and *consequences* that the other person's story might hold for oneself or the person who told the story. The participants act as a *resonance* or *sounding board* for each other. They resonate with each other and enrich the dialogue by offering their own reflections without presenting any assessment or judgment of what the other person said. These reflections focus mainly on values and on the way in which the statement makes sense as viewed from the point of view of one's own life universe. Without much complication, this approach can also be applied in larger meetings – the only requirements are that the person chairing the meeting introduces the procedure carefully and that all the participants accept it.

My comment to Patrick and my follow-up question to him should be understood in this perspective. First, I express my basic appreciation of his contribution and engagement. Next, I express my interest in hearing more from him by asking, "What does that involvement say about you and who you are?" Here I ask him to shift his perspective from assessment to self-reflection – a reflection in the identity landscape where he is invited to focus on personal values, convictions, aspirations, dreams and wishes that form the foundation of his own self-perception and identity. And Patrick accepts the invitation in a way that surprises all the participants. The intensity and the frankness in Patrick's story and its meaning for him, his self-perception and his fundamental action orientation affect all the participants in the coaching session. Patrick's story describes his most fundamental beliefs. His story becomes a living expression of his identity; an identity that has given him confidence, personal strength and goal direction, and which is ultimately the source of his impressive athletic achievements. The other participants know him in many regards, but mainly through his more visible actions and achievements. In his reply to my question he presents a story that not even his closest friend is familiar with. In Patrick's engaging and gripping story, the participants perceive a degree of *authenticity* that has a contagious effect on all the participants. Authenticity means *being real* and *being oneself*; it reflects a personal experience of one's own stance, attitude and behaviour, which others perceive as similar to one's own level of experience and reflection. Thus, the more aware one is of one's feelings and goals in relation to others, the more authentic one can be.[7]

This form of authenticity forms the basis of *relational attunement*, which I consider a prerequisite of developing reflective processes among two or more participants in a collaborative coaching process (see also Sect. 3.4.1.7). Sharing like this creates a reflective learning and developmental space, where new knowledge is co-created; knowledge that is meaningful to the individual and which can be shared with others. The development of this shared reflection space and co-created meaning universe is a characteristic feature of the witnessing process. Individually meaningful elements can be tested in relation to others, who take in the individual contributions in an appreciative spirit and adapt them to their own personal reality and life context. Group coaching as a narrative collaborative practice thus becomes a forum where the participants develop empowerment,[8] a personal strength that is based on the establishment of social capital[9] (Bourdieu, 1983; Putnam, 2000), a cohesive force that develops in social networks, and which the specific coaching session facilitates (Stelter, Nielsen, & Wikmann, 2011). Many of the group coaching participants mention that after the coaching process, they continue to draw on the other group members in conversations and for advice and support, something that previously seemed unthinkable, and which generates new possibilities in relation to their personal, relational and career development. These personal statements are further corroborated by significant findings from a study that was carried out 5 months after the completion of the intervention. More on that later (Sects. 5.2.2 & 5.3.1).

---

[7]I would like to thank my good colleague Ole Fogh Kirkeby for his insightful reflections on the concept of authenticity, which he has shared with me, and which have inspired this brief description. From a social-constructionist perspective (see Gergen, 2009a), the concept of authenticity is controversial. My presentation, however, integrates the individual and the relational perspective.

[8]In community psychology and socio-cultural theories, empowerment is used as a concept that highlights people's ability to counteract powerlessness and prove themselves able to affect their life situation. Group coaching focuses especially on the collective and collaborative awareness processes, which aim to enable all the participants to act in a competent and engaged manner in challenging situations.

[9]Social capital is a cohesive force that is present as a latent resource in social relations and networks in the form of trust, reciprocity and cooperation, where we learn from each other's knowledge and experiences on an ongoing basis, and where we use our reciprocal relations for the purpose of personal and common development.

5.2 Perceived Effect: A Narrative Analysis

The practicing coach or psychologist has virtually no possibility of studying effective factors in coaching or psychotherapy systematically and research-based in his or her own practice. Most practitioners do not use special evaluation methods that are capable of systematically tracking the effect of their work, neither in the form of interview studies nor in the form of quantifiable assessment/evaluation. The coach cannot step outside him/herself and the context he or she is a part of in order to ask the clients. Normally, the practitioner does not have access to any in-depth insight into the effects of the intervention based on the individual coachee's subjective experiences. The coach is too involved as a co-creator of the process. A coach or psychologist cannot ask their clients how the process went, for example by means of a qualitative interview.[10] One possibility is the use of questionnaires or evaluation forms. But in my opinion, supervision and reflection based on one's session notes, client files or even video or audio recordings offer a good and engaging way of developing one's practice. Generally, one develops a sense of what is going on and of the coachee's experience in his or her change process. But only rarely does a practitioner have the opportunity to carry out a systematic assessment of the long-term effect of his or her work.

I have taken advantage of this opportunity by involving a number of students working on their final thesis. As part of their thesis work, the students have carried out interview studies with a large number of group coaching participants from the project that the case above comes from. First, I will describe the narrative analysis method that was applied; next, selected group coaching participants will take the floor to tell their story about their experience of the process and how group coaching has affected them. In Sect. 5.3, I present the findings of a randomized controlled study, where the intervention group was compared with a control group.

5.2.1 The Narrative Analysis Method

The qualitative study of the perceived effect of group coaching is based on a narrative analysis of participant interviews that were carried out and analyzed by a group of students as part of their final thesis work. Narrative research aims to uncover how the participants create meaning in particular life contexts, in this case specifically in relation to the intervention that they participated in (Clandinin & Connelly, 2000; Czarniawska-Joerges, 2004).

To facilitate the intended presentation, the transcribed interviews were subjected to a combination of *interpretive phenomenological analysis* and *critical narrative analysis* (Langdridge, 2007). In the subsequent narrative text presentation of the

---

[10]Miller et al. (2003, 2006) present a strategy where feedback is an integrated part of their treatment/dialogue. They call this *feedback* or *outcome informed treatment (FIT)*.

individual participants, it is important to allow the individual to step into the light with his or her own words and personal expressions. The stories presented here are therefore based virtually exclusively on the participants' own words. The researcher's interpretation lies in identifying key units of meaning and in arranging the interview text into a story with a specific plot and storyline.

Narrative studies set a new agenda for social research by giving the participants a (personal) voice. The readers will be able to hear this voice and thus expand their own perspective in relation to challenges and contexts resembling the ones they read about. With clear reference to post-structuralist thinking, an acknowledged narrative researcher says,

> The narrative turn moves away from a singular, monolithic conception of social sciences toward a pluralism that promotes multiple forms of representation and research (Bochner, 2001, p. 134).

This suggests the benefit of working with multiple perspectives simultaneously and of recognizing the importance of having not just a single researcher's voice but multiple voices from researchers and project participants. Each in their way and from their individual theoretical or practical fields of experience, these voices qualify our knowledge about, for example, group coaching as a phenomenon.

5.2.2   Stories by Coaching Participants

In the following I present two stories. One is told by Maria, whom we already met in case study 3.[11] Maria was interviewed shortly after the end of the process, so some of the sessions she refers to took place 2–3 months prior to the interview. Certain experiences from the group coaching are interwoven with some of the subsequent actions and events, which suddenly take on new meaning – and thus may also alter the 'facts' of the original event. Hence, my description in case 3 also differs slightly from Maria's descriptions below.

The second story is told by Thomas, who was interviewed by one of my students[12] 6 months after the completion of the coaching process. In planning the thesis project I was unsure whether I could encourage a student to write a thesis involving participants who might not even recall the process any longer. I expected that many young people probably lead a life with so many different experiences that a coaching process of eight one-and-a-half-hour sessions over a period of 12 weeks would soon be forgotten. But I was wrong. Thomas' story is included here because he speaks so vividly about the changes that the group coaching has led to in relation to his sport, himself and his way of handling certain challenges.

---

[11] I would like to thank my two former graduate students Louise Emil Clausen and Thomas Høgh Henriksen for their permission to print Maria's story. The name is anonymized.

[12] I would like to thank my former graduate student Andreas Rytsel Nielsen for his permission to print Thomas' story. The name is anonymized.

The stories reveal the significant influence that group coaching has had on the participants' self-perception and identity, and how it has made the participants empowered, decisive and capable of creating new meaning. The stories speak for themselves. The individuals appear in the light of their own descriptions of their experiences during the coaching project. In the following, the reader is invited to imagine how such an approach might be useful in their life and work context.

5.2.2.1 Maria: My Sport Is Who I Am. It's My Lifestyle

My name is Maria, and I'm sixteen years old. I do sports[13] on an elite level. I spend about 25 hours a week training, and in addition I do fitness and workout. Mentally, my sport is a huge part of my daily life. I think about my diet a lot, what I do, and whether it will affect me later in terms of training.

At first, I was actually a little negative toward this process. The idea of sharing a lot of stuff about myself, opening up and sharing things that are really personal, I felt that was hard. But once we got going, I find it kind of interesting. It was interesting to hear how others deal with their problems. In fact, we've begun to talk more in the group, and I pay more attention to the others, like if they're having a bad day, or they've done something great, I ask about it. You could say that we've gotten to know each other in a new way.

I think it was a good process, because I learned to think about why I do things instead of just doing them. If I train really hard, I stop to think about why it is I'm doing this; it's because I want to be really good at it. Or sometimes in school, I think, why is it I bother to pay attention to class right now, if I could be chatting with the others instead; it's because I want good marks. I was surprised to be able to learn so much about myself, because I thought that I knew myself really well.

The conversations with the other athletes also made a big impression on me. Like the one with Patrick, where I said that my sports coach did not expect me to be able to qualify for the world championship group. Patrick told me to stop worrying about what my coach said, and that if I wanted to be in that group, I simply had to train to get in. After that, my training was much better than it used to be, and it just sort of became natural for me to train to get in, so I told him, and he said, 'well, do it, then.' That helped me a little.

Also Laura, who had injured her elbow and needed surgery. She was also wondering whether the sport was really worth it, because she also wanted to be able to hold her baby one day. That got me thinking, like, hey, think about how much time you're spending on this; you really have to want it. Just think about what any other teenager would be doing on a normal Tuesday, and there I am, training again tonight. That has made me more conscious of why I do certain things. For example, I only eat sweets on Fridays, so all the other days, I might think, why is it again that I'm doing this? It's because I have to do it to excel. I have learned to accept that my sport is not just a sport, it's a lifestyle, and you have to acknowledge that. Before the coaching process I used to think that I would just compete until I didn't enjoy it anymore. But now I think that I'm doing this because I love this lifestyle. But that has its drawbacks too, because when you have a poor training round sometimes, it can feel like my world is coming to an end, because I do spend so much time training.

But all the training, a lot of homework and time pressure sometimes stress me out. In the past I would just say, 'fuck it', and then I would go to bed, pull the blankets over my head, and then I wouldn't come out until I couldn't sleep any longer. After group coaching I am better at dealing with my problems, and I try to solve them by making a plan. I've become

---

[13]For the sake of anonymity, the specific sport has been omitted.

more aware of what it is that I want to achieve with my sport. So I think that I can use it to make the whole thing more structured, like, make a plan, where I used to be more of a mess. I didn't have the time to think about how to deal with a particular problem. Now I'm better at approaching my sports coach and saying, I have a problem, and I need to find a solution. I think that's pretty cool – that I'm not afraid to admit it when I have a problem now. It's cool to admit that sometimes you don't have everything under control – and then ask for help. It takes some of the pressure off if you tell others about your problem. If I tell people at training that I'm tired, it's nice, because then they have a basis for understanding why I am the way I am.

It's been great to receive feedback and to hear the others' opinions, because they're all my age, and they do more or less the same as I do, instead of talking to a sports coach. Like, I used to only talk to the two girls, but now I've begun to talk to the boys as well and getting to know them, compared to the others in class, because we know each other in more of a sports context and in a different way. I mean, I've learned more about how the others think when they train, or when they do really well.

5.2.2.2   Thomas' Story: Just Do What You're Good at

My name is Thomas, and I'm eighteen years old and in my third year of upper secondary school. I have played __[14] for 13 years. I started when I was five, because my whole family played: my mom, my dad and my little sister. So I thought, 'I'll give it a go.' I mean, they just dragged me along to the gym.

The first thing I remember from group coaching is that the focus was on how we were doing as a team. Since I'm a team player, we talked about how things were working in the team, and how the team could improve. Especially in situations when we are under pressure. Then we talked about how to deal with these situations, individually and as a team. And what you might think in those exact situations. What you could do to be sure to score.

The next thing I remember is that we talked about having that sense of victory. And how we felt in the group in the situations where we think, 'okay, we have this in the bag now.' I remember a game, like a month ago. The score was tied. We played four times ten minutes, and there were only 20 seconds left or something like that. I had the ball on top, and we're down by one point. In that situation, of course, you have to stall for time to make sure the others don't have time to score. So I'm on top, and I call one of my team mates, and then I feint. I make my move, and then I score. The game ends in that same second. We win. Compared to the time before group coaching, it's a very relaxed feeling. Before, I would have said, 'now I just have to score, otherwise we're screwed.' The good advice Reinhard gave me was to try to be relaxed and just do what you're good at. In the past six months, I have used that a lot in my training and my games. Especially in those high-pressure situations, where you're not quite sure what to do. Now I just take it nice and easy and relaxed and do what I do best. I have thought about how you could use the same approach in exams, especially when you're under pressure, and you're super nervous. Then you should just do what you do best, just do what you can. But that wasn't something we talked about in group coaching, that was mainly about sports. At least, I don't remember us talking about anything to do with school.

I have been much better at accomplishing my goals after group coaching. I don't know if you could say that it's because of the coaching. But it probably is, one way or another. I mean, before I only trained with my own team. Now I've begun to train with the elite

---

[14]A team sport.

team in the club, where we play for the Danish championship. I train much more now and on a higher level. I joined the elite team a month ago. That was pretty cool. Their coach came over and said that he had watched me train with my own team. Then he came up after training and asked if I wanted to have a go at training with the elite team. So I said, 'yes, sure I do.' Then he gave me the schedule, and I showed up for training. After two or three weeks with the elite team, he said, 'okay, you can join the team,' and then I was allowed to train with them regularly. It's super cool. I don't get much playing time with this team, they are a lot bigger, stronger and older than me, and they're more experienced. But it's great practice for me. You're pushed much harder than in your own training, and you learn much more from it. People are faster and better, and of course that helps a lot – that makes you a better player. Of course, it's a little hard, the fact that they're better. I think it makes you look worse somehow.

I don't know if it's just the amount of training that has made it so that I get to train with the elite. But coaching has affected me, especially in those high-pressure situations; it's really helped me out. I think it makes me a better player that I received coaching, in some ways I think it does. I think group coaching has helped me take a step up. Reinhard was thinking a lot about this thing of doing what you can and what you do best. And I think that I have really focused on that. In that sense I guess I've been rewarded by moving up a step, like, in the hierarchy in one of the top series. Especially in those high-pressure situations where you have to go in and decide a match. If there is very little time left, and the score is tied, and I need to place that one shot for us to get ahead. In those cases it definitely helps me. It really helps me score more often in high-pressure situations.

But it wasn't just Reinhard who helped me. I mean, you get a sort of group feeling, where you think 'okay, I'm not the only one doing this.' There were five of us in a group plus Reinhard as the coach, and then we took turns. For example, the swimmer explained when she did what she does best, and of course that's when she is swimming. The fencer described what he does best, and then we just took turns. So, there are other people who think like, 'okay, now I just have to go in there and do what I'm good at.' That actually gave me more confidence; yes, confidence is a good term for it. Yes, it definitely gave me confidence, I thought, 'okay, I can do this shit,' I just need to go and do it. It was especially hearing the others say it and also the fact that they felt the same way. I don't know if it's because we are a Team Danmark class, and we are all elite athletes. But I do think that the fact that there are more of us makes you think, 'okay, they can do it, they're doing what I'm doing, and they feel the same way.' It creates a little community, the same interest, even if it's not the same sport. It was nice that there were others who felt the same way.

Hans, who also did this coaching thing, he was up against some Italian bloke. He said that the Italian nation is just so much better than the Danish. Somehow, he just thought to himself before the fight, 'okay, I've lost this one,' and he approached the fight with that attitude. Then he got into the fight, and I think he was ahead for much of it. And then he came under pressure, and eventually he lost. I think it's a pretty interesting story, this thing where you're down, or you're up, and then you still lose. Of course, the outcome was not so good, but it was pretty interesting to hear about. I think that I could put myself in his shoes with this thing where he's under pressure. It's also this thing where somehow you don't defend your lead. Of course, you have to try to equalize, to get even farther ahead. You can go in there and go toe to toe with the best. That's what I took home from the fencer's story. At first, of course, he was really, really pissed off and really, really bitter about the fact that he had lost. But afterwards, when he'd had time to think about it, he was proud, of course, that he had fought so well. Against an Italian too; that made him pretty proud.

I had an experience myself, where the fencer's story sort of affected me a little. It was a tournament in Sweden, where we go up against the best team, the best team by far. We pull ahead, and then we still end up losing – not by as much as we had imagined, but we still lost. Of course that really sucked, especially because we had just been ahead. In the changing room after the game, we talked about it, like, 'okay, everyone actually did pretty well. We only lost by like ten points or something, where we could have lost by a lot more, to this really great team.' I don't recall if I was the one who said it – yes, it was me. I said to the guys in the changing room, 'look, guys, we played pretty damn well, we only lost by ten, and we could have lost by a hundred to this great team.' So everybody nodded a little. They were still pissed off, but still, they were nodding, like, 'yeah, you're right about that.' It was the fencing story that just came up and nudged me there.

I used one of the swimmers' stories, Lene. She said that you should be able to accept criticism and then of course use it constructively. The way we talked to each other in training, we're not pulling any punches, of course. We felt that we could get in each other's face more, in a good way, of course, to help each other improve. You can push people a little more in training and still mean it in a good way. Like, yesterday, in training, someone in my team didn't pass very well. I yell at him a lot, but I also give him praise: 'nice one' and stuff like that. That's something I think I've taken home from our talks with Reinhard. You're hard on each other, but it's still well intended, so that he'll learn from it and get better.

In training, it's almost all competition, but that's great. You push each other more, because you want to keep your place on the team and get extra minutes and stuff. But you can still be friends. It's like, when you're on your way to training, you're best friends. In training you're at each other's throats. And then a little later, you're best friends again, in a good way.

A story that made a big impression on me was someone from my class who does judo. He spends a lot of time worrying about being in a particular weight class. So often, when he weighs like a kilo too much or something, then he has to lose weight before some big event. It has made a big impression on me, the way he lost weight. Like, the way he would lie in bed, sweating, wearing a wool cap and mittens, under two blankets. He took saunas, and he just needed to get all this liquid out of his body. He didn't eat much, and then he had to be ready to fight in the competition. Of course it was something he had to do, but I thought that was pretty cool. That's pure willpower; it's cool to know that he is so committed to his sport, and that he does all this to perform. If I have to push myself, I sometimes think about this story, and I say to myself that if he can do it, I can do it too.

Like, we have these timeouts, where they put you on the bench. I think that I deal with that differently than I did before group coaching. Somehow I think that I listen more to what the coach has to say. After all, he's in charge, and you sort of feel that you have to listen to him a little more. He knows more than we do. Before, I'd be drinking water, and I wasn't really listening. I think there are many situations where you're like, 'okay, focus now,' because he's giving good advice. Reinhard said that you have to be focused all the time and pay attention and stuff. So when I was sitting there on the bench during timeout, tired as hell, and then I thought, 'oh, no, what was it Reinhard said . . .' So I would think back to when we were talking about focusing. I also remember that the judo fighter, he had a really hard time focusing when he had to lose weight. I don't know if you can really compare it, but he really had a hard time focusing. It's usually when you're behind that it becomes hard to maintain focus, I mean, on some level you're really pissed off, precisely because you're behind. You get sort of grumpy inside, and you often say shit to and about your team mates. I get more aggressive, and I yell at people, like 'pass the ball, damn it!' Then it might help to think back, 'just do it like we talked about it at group coaching.'

So I think my daily life has become more structured after group coaching. Like, I'm better at knowing when to do what. I know when it's time to do homework, when to train, and when to spend time with family and friends. I feel that it has provided a good structure. My daily life is more structured thanks to group coaching. We talked a lot about how we all felt, especially as individuals. We talked about how we felt about friends, family and our sport. Then this thing came up, that we had to make sure to have time for everything, so it's not all about the game all the time. Not to cut out your family and your mates, because you're so worried about school. I have much more structure now, which gives me more time with friends, family, ball playing and school. It's important for me to focus on all these things. I have to admit, I've begun to use my calendar a lot more. Writing things down, like when I have an appointment with my mates, and when I have class.

Afterwards, we haven't talked so much about the coaching as such. But personally, I feel that I have taken many of the stories or some of the stories with me. Like the stories I mentioned about fencing and the judo fighter. But we don't talk much on a daily basis. We're not like, 'do you remember that time in group coaching?' We don't do that. We don't use each other much. I don't know if we remember to ask, 'hey, Frank, how did that tournament go?' Well, in fact, we might ask more questions, 'Frank, how did it go this weekend?' and things like that. Maybe we ask a little more about the people who were in our group – about their results and stuff. Then they get some feedback, like 'all right, well done, definitely.' Yes, I think we ask more about the people who were in our group. Probably also because you take an interest in their sport, like, you get an insight into how they feel, and what they do. In coaching we also talked about the times when things don't go well. Like, you might say, 'okay, things didn't go so well this weekend.' Frank came up two weeks ago, so I asked him how the Nordic championship had been, and he said, 'ah, I got clobbered.' Then I said something like 'okay, too bad,' and 'who did you go up against in your first round?' Then he tells me a little, and I say, 'man, that sucks,' in order to be supportive. I asked because he hadn't been there that weekend, when we were supposed to go a party. He knew that he'd been beaten, and then you know you just have to train harder and do better. He wasn't embarrassed. I think everybody in our class has lost sometime. THAT'S THE WAY IT IS. It can be hard to stay positive, but if you take the example with Frank: He'll tell you that he lost, but then he'll also tell some story where he just completely wiped out his opponent. Where he just totally kicked arse in a fight. In order to get over the bad stuff you can come up with a good story, and that helps you get back on top again.

Generally, I think it's been really good to take part in the coaching sessions. I think it's been great, and I've used it over the past six months, for example this thing about structuring my time. I also think there are some of the special situations from group coaching that you can use in your sport. Like, you can use the situations the others talked about to plug into your own training or fights or whatever you do. I think it has given me a lot, even if I've probably forgotten some things. But there are still things that just stick, and which you have made part of your daily life and part of your training schedule and stuff. That's really cool. I also think, psychologically, that we've discussed things. We have shared our experiences with others, like trips abroad, tournaments and things like that. The fact that we've been able to share with others, I think that's nice. I think it's really nice to tell your stories to others, because the others are listening to you, thinking, 'okay, that was pretty cool' and things like that. They also ask, 'how did it go?' and so on. Throwing that out there to share with the others, that's neat, I think. Like, before group coaching, I used to keep things more to myself. I didn't really have anyone to share it with. Like, somehow, things improved a little when I joined the Team Danmark class. Here I could share a little more. But in coaching, in a way I was forced to do it – in a good way – to tell my stories to others, and people were listening. Group coaching has helped me focus on the good situations, and that is motivating for me. If I have a poor training round, it just sucks. But of course, then you try to think, 'okay, that was just a bad day,' and then you're back on again the next day. I think coaching has been extremely helpful. Especially in some of those situations, and I would like to find out how to become a sports coach. It's pretty awesome that you can help people improve their performance. Like, the way it helps people in all these different situations.

5.2.3 Reflection on Perceived Effect

Psychotherapy research has identified four key effective factors (Grawe, Regli, & Schmalbach, 1994): resource activation, problem activation, motivation clarification and problem management. These findings and the research into the success criteria for the coaching process (see also Greif, 2007, 2008) can serve as a guide for the effectiveness of coaching (we will return to this topic in Chap. 7).

The three presented case stories and the qualitative studies I have conducted in connection with my research[15] have produced findings that can also generally be associated with the key effectiveness factors from Grawe et al. (1994):

- The participants are able to develop action strategies to handle challenges in their daily life and athletic career. That activates the participants' own resources and capacity for problem management.
- The participants experience significant value through the shared process of meaning-making by exchanging perspectives on various challenges and by learning from their peers. That leads to a form of problem activation and enhances their motivation.
- The participants state that group coaching intervention improves their attention, and that others can support their developmental process. That leads to the establishment of social networks and becomes a clear factor in their resource activation.
- The participants experience renewed enjoyment from their involvement in their sport by focusing on meaning-making and personal values. That leads to resource activation and enhances their motivation.
- Finally, the participants mention that they have developed a specific strategy for managing stress by focusing on the present.

5.3   Statistical Effect: Social Recovery and Well-Being as the Main Outcomes

Studies that are based on a randomized, controlled research design are rare in coaching research so far (see e.g. Fillery-Travis, & Passmore, 2011; Spaten, 2010), and in my assessment, the study presented here is the first of its kind to evaluate the effect of the narrative collaborative intervention. A quantitative study, however, only allows for a very general assessment; therefore, the research project has also included several qualitative studies. The previous section has already outlined some of this research. A randomized, controlled study is often viewed as the highest approved method for documenting effect. It is standard procedure in medical research, for example. The basic principle is that the participants are randomly divided into two groups: an intervention group and a control group (see my critical comments about evidence in Chap. 6). Both groups are subjected to the same procedure for effect measurement, in our study a validated questionnaire that measures various aspects of *stress* and *motivation*, two psychological constructs that we have considered especially important for intervention effect. Thus, we cannot

---

[15]This refers to three Master theses as part of my research project. These were written by Thomas Behrens & Lene Gilkrog, Thomas Høgh Henriksen & Louis Emil Clausen and Andreas Rytsel Nielsen.

rule out measurable effects in other areas that simply were not included in our assessment. The research design is very appropriate and widely used in medical science, for example in connection with testing new drugs and procedures, where one group of patients receives the test drug, while a control group receives a placebo.

However, using this procedure to study a coaching intervention is more complicated than a traditional medical study. What is it that makes this research approach so much more complicated and the randomization procedure and the use of a control group more complex and possibly less ideal? Earlier, I mentioned that the coaching relationship and the coachee's readiness and commitment are key factors for a positive outcome of an intervention (see Chap. 3). I will briefly address these two factors in relation to the study that was carried out:

1. The *coaching relationship*: Our study involved five coaches, three women and two men,[16] each with their unique appearance and style. In order to minimize biases we have used common guidelines (see Chap. 4, Sect. 4.3.1.2.) and frequent collegial supervision meetings to coordinate our approach.
2. The *coachee's readiness and commitment*: With regard to the coachee's readiness, this study design clearly has a slight drawback. The participants originally gave their full consent to take part in the study, but they did not know ahead of time which group they would be assigned to or the specific implications of coaching in this context. They did not deliberately choose to change their life situation by taking part in coaching, a factor that is normally considered crucial for a successful outcome. The involved coaches therefore had to compensate by means of motivation measures, especially in the beginning of the process.

The impact of these two factors should be considered in the critical assessment of the findings that are presented below. It is however, undoubtedly positive that the study is able to document positive effects, particularly with regard to the long-term effect of the group coaching intervention.

5.3.1 Research Design and Findings

The research project and the intervention itself were carried out under the leadership of the author in cooperation with a larger number of project partners.[17] The overall

---

[16]The coaching intervention team included M.Sc. (physical education and sport), coach and consultant Lotte Ellebjerg Møller, M.Sc. (psychology) and coach Shereen Horami, M.Sc. (psychology), M.Sc. (physical education and sports) and Industrial Ph.D. Morten Bertelsen, M.Sc. (psychology) Sofie Ejlersen and project manager, Professor Reinhard Stelter. The study is published in Stelter et al. (2011).

[17]In addition to the previously mentioned coaches I would like to thank Rector Kirsten Cornelius and Head Teacher and Team Danmark coordinator Christina Teller, Falkonergårdens Gymnasium, Frederiksberg/Copenhagen, colleagues at the Department of Nutrition, Exercise and Sports, University of Copenhagen, Ph.D. student Johan Wikmann for his contributions and for his own research carried out in the same department, Associate Professor Anne-Marie Elbe for her expertise in the use of questionnaires, administrative officer, Ph.D. Glen Nielsen for his help with the

goal of the study was to examine the influence of narrative collaborative group coaching in the career development, self-reflection and general well-being of young sports talents with the purpose of facilitating the integration of their athletic career, educational requirements and personal lives. The young people who took part in the research project typically had very high ambitions for their career and therefore tended to spend many hours on training and in competitions, often associated with considerable travel time.

Taking part in elite sports is extremely demanding. The participants in this study all attended upper secondary school and therefore had classes, homework and exams to deal with in addition to handling a potentially challenging transition to adult life. Furthermore, they also had to manage long training hours as well as their own and others' performance pressures, performance demands and athletic ambitions. This combination and the number of challenges they were facing has been recognized a key source of stress in elite athletes (Cohn, 1990).

The statistical study[18] is based on a randomized, controlled design with 77 subjects, 31 of whom participated in group coaching, while 46 were assigned to the control group. All the participants filled out a validated questionnaire prior to the study, at the midway point, immediately after the final intervention session and 5 months after the end of the intervention. The coaching participants were divided into groups of four to six athletes, who received group coaching on a narrative collaborative basis (see description in Chap. 4). The control group did not engage in any specific activities. The questionnaire aimed to rate changes in stress management and well-being (Elbe, 2008).

The findings showed significant improvements among the subjects who partic-ipated in group coaching. Figure 5.1 illustrates how the 12-week-long coaching intervention influenced the level of *social recovery*[19]; this positive effect was also present in comparisons between the situation before the intervention and the situation 5 months after completion of the intervention. However, no significant improvement was found from the completion of the intervention to the measurement 5 months later. Social recovery is a construct in the questionnaire we used (Elbe, 2008) that reflects a return to a higher level of social functioning and the participants' growing awareness and inclusion of others in their life.

There were similar positive findings with regard to the participants' general well-being. Figure 5.2 illustrates that the 12-week-long coaching intervention

---

statistical analysis, administrative officer Marianne Brandt-Hansen and student Daniel Hundahl for their administrative support, psychologist and supervisor Mette Amtoft and, finally, Team Danmark, the Danish elite sports organization that funded the project.

[18] I owe a special thanks to Ph.D. Glen Nielsen for his assistance with the statistical analyses.

[19] In order to measure social recovery, a form of social satisfaction, the participants were asked,

"*In the course of the past three days,*

... *I have laughed*

... *I have had fun with friends*

... *I have seen close friends*

... *I have enoyed myself*"

Scores of 0–6 corresponding to never, rarely, occasionally, several times, often, very often, always.

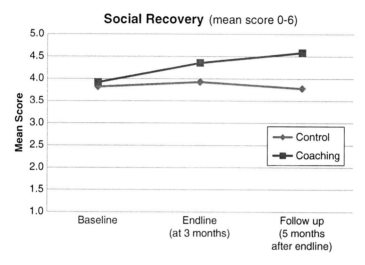

Fig. 5.1 Positive development in social recovery among the group coaching participants (**positive effect of group coaching** (measured immediately before the beginning of and immediately after the completion of the intervention). Adjusted for baseline scores **coaching group had 0.381 higher social recovery score after 12 weeks compared to control group**. Effect size was medium ($r = 0.24$, $p = 0.038$). **Positive long-term effect of group coaching** (measured immediately before the beginning of and 5 months after the completion of the intervention). Adjusted for baseline scores **coaching group had 0.584 higher social recovery score at follow-up compared to control group**. Effect size was moderate ($r = 0.275$, $p = 0.035$). **No long-term effect of group coaching** (5 months after completion). Adjusted for week 12 scores **coaching group had 0.359 insignificant ($p = 0.247$) higher social recovery score at follow-up compared to control group**. Effect size was low ($r = 0.163$) and insignificant ($p = 0.247$))

influenced their level of general well-being[20]; this positive effect was also found in a comparison between the situation before the intervention and the situation 5 months after completion of the intervention. However, no significant improvement was found from the end of the intervention to the measurement 5 months later. An increase in someone's general well-being means that the person perceives him/herself as being in a better mood, more relaxed and more at ease.

The most surprising finding in this research project is the long-term effect of the intervention on the former participants, a finding that is relatively rare; first of all, because most studies do not collect data several months after completion of the intervention, and secondly because it is rarely possible to document any significant long-term effect of an intervention.

---

[20] In order to measure general well-being, the subjects were asked,
  "*In the course of the past three days,*
  ... I have felt confident
  ... I have been in a good mood
  ... I have felt happy
  ... I have felt satisfied"

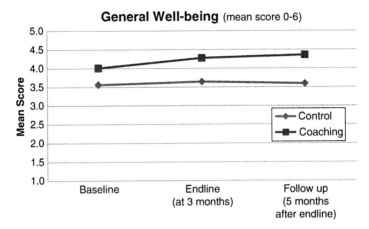

Fig. 5.2 Positive development in general well-being among group coaching participants (positive effect of group coaching (measured immediately before the beginning of and after the completion of the intervention). Adjusted for baseline scores **coaching group had 0.311 higher general well-being score after 12 weeks compared to control group.** Effect size was small (r = 0.22) and borderline significant (p = 0.059). Positive long-term effect of group coaching (measured immediately before the beginning of and 5 months after the completion of the intervention). Adjusted for baseline scores **coaching group had (borderline significant) 0.602 higher general wellbeing score at follow-up compared to control group.** Effect size was moderate (r = 0.23, p = 0.077). From intervention end-point to follow-up: no effect. Adjusted for week 12 scores **Coaching group did not have higher general well-being score at follow-up compared to control group.** Effect size was low (r = 0.130) and insignificant (p = 0.355))

Let us therefore look at the effect of the group coaching intervention on the participants 5 months after completion of the intervention. As mentioned earlier, the study did not find any lasting effect on *social recovery* and *general well-being* after completion of the intervention. But suddenly, we see findings pertaining to effects that only seem to occur after completion of the intervention. Effects are found in two new dimensions in relation to stress management and well-being: physical recovery[21] and perceived success[22] (see Figs. 5.3 and 5.4).

---

[21] In order to measure physical recovery the participants were asked,
   "In the course of the past three days,
   ... I have felt physically relaxed
   ... I have felt comfortable
   ... I have felt physically fit
   ... I have felt physically strong."

[22] In order to measure perceived success, the participants were asked,
   "In the course of the past three days,
   ... I have completed important tasks
   ... I have been successful
   ... I have made important decisions
   ... I have had good ideas."

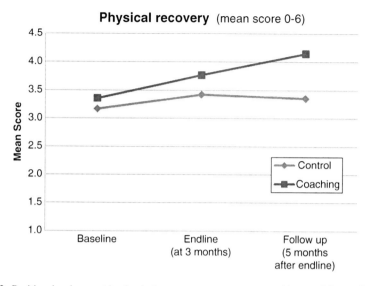

Fig. 5.3 Positive development in physical recovery among group coaching participants 5 months after the intervention (No short-term effect of group coaching (measured immediately after the completion of the intervention). Adjusted for baseline scores **coaching group had insignificant (p = 0.207) 0.228 higher physical recovery score after 12 weeks compared to control group.** Effect size was low (r = 0.14, p = 0.207). **Positive long-term effect of group coaching** (measured immediately before the beginning of and 5 months after the completion of the intervention). Adjusted for baseline scores **coaching group had 0.666 higher physical recovery score at follow-up compared to control group.** Effect size was moderate (r = 0.346, p = 0.008). **Positive long-term effect** (measured immediately after the completion of the intervention and 5 months after the completion of the intervention). Adjusted for week 12 scores **coaching group had 0.582 higher physical recovery score at follow-up compared to the control group.** Effect size was moderate (r = 0.306, p = 0.026))

5.3.2 Discussion of Findings

The findings clearly show that group coaching had a significant effect, both immediately after completion of the intervention and 5 months later. The findings show a significant increase in the level of social recovery, a form of social satisfaction; this can be interpreted as consistent with the overall intention of narrative collaborative group coaching. One of the main purposes of this form of coaching is for the group participants to learn to share experiences, thoughts and reflections in order to stimulate and learn from each other. In doing so, they help both the group as a whole and the individual athlete form new, uplifting stories about unique events and challenging situations. The simultaneous and significant increase in the participants' general well-being is undoubtedly associated with their growing sense of social satisfaction. By reinterpreting key events and situations in a more positive light in the coaching session, the participants are also more likely to perceive present and future events as less stressful. As a result, the participants' general well-being improves.

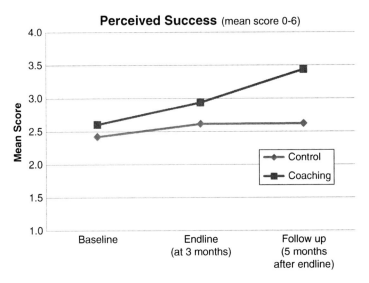

Fig. 5.4 Positive development in perceived success in group coaching participants 5 months after the intervention (No short-term effect of group coaching (measured immediately after the completion of the intervention). Adjusted for baseline scores coaching group did not have significant different score for success. **Positive long-term effect of group coaching** (measured immediately before the beginning of and 5 months after the completion of the intervention). Adjusted for baseline scores **coaching group had 0.597 higher success score at follow-up. compared to the control group.** Effect size was moderate (r = 0.34) and highly significant (p = 0.008). **Positive effect of group coaching measured from the end-point of the intervention until follow-up:** Adjusted for week 12 scores **coaching group had 0.470 higher success score at follow-up compared to control group.** Effect size was medium (r = 0.275) and borderline significant (p = 0.051))

In the final evaluation at the end of the sessions, many participants stated that their behaviour had changed: They had begun to include some of the group members as dialogue partners, also outside the coaching context. Some of them also modified the way they related to team or club mates and became more interested in cooperating with the sports coach in their club in a new way. These developments all clearly reflect the essence of social recovery.

The participants' new modes of interacting, where they use each other as dialogue partners in what are, for them, meaningful life contexts, is also found to influence the findings in the statistical analysis: The former group coaching participants experience a significant increase in perceived physical recovery and perceived success. Thus, it appears that the participants have learned something in group coaching that has improved their subjective experience of their own physical resources and success.

The qualitative study in particular has shed light on how the participants have perceived the importance of others in their personal developmental process. Hence I link the group coaching process to the concept *community of practice*

(Lave & Wenger, 1991; Wenger, 1998), which I consider a key theoretical concept for explaining what has also emerged in group coaching as narrative collaborative practice. Wenger (2011) offers the following description of the term on his website:

> Communities of practice are formed by people who engage in a process of collective learning in a shared domain of human endeavour: a tribe learning to survive, a band of artists seeking new forms of expression, a group of engineers working on similar problems, a clique of pupils defining their identity in the school, a network of surgeons exploring novel techniques, a gathering of first-time managers helping each other cope. In a nutshell: Communities of practice are groups of people who share a concern or a passion for something they do and learn how to do it better as they interact regularly.

Wenger (1998) points to three aspects as essential for the development of a community of practice: mutual engagement, a joint enterprise and the development of a shared repertoire; these factors can be described as follows:

- *Mutual engagement*, which exists because the participants are engaged in actions whose meaning is mutually negotiated. To achieve mutual engagement the participants must be able to *supplement each other*, and they must have overlapping competences in order to act as participants in the same community of practice.
- A *joint enterprise* promotes bonding – based on a shared negotiation process that all the participants are involved, in one way or another, and where everyone seeks to convince the others. Furthermore, everybody has a shared responsibility for the situation.
- A *shared repertoire* includes routines, concepts, tools, action strategies, stories, gestures, symbols, procedures, actions and concepts that are a condition of and a result of the development of a community of practice.

A community of practice develops a common basis for meaning-making based in a culture that is shared or developed in the group process. Bruner (1996) offers an excellent description of culturally situated meaning-making or meaning production, which goes to the core of what happens in narrative collaborative group coaching:

> Culture ... is superorganic. But it shapes the minds of individuals as well. Its individual expression inheres in *meaning making*, assigning meanings to things in different settings on particular occasions. Meaning making involves situating encounters with the world in their appropriate cultural contexts in order to know 'what they are about.' Although meanings are 'in the mind', they have their origins and their significance in the culture in which they are created. It is this cultural situatedness of meanings that assures their negotiability and, ultimately, their communicability. Whether 'private meanings' exist is not the point; what is important is that meanings provide a basis for cultural exchange. (Bruner, 1996, p. 3)

The final theoretical cornerstone I would like to present is the following: The social processes that led to social recovery, and which are the result of shared meaning-making in communities of practice, have led to the accumulation of social capital – a key term that explains how people in society and in certain social contexts can cooperate successfully and achieve a higher degree of social integration and satisfaction. Social capital (Bourdieu, 1983; Coleman, 1990; Putnam, 1995) is a theoretical concept that is helpful for understanding the importance of social relations and the formation of civil society. The French sociologist Pierre Bourdieu (1983) defined social capital as follows:

> The aggregate of the actual or potential resources which are linked to possession of a durable network of more or less institutionalized relationships of mutual acquaintance or recognition (p. 248).

When moving from the individual's personal development to a broader social perspective, one should include Putnam (1995) and his position as a political scientist. He views social capital as a crucial necessity for the development of civil society on a larger societal scale. Putnam says, "'Social capital' refers to features of social organization such as networks, norms, and social trust that facilitate coordination and cooperation for mutual benefit" (p. 67).

The main goal of narrative collaborative group coaching has been to develop the participants' mutual engagement in order to stimulate social trust and thus help them navigate in their current life context. The participants have not belonged to the same sport or club, but they do have a shared point of departure, and they are learning to appreciate other people's reflections despite differences in their specific conditions in the various sports. Included are many issues concerning psychological challenges within the sport (e.g. preparing for competitions, training schedules) and academic demands from the school where they have shared experiences and interests, and where the group's dialogues have been seen as encouraging and developing for their engagement and meaningful participation in the various contexts (school, sport, family etc.).

5.4 Conclusion in Relation to the Research Project

Narrative collaborative group coaching has had an effect on social recovery and well-being in the young sports talents, and 5 months after the process, a significant increase was found in the participants' subjective perception of physical recovery and success. Based on these findings and the discussion above, where I have attempted to broaden the perspective by outlining the general principles concerning social recovery and the development of social capital, this form of intervention can arguably be applied successfully, also in other domains and social contexts. Narrative collaborative group coaching can be seen as a community psychological intervention (Orford, 2008) that promotes the development of social networks and enhances the individual participant's capacity for handling challenging career situations and life in general.

Based on these findings, narrative collaborative group coaching can arguably also be successfully applied in other contexts. A few examples: In collegial groups, the participants (e.g. leaders on the same level or professionals in the education or healthcare sector) support each other by reflecting together on specific challenges that they might encounter in their professional lives. In education, teachers or other professionals can encourage young people to engage in group coaching sessions to reflect on specific challenges related to career decisions, learning strategies etc. In healthcare or social services, nurses, therapists or social workers can use group coaching to support their patients or clients in relation to prevention or rehabilitation challenges. It should be emphasized, however, that the role of the coach is not to be an expert but to be present as a fellow human being who joins the group conversation as an open-minded and interested partner.

5.5 Closing Comments

The purpose of this chapter was to introduce a wide range of research approaches: In the first part of the chapter I present examples of process research that one can carry out as a reflective practitioner, and in the second part I present findings that document the effect of coaching, both in the form of the coachees' subjective experiences and in the form of more objective statistical data. The chapter revolves around the author's own research and practice as a coach. It is not intended as an exhaustive description of coaching research and its findings in general. For anyone who wants to stay updated on new developments within coaching research, the best source is the professional and peer-reviewed journals within coaching, coaching psychology and related fields.[23]

---

[23] A selection of journals: *The Coaching Psychologist, International Coaching Psychology Review, International Journal of Coaching in Organizations, International Journal of Evidence Based Coaching and Mentoring, The International Journal of Mentoring and Coaching* and a new Danish journal, *Coachingpsykologi.*

Chapter 6
Professional Practice Between Research, Knowledge and Reflection

Coaching and coaching psychology form a relatively young practice field. Until now, there have been no clear guidelines for coaching as a profession. There are many competing societies, associations and interest organizations[1] in the field of coaching and coaching psychology, and users and clients are fairly bewildered and confused about what they can expect from coaching.[2] Users do have some degree of assurance with regard to training and professionalism when they contact a psychologist specializing in coaching, a coaching psychologist. Generally, however, the coaching market is characterized by a high degree of uncertainty and doubt, although there are many competent coaches, coaching psychologist and consultants in the market with lengthy academic training in a relevant discipline (for example from business colleges or university programmes within the humanities or social sciences) in combination with supplemental training in coaching. Uncertainty prevails because there is also an unknown and presumably large number of people with disconcertingly little training and experience, who discredit the entire field. These quacks with their dubious expertise generate a sense suspicion in the market. Although coaching is becoming much more widespread, we are still a long way from having established a proper profession (see also Lane, Stelter, & Stout-Royston, 2010).[3] In the effort to secure a good reputation for coaching and coaching psychology as well as professional and economic development of the field, documentation of the *evidence* that underpins interventions and the establishment

---

[1] For example International Coach Federation (ICF), International Society for Coaching Psychology (ISCP), International Coaching Community (ICC), European Mentoring and Coaching Council (EMCC), Worldwide Association of Business Coaches (WABC) – to mention but a few. Naturally, every organization has its own accreditation system.

[2] As the first chairman of Selskab for Evidensbaseret Coaching (Society for Evidence-Based Coaching), Lavendt (2010) has offered an overview.

[3] Still, it should be noted that coaching can and often does form a very useful component in other professions and disciplines, for example in nursing, teaching and management.

R. Stelter, *A Guide to Third Generation Coaching: Narrative-Collaborative Theory and Practice*, DOI 10.1007/978-94-007-7186-4_6,
© Springer Science+Business Media Dordrecht 2014

of *evidence-based practice* in coaching and coaching psychology are seen – by coaching organisations as well as leading practitioners and researchers – as the proper tools for gaining professional recognition and development.

In this chapter, I examine the concept of evidence-based practice and its scope, possible limitations and pitfalls. My intention is to expand the perspective and clarify that the pursuit of research-based evidence is not the only and possibly not even the best way to achieve quality assurance. We should remember that calls for evidence are currently putting all fields under pressure, from medicine to education. And all fields do not lend themselves equally well to very generalized forms of outcome measurement and effect evaluation. Therefore I will later offer a practitioner's perspective. Here I want to discuss how *practitioners* can improve their professional competence and, specifically, how coaching practitioners or coaching psychologists can strengthen their professional competence. Within the fields of psychology and education in particular, there is a significant gap between researchers and practitioners, and it is crucial for the development of practice to achieve closer contact and even integration between research and practice.

6.1 Evidence-Based Practice and Practice-Based Evidence

Since the 1980s, a development has been unfolding that might be described as a *battle for evidence*. According to the French sociologist Foucault (1972), recognized *evidence* can be used as the main argument for claiming a sort of regimen of truth, which may lead to the exclusion or marginalization of alternative forms of knowledge and perceptions of reality. Based on its positivistic view of science, the prevailing *evidence discourse* favours certain truths and thus practice forms while simultaneously suppressing other truths that emerge as a result of alternative means of knowledge generation, for example the knowledge that is generated in the practice context itself. The evidence concept in the prevailing discourse strives to generalize practice and thus contributes to suppressing the focus on individual characteristics, culture, context and complexity that are inherent factors in any situation. A generalizing research perspective based on gold-standard studies (that is, from meta-analyses or randomized, controlled trials) rarely fosters practice innovation.

The currently prevailing evidence discourse has its roots in medicine. The development began in the 1930s with the introduction of a particular research approach: randomized, controlled trials (RCTs), where patients are randomly divided into two groups, an intervention group and a control group[4]; I actually used this research design in the study on group coaching that is discussed in Chap. 5. A unique characteristic of this approach is the effort to control every aspect and

---

[4]I also discuss this randomized controlled trial (RCT) approach as part of a coaching research project that is described in Chap. 5.

maximize uniformity in the intervention in order to document that a particular drug or therapeutic (or coaching) intervention can be characterized as effective. This development is associated with the English doctor Archie Cochrane (1972), who in his way was a very dedicated individual striving to increase the efficiency of the healthcare system, in part by reducing the use of ineffective and often costly therapies (see also Thorgård & Juul Jensen, 2011). His book took on myth-like status for the subsequent Cochrane movement (see www.cochrane.org). As a result of this understanding, the medical profession has developed the following definition of evidence-based medicine:

> ... conscientious, explicit, and judicious use of current best evidence in making decisions about the care of individual patients. The practice of evidence based medicine means integrating individual clinical expertise with the best available external clinical evidence from systematic research. By individual clinical expertise we mean the proficiency and judgment that individual clinicians acquire through clinical experience and clinical practice (Sackett, Rosenberg, Gray, Haynes, & Richardson, 1996, p. 71).

The discourse about evidence has spread to a diverse range of fields including nursing, social work, education, human resource management, psychology and psychotherapy (see Trinder & Reynolds, 2000).[5] In highly context-dependent fields, especially education and social work, a positivistic emphasis on evidence can completely block the emergence of creative and situationally adapted solutions. The definition outlined above has also been embraced by many in the field of coaching. As pioneers in coaching psychology, Grant and Cavanagh (2004) have transferred it to a definition of evidence-based coaching – and in Denmark, the interest group for coaching under the Danish Psychological Association is actually called 'Selskab for Evidensbaseret Coaching' (Society for Evidence-Based Coaching). However, the definition of 'evidence-based' seems too narrow and restrictive to me, and in the following I offer my objections, reflections and constructive proposals:

- It is more than understandable that attempts to brand a new practice field such as coaching (or coaching psychology) rely on the concept of 'evidence', which is so dominant in the public debate. Scientific evidence seems to ensure the justification and legitimacy of the field by referencing research that documents the effectiveness of coaching (see, for example, Greif's review of coaching outcomes from 2007). There is no doubt that research is important for the development of a professional field. Or that development, documentation and quality assurance can be achieved by means of research and practice development activities. However, describing coaching as an evidence-based practice may be doing the field a disservice, as there is no strong direct evidence related to coaching and coaching psychology, especially not when applying the gold

---

[5]There has been intensive discussion among Danish psychologists with Hougaard (2007) and Zachariae (2007), both highly esteemed researchers, as advocates, and Ramian (2009), a highly esteemed practitioner, as critic. See also the statement on evidence-based practice from the American Psychological Association from 2006, which contains more nuance than the medical concept of evidence, also with regard to the types of research that may contribute to evidence.

standard of research, meta-analyses and RCTs, which are relatively rare in the field. Hence, coaching and coaching psychology should steer well clear of relying exclusively on advertising itself as evidence-based.

- A focus on evidence is mostly helpful for determining *which* form of treatment to implement and apply, for example in healthcare. But focusing on evidence does not really help the practitioner exercise the chosen 'treatment', in our case the coaching dialogue. Thus, we often hear practitioners object to the use of evidence, despite their dedication to providing 'best practice' (see, for example, Nay & Fetherstonhaugh, 2007). In the debate about evidence-based practice, the practitioner is positioned as a research consumer, not a generator of knowledge. This represents a clear misapprehension, which is frustrating for the practitioner and does nothing to improve the quality of the practice.

- The strong relational character of coaching makes other perspectives essential, especially the factors that apply to all dialogues and which are so crucial for the transformative effect of the dialogue; these common factors include the coachee's willingness, readiness and hope, the coach's capacity for sensitive responsiveness and the safety and depth of their mutual relationship.[6] These factors are not captured in an RCT, which aims to control for deviations (for example with regard to the coach's personality or the coachee's particular interest in and willingness to change).

- There is growing dissatisfaction, especially among practitioners, with the lack of bridge-building between researchers and practitioners. However, since the beginning of the twenty-first century, we have seen the emergence of new research initiatives based on *practice-based evidence.*[7] Researchers and practitioners need to work together to ensure the optimal development of practice under the very different conditions and contexts that occur in the helping professions – including coaching. Evidence pertaining to one field and one group of people (for example my study involving talented young athletes) offers no guarantee that the method in question will also be effective in other contexts, which involve other challenges. Coaching and other practice contexts where personal and interpersonal factors are paramount require a different research approach, often a strong qualitative or action research element – we need research that both

---

[6]Here I refer to Lambert and Barley's (2002) summary of research into the therapeutic relationship and psychotherapy outcomes. Similar factors in coaching have not yet been documented, but we may assume a high degree of similarity between coaching and psychotherapy with regard to the relational aspect.

[7]We have the following definition: "Practice-based evidence is the conscientious, explicit, and judicious use of current evidence drawn from practice settings in making decisions about the care of individual patients. Practice-based evidence means integrating both individual clinical expertise and service level parameters with the best available evidence drawn rigorous research carried out in routine clinical settings" (Barkham & Margison, 2007, p. 446, quoted from Barkham, Hardy, & Mellor-Clark, 2010, p. 23). Initiatives are seen especially within the field of public health, see: Green, 2006; McDonald & Viehbeck, 2007. Ramian (2007, 2009) has indicated new ways of working with psychological research and development as a practitioner.

develops the actual practice and broadens our understanding of coaching as a phenomenon and its effect and influence on the coachee's thoughts, feelings and actions.[8]

- And finally, I would like to offer the following general and concluding invitation: Strengthening coaching (or coaching psychology) practice directly, together with the practitioner, requires the use of additional means: education (and accreditation), continuing training, mandatory supervision, training forums for practitioners and practice researchers, exchange between researchers and practitioners, the development of practitioner research and new forms of collaboration between practitioners and researchers.

Criticizing the concept of evidence, as I have done, while still wishing to discuss evidence means entering a *political and new professional discourse* about evidence and the roots of the concept in research and practice. The question, then, is what we mean by evidence. How can we use 'evidence' to improve and develop practice? David Drake (2009a), a narrative-inspired coach from the USA, attempts to expand the common understanding of evidence by incorporating a relational perspective. In doing so, he is rejecting the narrow and highly positivistic discourse on evidence and enabling a new understanding of evidence that is closely tied to practice. He arrives at the following:

> Instead, I share the interest of Tanenbaum (2005) and others in aspiring to decision-making patterns in coaching that openly draw on valid research, personal reflexivity, professional experience, and contextual awareness on behalf of the client. I observe that there is a growing sophistication in the coaching community in making finer distinctions among the types and sources of knowledge and the implications of evidence (Corrie & Callahan, 2000) for an integrated and masterful approach to coaching (Drake, 2009a, p. 2).

Focusing on knowledge and its unique influence on the coaching process sets a new agenda for talking about evidence in practice. By clearly structuring and developing their knowledge field, practitioners become personally involved in strengthening the *practice-based evidence* of the coaching dialogue. In the following, I will therefore briefly outline the broad knowledge base of coaching.

6.2   The Knowledge Base of Coaching Practice

I view coaching as an interdisciplinary field with multiple knowledge domains, which are partly determined by the work context and by the coachee or client in the dialogue. It draws on knowledge from a variety of knowledge fields and sciences,

---

[8] As an example I point to my Ph.D. student Morten Bertelsen, who is currently investigating the relationship between coach and coachee through video recordings of nine long-term coaching processes in different contexts. This research process enhances the understanding of all the actors involved – researcher, coach and coachee – and, later, fellow researchers, practitioners and users of coaching. The project is scheduled to be completed in early 2014.

and this diversity affects the course and development of the coaching process in a number of ways. Whether we are talking about coaching psychology or coaching as the overarching concept, we should remain open to all the related disciplines and knowledge domains. That is also why coaching requires such a wide range of competences, with psychology and dialogue as key among them. A coach's choice of knowledge base also depends on the form of coaching that he or she is striving for. Here I will introduce the key knowledge/scientific fields affecting the specific handling of the coaching dialogue and thus defining the coach's (or coaching psychologist's) professional field. In this presentation I focus especially on the areas that have a significant impact on third-generation coaching. By necessity, I keep the presentation brief – the topic easily warrants an entire book on its own. My goal is not to unfold the entire knowledge base in this context. Much has already been presented in the first chapters of the book. Instead, the following summary aims to illustrate the complex and interdisciplinary nature of the knowledge base that coaching rests on.

6.2.1 *Knowledge from Philosophy*

Philosophy has a special place in the development of third-generation coaching. I will therefore outline some selected topics that I consider especially important in relation to the coaching approach that is addressed here.

(a) Philosophy has always dealt with *dialogues* and *reflection processes*. In Greek philosophy, the goal was to become skilled in thinking and dialogue. In particular, Aristotle's dialectic understanding can be said to have affected the dialogue processes in coaching. The dialectic method relies on two key factors, which help the reflecting person find an answer to the challenge he or she is grappling with: Determining (1) what premises lead to the desired conclusion and (2) what premises are acceptable in the dialogue with the other. This art of dialogue has its modern parallel in Ole Fogh Kirkeby's (Kirkeby, 2009) protreptic dialogue, a form of coaching that encourages the other (1) to ask *why* he or she lives, acts, thinks and feels the way he or she does, (2) to become the master of his or her own life by confronting his or her own fundamental values and (3) revealing his or her own possible self-deception and strengthening his or her self-confidence. Protreptics is a form of third-generation coaching, although it differs from the form presented in the present book by not aiming directly for an action perspective. In their true form, protreptic dialogues operate almost exclusively on the level of reflections and values, and the focus is not on consequences for future desired actions – in contrast to many goal-oriented versions of first-generation coaching (such as the GROW model, for example).

(b) Through an *ontological lens* one examines the basic structure of reality and being.[9] Incorporating an ontological perspective in coaching means focusing on fundamental and sometimes existential questions: Who am I? What makes me who I am? How do I become who I would like to be? What influence does the other – my interlocutor – have on my becoming? How do my thoughts and feelings find the proper words and the right language? A number of philosophers have addressed the role of the other's (the interlocutor's) influence on the development of the self: Martin Buber was mentioned earlier. Another important philosopher is Søren Kierkegaard: To Kierkegaard (2010, SKS 11; "Christian Discourses" is one of the first books in the second phase of his authorship; published on April 26, 1848.) the self is a task, a problem, a process and a relationship that relates to itself. A human being is never finished with him/herself and must be permanently driven to self-reflection and self-development: One must choose oneself – a fundamental ethical requirement for any human being – by distancing oneself and subsequently returning to oneself. In his writing as an existentialist philosopher and theologian, Søren Kierkegaard (1813–1855) addressed what one person (whom he calls the informant) can do for the other (the recipient). The informant can ask questions in order to raise the recipient's awareness. Eventually, however, the recipient is thrown back on himself and forced to make up his own mind.[10] Kierkegaard (SKS 7; "Concluding Unscientific Postscript to Philosophical Fragments" from 1846) speaks about the double reflection of the message, which is another characteristic of third-generation coaching and of teaching and other forms of developmental processes: The informant (in our case, the coach) also develops as a result of the process (see also Kling-Jensen, 2008). Essentially, this process of double reflection is also characteristic of the coach's own development as a practitioner as expressed through reflection-in-practice, to borrow Schön's (1983) term.

(c) The *phenomenological-experiential discourse* in philosophy focuses on man's being-in-the-world (Merleau-Ponty, 2012). As human beings we are always anchored bodily and intentionally in our world, that is, in our current context. Due to the body's central position as a mediator between person and environment, phenomenology has overcome the classic distinction between subject and object that characterizes the traditional and positivistic epistemology and perception of science. In this *non-objectivist* approach, perception/sensation is understood as a construction process where the individual creates *meaning* in relation to the specific environmental situation. The person and the situation are interconnected or, to use a more apt term, *co-dependent*, that is, mutually dependent and linked. Perception/sensation occurs via the lived body and is

---

[9]Morten Ziethen of Aarhus University/Rambøll Management Consulting/Attractor is one of the philosophers and coaches who bring considerable professional substance to the development of an ontological approach to coaching; see e.g. Alrø, Nørgaard Dahl, and Frimann (eds.) 2011.

[10]Read more about 'Kierkegaard as coach' in Søltoft (2008).

thus always associated with movement and action. Perception/sensation is an active process and has nothing to do with a passive world perception. The lived body is a condition for the person's ability to sense and act. This philosophical *and* psychological understanding may fundamentally impact the way in which the coach and the coachee speak about certain situations and events. The experience is there, but they may not have a language for describing it. In the coaching dialogue, both parties are therefore challenged to move gradually toward articulation. This gives the coachee an opportunity to learn to understand him/herself and his or her actions.

6.2.2 Knowledge from Psychology

With its historical roots in both philosophy and natural science, psychology is a scientific field that continues to develop with relations to both camps. As a consequence, all psychologists do not necessarily understand each other or share the same understanding of science. Nevertheless, I would claim that the psychology that guides the development of coaching psychology and coaching is mainly anchored in the tradition of the humanities and the social sciences. In the future, however, neuropsychology and neuroscience may come to play a greater role in relation to coaching (see Rock & Page, 2009). In the development and understanding of third-generation coaching, psychological theories on learning, identity and self play an important role. These theories were introduced earlier in this book. In relation to team and group coaching, models of group dynamics and social learning theories (for example Wenger, 1998) occupy a special position. In addition, any well-founded coach must have knowledge of the major psychological schools (psychodynamic, cognitive, existential, systemic, social-constructionist-narrative etc.). In specific coaching situations, these theories may influence the coach's way of asking questions about the situation. Awareness of testing in theory and practice can also be helpful, not least for someone who takes a critical stance toward the use of testing.

6.2.3 Knowledge from Education, Adult Learning and Personal Development

Social developments in recent decades have led to a completely new understanding of learning and development, which is rapidly taking root in many educational environments, in our personal lives and in the labour market. Learning is increasingly associated with development and the generation of knowledge in specific contexts. In society in general, there are growing demands to continuing personal and professional development: Learning has become a life-long process. In this developmental process, coaching and coaching-based dialogues have taken on increasing prominence. The particular challenges related to learning and key theoretical approaches to learning were addressed previously in this book and argue directly in favour of the necessity of developing third-generation coaching. Any professionally ambitious coach has to understand these learning-related and developmental challenges and thus demonstrate his or her competence in supporting individuals and groups in their continuing professional and personal development.

6.2.4 Knowledge About Specific Professional Contexts

It is often an advantage to have specialist knowledge about the fields where one operates as a coach. Compared to Denmark, in Germany there is a much greater emphasis on the need for business coaches to have an academic degree, for example in business economics or HR. In Denmark, on the other hand, there is a stronger emphasis on expertise within organizational psychology. For anyone working as a coach or a coaching psychologist in a business context, it is clearly an advantage to have sound professional knowledge of theories and research related to management theories, leadership, organizational development, learning in organizations and human resource theories. If one's work mainly takes place in the field of sales and marketing, knowledge and perhaps work experience within these areas will definitely be useful.

Coaching is increasingly spreading to other areas such as healthcare and preventive efforts, rehabilitation, social work, education, unemployment rehabilitation etc. Coaches and coaching psychologists working within these areas must have professional expertise and often also work experience within these or related fields. That is a necessary condition for being a good sparring partner in a collegial work community and a competent coach. If one's work revolves around basic questions, that is, value-oriented questions that encourage self-reflection processes, which is also characteristic of third-generation coaching, expert knowledge about the coachee's specific work context will be less crucial for the coach's ability to conduct a meaningful and developing coaching dialogue.

6.2.5 Knowledge Domains in Dialogue Practice

If we look, in conclusion, at the knowledge domains that impact the coaching dialogue directly, we can distinguish between four different forms, each with a unique role as a competence basis for the way in which the coach or coaching psychologist conducts a coaching dialogue. I consider these four knowledge forms, which Drake (2009a) refers to in his definition of evidence, crucial for the further development of the practice-based evidence that I mentioned earlier. The first knowledge domain is the coach's *self knowledge* of him/herself as a professional. In the cases that are presented in Chap. 7, where coaching experts reflect on their own practice, the crucial role of self knowledge, especially in the form of intuition and relational understanding, is abundantly clear. As the second knowledge domain,

Table 6.1 Domains of knowledge (with inspiration from Drake, 2009a)

Coaching dialogue			
Self-knowledge	Foundational knowledge	Contextual knowledge	Professional knowledge
Awareness Maturity Self-reflection Wisdom Intuition Relational understanding	Theories, models and guidelines based on research and scholarship from basic and applied sciences	Subject matter expertise Organizational and contextual understanding Knowledge of the specific profession where the coaching is carried out Understanding of the coachee's life perspective, values and goals	Theories, methods and competences based on research and scholarship by practitioners engaging in coaching/coaching psychology

Drake mentions *foundational knowledge*. That is the domain of knowledge that is based on theoretical approaches and models, a knowledge domain that has also received considerable attention in this book. The need for *contextual knowledge* was discussed in the preceding section. The final domain of knowledge is *professional knowledge*, which is acquired through reflection on and the continued development of practice. This knowledge domain is generated by the practitioner-researcher, a type of researcher that I will return to later in the present chapter. Schematically, these four domains of knowledge can be presented like in Table 6.1.

6.3   Developing Knowledge, Practice and Profession

With this section I aim to illustrate how coaching and coaching psychology practitioners can act proactively and self-reflectively in relation to their own professional development and thus help to establish the professional knowledge that is necessary for developing their professional competence. The traditional perception of evidence-based practice appears to render the practitioner incapable. In order to ensure professional development that is anchored in real life, the practitioner has to step up to the plate. Professional development is generated by the reflective practitioner or 'scientist-practitioner'. Hence, my choice of the term 'professional edification' (German: Bildung) is quite deliberate. According to Danish philosopher Thyssen (2004), modern edification implies the "ability to handle second-order observations" (p. 331; translated for this edition), that is, developing from a self-reflective position in one's professional life – as in life in general. Today, individuals and professionals face the challenge of developing their own (professional) identity – in interaction with others and with changing environmental situations. Professional edification is not uniform

Table 6.2 Relationship between psychological theory and practice (according to Kvale, 2007)

Relationship between psychological theory and practice
1. **Theory➔ practice:** The 'engineering model' – interventions are based on manuals developed through research
2. **Theory➔/ /practice:** Practitioners resist using theory. Some practitioners consider research-based theory irrelevant to their work
3. **Practice➔ theory:** Practice is the primary driver of theory. Theoretical reflection is a sort of assistive tool for practitioners but not an absolute authority
4. **Theory ⟷ practice:** Theory and practice interact. Issues may spring from academic research as well as from the psychologist's practical work
5. **Theory =/= practice:** Theory and practice are mutually independent. Theoretical knowledge deals with invariable and context-independent aspects, while practice deals with what is variable and context-dependent
6. **Theory > practice:** Theory has little relevance for practice and is not a success criterion for good practice, but theory legitimizes the profession
7. **Theory <> practice:** Theory and practice are seen as unrelated but mutually legitimizing

in character; the key is to develop a dynamic form of professional knowledge and capital.

6.3.1 Relationship Between Practice and Theory

Reality is often different, however: In psychology and several related areas such as education, nursing, social work and definitely also coaching, one may observe academic theory and research on the one hand and professional practices on the other leading relatively unconnected lives, side by side. Kvale (2007) outlines seven models for understanding the relationship between psychological theory and practice, which are summarized in Table 6.2.

In my opinion, a desirable development of coaching and coaching psychology as a profession lies within categories 3 and 4. Category 3 describes efforts that promote a development toward a *reflective practice*. This approach appreciates the notion that in practice, one cannot simply transfer knowledge from research and theory; instead, the practitioner has his or her own concept of knowledge, which is unfolded in practice, respectively reflected-in-action, and developed further to qualify as *practice-based evidence*. In category 4, the goal is a higher degree of interaction between theory and practice. Here, the aim is to intensify the cooperation between academic research and professional practice to achieve a more dynamic interaction than is common today. Both environments have to approach each other with respect for their differences and openness to cooperation. Otherwise, the talk of evidence-based practice becomes a more or less empty discourse in real life.

6.3.2   Paths to Professional and Practice Development

Clearly, the main target group of this book is reflective practitioners. The efforts involved in reading this book and reflecting on the content warrant appreciation for anyone who undertakes the task. (Thanks for your interest, dear reader!) I am pleased and delighted to enable this encounter between myself and the reader. As a researcher, I consider it an obligation to enter into dialogue with practice and practitioners and in fact to have my own professional practice alongside my research activities. My ambition lies in having my own practice and thus be viewed as a respected fellow practitioner. However, I also have an ambition and a hope of stimulating practitioners and the professional development of the field in general, that is, to present 'evidence' to the practice field through the development of research, theory and practice. As a researcher I have a pronounced interest in connecting research and practice.

What can we do to develop the profession and practice? How can theory/research and practice enter into fruitful interaction? How can practice and the practitioner's professionalism develop? The literature list offers proposals, which I will briefly introduce in the following.

6.3.2.1   Developing Professional Knowledge by Means of Situated Learning and Apprenticeship Learning

In this area, Nielsen and Kvale (1997) and Nielsen (2006, 2008) stand out with works based on ideas that were originally proposed by Lave and Wenger (1991). The theory of situated learning shifts attention away from learning in scholastic contexts (for example formalized learning in school) and thus offers a critical alternative to functionalist concepts of knowledge and learning. Situated learning and development take place in practice communities in a new form of apprenticeship learning, where novices find a practice ground for specific situations and are thus able to develop in a learning community with others. This approach ought to play a greater role in education with a variety of training and learning forms, individual supervision, collegial supervision, video analysis of selected sessions and professional developmental forums. In this connection, it is essential that experts (researchers, experienced practitioners etc.) take on the role as 'masters', co-reflecting on the novice's practice. The 'master', for example the teacher or the group supervisor, should not appear as an external expert but should instead enter into a learning community where knowledge is seen as discursive in nature, and where everybody contributes to shared meaning-making and the development of knowledge. There is no final answer, as knowledge is contextual and situated. This form of situated learning produces knowledge that frames meaningful reflection on what the actor does. This knowledge can also be linked with existing theory and research that is not necessarily related to the same specific context. Further, it is possible to achieve a different form of second-order learning, where participants reflect on their manner of reflecting. In that way, everybody who is involved in a practice community will be able to contribute with their knowledge and experience, which in many ways complements the creation of a developmental space that benefits everybody.

6.3.2.2 The Reflective Practitioner

The notion of the reflective practitioner that is presented in the following lies in extension of this basic understanding of situated learning. Schön (1983), who was an educational researcher at Massachusetts Institute of Technology, MIT, takes his point of departure in a factor that several researchers have pointed out: "a gap between professional knowledge and the demands of real-world practice" (p. 45). This gap springs in particular from the fact that the basic and applied sciences are convergent, while practice is divergent and in many ways has a much greater complexity than can be captured in classic research and scientific methods and controlled trials. In that connection, Schön directs our attention to the spontaneous, intuitive execution of everyday actions that form the point of departure for the following conclusion and thus the introduction of the concept of *reflection-in-action*: "Our knowing is ordinarily tacit, implicit in our patterns of action and in our feel for the stuff with which we are dealing" (p. 49). The crucial point for the development of professional practices is contained in the following question: How do we get in touch with and articulate these often implicit and intuitive 'reflections', which initially are only sensations in relation to specific situations?

The answer to this question falls into three parts:

1. *Reflection-in-action must be part of the actual dialogue between the coach and coachee.* Reflection-in-action is thus a joint project involving both parties in the coaching relationship. If this ongoing reflection is successful it serves to intensify the relationship, which is likely to enhance the coaching process and the positive and constructive outcome of the coaching intervention (see de Haan, 2008; Miller et al., 2004; Norcross, 2002; Wampold, 2001). In his understanding of *relational coaching*, de Haan (2008) speaks about going from intervention to interaction. An application of Schön's basic understanding in coaching leads to the following: Through reflection-in-action or, better, *reflection-in-interaction* the coach and coachee achieve, among other things, agreement about the degree of control and intimacy, agreement about the procedure and process and agreement about what goals and tasks to work with. The *shared contribution* that coach and coachee(s) make in the dialogue has been identified as one of the most important *common factors* for the success of interventions in psychotherapy. To ensure that the dialogue leads to shared negotiation and clarification, the coach should act as *process manager*. Thus, the coach should be the one to check, by means of questions, whether the relationship is developing appropriately and to initiate the process of reflection-in-interaction. A mature coachee will also

be able to put his or her reflections-in-action/reflections-in-interaction on the agenda, but essentially that is the responsibility of the coach.

2. *Reflection-in-action should also serve as a learning and reflection process* that the coach engages in before and after the intervention, a continuous developmental process where the coach works on his or her own development with a view to refining and improving his or her approach to the dialogue. Julie Hay (2007), the former president of EMCC (European Mentoring & Coaching Council), has worked especially with reflective practices in coaching, and she divides this development and learning process into six phases: *First*, one captures key events by taking notes, becoming more aware of what happened and, possibly, by recording the events (audio/video). In *phase two*, one reviews selected events from various positions and angles (including one's own perspective, a meta-perspective, the coachee's perspective and a collegial perspective). *Phase three* involves searching for patterns by comparing events and examining them for similarities and differences. This may include going over one's files or using one's intuition about certain recurring events where the same challenge occurs again and again without leading to appropriate actions. *Phase four* involves planning one's own learning and renewal by going over notes and files in order to identify possible interventions that proved particularly useful. A helpful element in this phase is to search for inspiration in literature. In *phase five*, the coach plans certain events for a particular client (to the extent that these events can be planned), for example by trying out particular types of questions, methods or procedures. Finally, *phase six*, aims for implementation. Let me offer an example: A coach has the sense that she is too easily caught up in the coachee's issues and dilemmas. In extreme situations, she has repeatedly noted a sense of feeling trapped and powerless in her role as a coach. In order to plan a new strategy, she turns to the literature in a search for books and articles that might help her move past this impasse. She might also discuss the matter with a colleague. She identifies questioning strategies (for example circular questioning from the systemic approach or externalization from the narrative approach) that might be helpful in the situation by inviting new perspectives into the dialogue. In this process, the art is for her to *integrate* a particular new perspective in her action repertoire without reducing her intervention to a mere 'technique', which may not be wholly appropriate for the case and her general approach. This latter dimension is not sufficiently addressed in Hay's approach (Hay), however. In her planning, the coach attempts to find a 'good' client among her current clients, where she has had this feeling of an impasse in the dialogue, and where it would be appropriate to implement this type of intervention the next time the issue comes up. The case with the expert coach Martha in Chap. 7, however, also illustrates the limitations of this approach. Martha says explicitly that she sometimes has to avoid focusing on her technique and instead trust her intuition and relational understanding.

3. *Reflection-in-action can be continued in and form the basis of supervision.* In this way, supervision becomes an essential professional development tool that lets the coach reflect on his or her practice from a meta-perspective together with one or

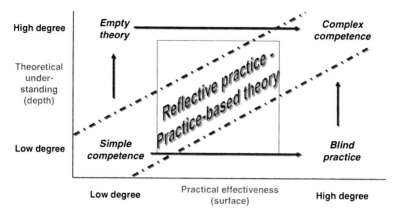

Fig. 6.1 Complex competence by means of reflective practice and practice-based theory

more companions who keep a hold on him or her and are able to offer inspiration from new theoretical and professional angles. The person receiving supervision may for example choose a particular situation from a recent dialogue or a pattern in a set of recurring situations (see the previous point). The supervision may also be based on selected recorded video or audio sequences – a method that will seem especially natural in an educational context. In many regards, the supervisor acts as a coach and professional mentor but never as someone who knows best. The supervisor is a sparring partner and travel companion, at times even a professional expert, but always someone who is interested in pursuing his or her own personal development. In that sense, supervision can be viewed as shared learning. It is often helpful to approach colleagues for collegial supervision, which can also take place in groups.

The key factor in professional development is that the reflective practitioner learns to link the specifics of his or her own practice with the often generalizing theoretical and research-based input. The reflective practitioner never assumes the role of 'expert' but instead as someone who "engages in a continuing process of self-education" (Schön, 1983, p. 299). The complexity of one's competence only develops when practice is linked with theory in a specific and meaningful manner. With Schön in mind, this can be illustrated as follows (see Fig. 6.1):

In the following statement, Schön (1983) describes the reflective practitioner as engaged in permanent searching: "I am presumed to know, but I am not the only one in the situation to have relevant and important knowledge. My uncertainties may be a source of learning for me and for them" (p. 300). The reflective practitioner seeks to integrate practical and theoretical knowledge (see Brinkmann & Tanggård, 2012), knowledge that is often not reflective in the actual dialogue situation but which surfaces as implicit knowledge, often described as *intuition*. Schön (1983) offers the following description of the reflective practitioner's capability:

> It is our capacity to *see-as* and *act-as* that allows us to have a feel for problems that do
> not fit existing rules. The artistry of a practitioner [. . .] hinges on the range and variety
> of the repertoire that he brings to unfamiliar situations. Because he is able to *see* these *as*
> elements of his repertoire, he is able to make sense of uniqueness and need not reduce them
> to instances of a standard category. (p. 140; italics in original)

According to Schön, all professional development is driven by a general search
for a personal and professional identity that can be described by means of two
questions: "What, in my work, really gives me satisfaction?" and "How can
I produce more experiences of that kind?" (Schön, 1983, p. 299). This describes
a reflection on essential values in one's work that ought to be key when articulating
one's general understanding of one's profession and actual practice in relation to
one's clients.

6.3.2.3 Scientist-Practitioner

In clinical psychology, there is a long-standing discussion about the relationship of
theory, science and practice and the related professional development; the official
international kick-off to this debate occurred at a conference in 1949 in Boulder,
Colorado, where attempts were made to describe how a psychologist could work
both as a practitioner and a scientist. The relationship between science and practice
is not always seen as unproblematic due to the gap between the world of science,
which is often far removed from practice, and the professional practitioners, who
are often wary of science. David Lane, himself a dedicated coaching psychologist,
and his colleague Sarah Corrie have been working on a *scientist-practitioner* model
for the twenty-first century (Lane & Corrie, 2006). They view professional practice
as part of a complex and dynamic system. Lane and Corrie view the professional's
development process in the framework of Kolb's experiential learning cycle (Kolb,
1984), which takes its point of departure in practice by defining certain challenges
in and reflections on practice and then includes and explores ideas, which in turn
form the basis of active experimentation with various strategies and eventually
implementation in the actual dialogue situation. Lane and Corrie define the *ability
to formulate the actual case* based on its inherent challenges as one of the most
essential qualifications of a psychologist or a coach. The authors view the ability to
formulate a case as a form of *psychological sense-making*. Lane and Corrie (2006)
offer the following description of the impact of theory on the articulation of the case
and the relationship between theory and practice:

> Seen from this broader perspective, formulation is less concerned with attempting to
> 'explain' a presenting issue from one theoretical perspective or another, and more organized
> around encouraging a capacity for creative thinking that is large atheoretical (although
> certainly not antitheoretical) in early stages. Theory is then combined with creative and
> reflective thinking rather than imposed upon it, with the formulation representing a story
> that is elaborated through gradually adding layers of theoretical constructs and ideas that
> can be examined for their implications. (p. 47)

Lane and Corrie point out that there are many ways of acting as *scientist-practitioner*, and in this they differ from more traditional thinking, which asserts that the practitioner must follow a particular procedure, for example with regard to the use of assessments, the testing of hypotheses etc.

6.3.2.4 The Practitioner-Researcher

In closing, I would like to introduce an approach that seeks to link practice and theory/research: the practitioner-researcher model. In this approach, the practitioner also essentially acts as a researcher, only in a different way than in classic academic research, which is often far removed from practice. When acting as a practitioner-researcher, the coach or coaching psychologist takes a clear step toward research by systematically exploring his or her own and others' practice. The English educational researcher Peter Jarvis (1999) in particular has developed and explored this research mode. He builds on Schön's work by examining the relationship between practice and research in a new perspective – for example within the fields of education and nursing. This approach can be expanded to other professional practices. The key question in Jarvis' approach is how a practitioner can go about engaging in research. He underscores that anyone who is receiving education and continuous professional development, for example in coaching, ought to operate – with greater or lesser intensity – as a practitioner-researcher. This involvement in practitioner-research should be continued in some form or other throughout the person's professional life. Jarvis highlights some benefits of *practitioner research*:

> Practitioner-researchers are able to report aspects of practice at a depth that traditional forms of research might well not capture, precisely because they are practitioners. Their research can be enriched if it undertaken in collaboration (p. 24).

I introduced the first steps toward becoming a practitioner-researcher in the previous sections, especially in my description of the process of *reflection-in-action*. In Chap. 5 of this book I systematically presented some of my own contributions as a practitioner-researcher. If one's daily work is most closely associated with practice, case studies are the most obvious approach to being a practitioner-researcher. Other modes include action research and collaborative research.

A competent reflective practitioner and, even more so, a competent practitioner-researcher will be able to link his or her own practice to theory and to other people's research findings. How can one best understand the relationship between theory and practice, and how can this relationship unfold in the work of the practitioner-researcher? Here Jarvis distinguishes between novices ("new recruits") on the one hand and experienced practitioners and practitioner-researchers on the other. Jarvis (1999, pp. 150–151) describes the relationship between theory and practice for new recruits in the following continuing loop:

1. The new recruits are provided with information.
2. They learn the information, which becomes theory for them (knowledge about practice).

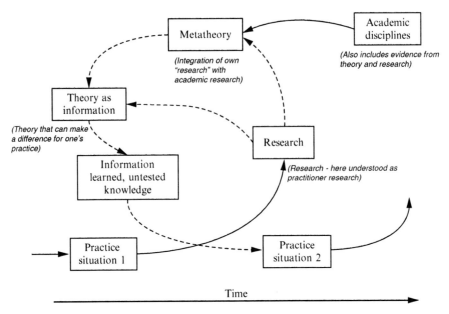

Note: Dotted lines indicate weaker links than solid lines.

Fig. 6.2   Theory, practice and research (Jarvis, 1999, p. 153, incl. my own additions)

3. They try it out in practice.
4. They reflect on their experiences.
5. They generate their own personal theory.
6. The loop continues...

For an experienced practitioner-researcher, this loop is more complex (see Fig. 6.2).

This loop ought to form the basis of education in coaching and coaching psychology. Educational curricula and professional development should be structured in accordance with this model. A clear and systematic understanding, a theoretical basis for one's own practice and its permanent development ensure the achievement of *expertise.* According to Dreyfus (1992), someone who has reached the expert level performs fluently and with ease, uninterrupted by analytical considerations. This is the level of the virtuoso, a level of intuitive, holistic and synchronic expertise. How this expertise is achieved has still not been fully explained by research. Ericsson (2006) notes, among other points, that expertise develops on the basis of many hours of *deliberate practice,* that is, an intense and reflective process of learning, development and practice. Here, one should maintain the distinction between the development of expertise in the fields of music and sports and the development of expertise in a professional practice. A practitioner-researcher moves toward expertise by understanding and developing his or her own practice and that of his or her colleagues. This constitutes the professional practitioner's *deliberate practice.* This course of development earns credit in relation to practice aimed at expertise but less so in relation to the world of academic research – much practitioner research is not published but is mainly intended for internal use in particular organizations (for example consultancy firms or collegial forums).

6.4 Knowledge Between Fact and Intuition

In this chapter I have attempted to clarify the complexity of the concept of knowledge. A coaching practitioner needs basic factual knowledge. It lays a foundation that is gradually embedded in practice over time. However, this form of reflective knowledge is far from sufficient for being a competent practitioner. In some situations, it can even be a hindrance if one attempts to articulate it as conscious knowledge. Several of the authors who have been mentioned here observe that knowledge is often expressed as intuition. However, we lack clear guidelines and action-oriented instructions for ways of developing intuition. Our education system is far too dominated by rationality, and the computer with its hard disk is held up as a metaphor for the 'good and diligent student'. It is fed with knowledge which it is able to recall at a later time. The knowledge that is applied in practice, however, is often elusive, as the 'computer' fails to capture the complexity and dynamics contained in the situation. As mentioned above, Dreyfus (1992) describes expertise as intuitive. One will only ever be able to attain a certain level as a professional practitioner by attempting to address a given situation by means of specific theories, reflecting on them and arriving at a rational decision. Such an approach is not appropriate in the situation. That has to wait till afterwards.

In fact, experts cannot fully account for how they arrive at their conclusions. The intuitive expert cannot analyse his or her procedure within the framework of the rules. According to Dreyfus (1992), intuition is defined as the ability to draw directly on one's experiences and recognize similarities between one's experiences and novel situations. Intuition may be viewed as an *intentional state of readiness*, where one is able to draw on knowledge and associate it with the demands of the current situation. Intuition may be defined as the action potential of personal, implicit (unarticulated) and tacit knowledge in relation to a given situation. Intuitive processes do not follow a sequential course but proceed in leaps and holistic units of meaning that are associated with particular situations and contexts, and which spring from embodied experiences in these situations. The role of intuition in relation to process awareness, relational understanding and agency will also be evident in several of the case stories involving coaching experts that are described in the following chapter. The importance of this intentional readiness is surely also part of the explanation for the relatively limited role of dialogue techniques in comparison with the influence of the so-called common factors on the satisfactory outcome of the dialogue.[11]

The emphasis on the importance of intuition for the coach's competence to act as an expert does not, however, diminish the role of science, research and factual knowledge. Without theory and factual knowledge, there can be no development for the expert. However, one develops expertise through *deliberate practice*, that is, by means of *reflection-in-action/reflection-in-interaction* and by means of continuing professional development, in part by efforts to act as a *practitioner-researcher*. The development of intuitive expertise cannot be forced, and expertise does not (unfortunately) follow as the result of a diploma or a degree. One acquires expertise in part by preparing for it, by 'proving worthy to the event',[12] by seizing moments and by being present in the moment and sensing the possibilities that the situation enables.

---

[11]So far, the role of these factors has only been well documented in the field of psychotherapy (see Wampold, 2010a). I assume, however, that similar connections apply within the field of coaching.

[12]I have borrowed this phrase from Ole Fogh Kirkeby (2004). I will not attempt a brief explanation here. The philosophy of the event is a universe that requires immersion. It takes time. Kirkeby's authorship offers rich opportunities for immersion.

Chapter 7
Reflective Practice Among Coaching Experts

This chapter offers an additional example of practitioner-research. In Chap. 5, I mainly presented my own research, in part with a systematic look at third-generation coaching practice. In this chapter I include other coaches' coaching practices, which are not necessarily in accordance with my own intervention theory, but which represent a broad selection of current coaching approaches. The purpose is to look at how practitioners reflect on their own practice and to see what general conclusions I can draw from these practitioners' reflections in light of existing pertinent research. In my choice of experts I have focused on professional coaches who enjoy national and international recognition, and who have extensive academic educational backgrounds – preferably also research training. In addition, they have been involved in coaching education programs, either as teachers or as course directors in addition to their extensive experience as coaching practitioners.[1] I have not focused on the specific form of coaching the four practitioners offer. Also, their practices are quite varied in terms of theoretical approach and method. Martha, the only Danish coaching expert among the four, is the only one to work with a specific form of third-generation coaching, although her approach has a stronger philosophical slant than the form that is the topic of the presented book.

With reference to the previous chapter, I pursue an intention of inviting the reader to act as a reflective practitioner and as a practitioner-researcher. My focus in reviewing the interview material is not on performing an in-depth analysis aimed at identifying specific intervention theories but mainly on uncovering possible common factors (Wampold, 2001, 2010a) that are important to the coaching experts and to the format and success of the coaching conversation. By presenting the

---

[1] Clearly, there are many others that I could have chosen with equal expertise to the ones who appear here. A contributing selection criterion for me was their perceived status; the recognition they enjoy among their colleagues and clients as well as the formal documentation of their status in the form of specific positions they have held in coaching or coaching psychology. Furthermore, the selected coaching experts are part of my personal network. Some have wanted to remain anonymous. As a consequence, all the coaching experts have been rendered anonymous – which is clearly also an advantage in terms of safeguarding the anonymity of their clients.

R. Stelter, *A Guide to Third Generation Coaching: Narrative-Collaborative Theory and Practice*, DOI 10.1007/978-94-007-7186-4_7,
© Springer Science+Business Media Dordrecht 2014

reflections of the four coaching experts I hope that the reader will feel inspired to do the same: engage in conscious reflection on their own practice by developing strategies of their own that match their particular conditions and resources. Below, I outline the structure of the developmental project, which also shapes the structure of the chapter:

- In order to get close to the individual practitioner's personal reflections while also relating the findings to some general theoretical positions and research findings, I have chosen a case study design.
- For this purpose I have carried out 50–70-min interviews with a number of highly qualified coaching experts. All the interviews were transcribed. For the final presentation here I have selected the four interviews that seemed the most appropriate for the purposes of this presentation.
- The interviews are based on a semi-structured interview guide with the following key points:

  1. Drawing on a specific coaching situation that the coach appreciates especially with regard to the format, course or outcome of the coaching process, and which says something about the coach's aspirations for his or her work.
  2. Intentions for the coaching process.
  3. Influences from and interactions with theory and specific coaching approaches.
  4. The crucial aspect of the coaching relationship.
  5. The coachee's learning and development in the course of the conversation.
  6. Evaluation of the conversation, the practical approach and the coach's own performance.

- Findings from the interview analysis will be presented in a form of a coherent narrative based almost 100 % on the coaching expert's own words.[2] Narratives are a new presentation format in qualitative research and offer a coherent way of analyzing and presenting qualitative interview material. It is a method that is finding growing recognition within research (Richardson & Adams St. Pierre, 2005).[3]

---

[2]Three of the four interviews were done in English. The analysis procedure in the three cases was also based on the English original transcript. The Danish narrative was translated into English by a professional translator for this edition of the book. In order to facilitate the comprehension of all four stories, a small degree of language editing was carried out. Other than that, the stories are in the interviewees' own words throughout. All the interview narratives were approved by the implied coaches.

[3]Here I owe a debt of gratitude to my academic research assistant in the department, Rikke Schou Jeppesen, who prepared three interview narratives and my Industrial Ph.D. scholar Morten Bertelsen, who prepared one of the narratives. Their efforts have contributed greatly to the quality of the chapter. The procedure behind preparing the narratives adhered to a clear set of guidelines: Essentially the intention of this analysis lies in coding the key interview passages based on selected coding concepts in order to structure meaning and develop a plot and narrative structure, which produces to the final narrative, which represents the interviewees' key experiences, thoughts and reflections, here in relation to their own practice.

Based on post-structuralist and social constructionist epistemology, my goal is not to glean the one acceptable truth from the interview analysis but rather to enable one possible version that offers a meaningful interpretation of these experts' interview material. Any research narrative aims to enable and facilitate ongoing reflection in a forum of interested parties to whom the research narrative might be relevant. In this way, the following narratives may help produce a wide range of new realities for the individual practitioner who wants to engage in a professional discourse with fellow coaches and colleagues.

In the following I present the selected coaching experts' four narratives after a brief introduction of their professional and educational background. Afterwards, I address some of the key topics that come up in the narratives and some topics that make an appearance in all four narratives. This cross-analysis forms the basis for some general theoretical reflections and discussions with reference to previous presentations based on relevant research.

7.1 Peter

Peter is a trained psychologist specializing in business, work and organizational psychology, an accredited coach and a trained coaching supervisor. He has earned a Ph.D. and has worked as a consultant, business psychologist and a management coach in a wide range of organizations. For a number of years, he held a research position at a university, but he is currently back working as an independent consultant and management coach. Peter has written a large number of books and scientific articles on coaching. Here is his story:

It was a project where I was coaching a management team in an organization. I had been involved in the leadership programme, and my role was to coach the management team. I think there were nine people in the management team, and I was coaching all of them. This case is about a middle manager. We had an initial explanation meeting about what coaching is, and how I might help him. He had a new role as responsible for the customer services and organization, probably just a couple of hundred people and a few million pounds – not a huge role but a reasonably substantive one. This was a promotion set for him. He had worked in the organization for a long time. And he was about five years, maybe less, away from retirement. He hadn't applied for the role, but because there was a restructuring in the organization he was placed into this position. As a personality type he was very enthusiastic. We had four coaching sessions, which for me is pretty typical.

The Working Relationship
He had a lot of experience as a leader, but given this new power, he brought two particular challenges, from my memory, to the coaching conversation. One was that he had a large number of staff to manage, and he was wondering whether he was able to manage that many people, in particular some of the younger managers who were his direct reports: people who were in their late 20s or early 30s. The second issue I remember him talking about was, with just a few years to go, what was going to be his legacy?

I guess I liked him. Whenever I think about him, I smile. I have a very warm feeling towards him. I like his positivity and the way he always finds the good in other people. I think those qualities are very nice qualities, which I admire, which I like, so he is a nice client to work with. We are drawn to people that we like, and that is probably why I thought of selecting him as a concrete example.

My Approach

If I were to describe what my normal model is, and how I apply that model I would say that I use quite an eclectic or integrated approach. It combines humanistic positive psychology aspects with behavioural problem-solving approaches, with cognitive behavioural, with little bits of psychodynamic, and, where it's appropriate, strong bits of motivational interviewing. I tend to use that blend of different approaches, depending on the individual and the problems that they want to talk about, and to move between those, either within the session, or often between sessions, depending on the issues they want to discuss.

Okay, so as a general rule, I would start with building the relationship, so it's, "Tell me about what you have been doing." Get them to tell some stories, get them to talk and build a relationship through listening skills, through empathizing, through affirming. That's the usual places I would start, specifically if I've got four or six sessions.

If the problem is a "how-do-I-do-this"-problem, problem-solving, you know, it's about getting the person to generate some of their thinking about what they could do and evaluate that thinking, pros and cons and then come up with a plan that they could go and take away, understanding the possible downsides of that plan. If it's an issue about confidence or if it is an issue about feelings, then I tend to go into a cognitive behavioural approach. I tend to drift into psychodynamic when I think that, usually it's to do with body language aspects that I may be picking up, something that I think, hmmm, that may be an issue. It's outside their awareness, and I might then introduce that into the conversation. I also think about how people then view others, sort of archetypes, or parental type relationships. So my mind is on some of those sorts of aspects. And that happens for me, 5%, 10% of the time of a coaching conversation, so it is a small amount of how I tend to operate.

And I think maybe 10 to 20% of the time I use motivational interviewing. I would tend to pick it only for people who are not fully engaged in the topic or for people who do not recognize that there is an issue here. So I get them to identify that there is an issue for themselves and then explore whether they should be taking some action around the issue and plan about what they are going to do. But we would also work on the fact that behavioural change is quite difficult, so future sessions are often much more about helping the person to cope with the fact that "I wanted to do this, it didn't happen," and how can they now put that plan back in place? So there is that part of what I do. And also running through that is the positive psychology aspect of people building confidence and self-belief. So, remembering good things and focusing on successes – that type of work.

This is a certain or sort of general model I like to hold in my head, and how I make choices between what I would do, and I think that it is something that emerges.

I may test something that doesn't seem to work, then I'll test something else, and if that works, I will do more of it. So there is that process that's going on in the coaching. About coaching being a science . . . in other aspects it is very much an art where there is never a perfect solution. Because sometimes it works, and sometimes it doesn't, and then I need to do something else and be able to spot what works. That is as important as being able to use the skills.

Practice Is Relationship
I think that practice is always a relationship, some form of a relationship with the individual. So I usually have a pre-meeting or a pre-coaching telephone conversation with the person, to form an impression about them. And that gives me a view of how we might be working together. And the sort of person they are. So for example, I might think about how challenging does this person want me to be? The more relational they are, the more relational I will be. The more formal and the more of a mask that I feel they have put forward, the more likely I am to want to challenge them and be more formal with them. So that is one dimension that I think about. A second dimension I often think about that relates to practice is, "What is it the person asks for, and what do they really want?" And what people ask for is not what they always really want.

A third thing I probably would be thinking about – this is all before meeting them, based on that initial conversation – is my emotional reaction to them. Do I like them, do I have some empathy, something in common with them? And I guess what I'm often looking for, in some people it's very easy to find. In some individuals I use the conversation to identify bridges between them and me. I try to build a bridge that leads to a personal relationship. If I'm able to like the person, empathize with the person, for me, that makes it easier to do the coaching work. But I have heard other coaches say that they look for the opposite; they prefer to work with people that they don't like because then they can be highly challenging with them, and they think they are at their best when they are highly challenging. I think I'm at my best when I am being empathetic, and when I have an understanding of the person and can empathize with them.

I believe that someone who is relational and someone who is authentic, who is genuine, and who is willing to build a relationship, to be vulnerable, to be human, to look at themselves genuinely in the mirror – for me that actually helps the process. I don't want to have to take a pickaxe to the person, or a hammer, to sort of battle through their mask, and try to wrest it off of them. And some clients are like that, some are very protective with their masks, and they may not even know they have a mask on, but you sort of see that.

Well, I think I would come back to the point that I was saying earlier: From my experience, what seems to work is me being authentic and genuine, me being someone who is genuinely interested in listening to them as a human being and the story they have to tell. And someone who is genuinely interested in helping them, with no agenda from me, who wants to help them come up with a plan or a new way to deal with that issue or that problem. I feel if I provide someone with the space to talk, the right questions to think about, and if I am affirming and positive and smiling and nodding and paying attention to them, that is more likely to lead to a positive working relationship quite quickly.

In the very beginning, I focus most on the relationship. As that changes, the relationship goes into the background, but it still provides the frame for the conversation. So very rarely would I be willing to sacrifice the relationship to help the person to make progress, but I would be willing to, or there may be occasions where I would be willing to do something or say something that threatens or completely undermines the relationship, if I felt that that intervention would be transformational for the point we are going toward. At the end of the session, I try as best I can not to hold in my mind, "Could I have done some extra work with this person?" Instead, I'm always thinking about, "Okay we agreed to four sessions, that's fine, that's the end of our four sessions, let the person go off," rather than look for another four sessions. And because of that I am willing, as the relationship goes on, to be more challenging, but usually not to the point where it ever jeopardizes the relationship, because as a general view, if you jeopardize the relationship you undermine the respect and trust that is the container for the coaching work that you are doing. And if you throw that away, you probably also throw away the transformational change that the person wants. Not always; sometimes there may be exceptions to that. So in the beginning, I think I work lots on the relationship, and that maybe, say, out of four sessions, that might be 85% of the first hour of the first session is on the relationship. In the second hour maybe a 50/50 split … and we then might move to a 70/30 split, and then the last session 80/20. Increasing the level of challenge, helping the person to come up with insight or solutions.

The Focus of My Work

I think there are two things that I tend to focus on. One is led by the client, and most of my work is about leadership, management and executive coaching. So they are people in organizations who want to do a better job. And in that environment, I find that people are quite goal-oriented, focused, so in general, they will bring what they want to talk about through three or four issues, which is quite broad issues.

My agenda in this is that I also try to give them personal insight. Not very many clients say, "I would like to understand myself better." So the subtext of my work, and I do not say that or talk about it until the end, is that I am always carrying it in the back of my mind, "How can I, through this conversation, towards that particular goal, help this person understand who they are, as an individual, in this culture, in this context, in this situation, with those people, better?"

7.2   Steven

Steven has worked with executive coaching for more than three decades. He is a trained psychologist and has a Ph.D. in psychology. For many years, he has been the director of his own consultancy and coaching firm, and he heads an educational programme in executive coaching. He has also authored a book and other texts on coaching. Here is Steven's story:

Background

I would like to give you an idea of my coaching practice by sharing experiences with you from coaching this particular client, who is the president of a large private organization. I started coaching him when he was the vice president there, and the board was trying to decide whether or not they wanted to consider him seriously for the presidency. The president at the time would be retiring within two years. I coached him for a total of two years, and the first year was to help him and the firm decide if he would become president, and the second year was to help him transition into the presidency and then for the first six months of his presidency. The session I have in mind is from when he had been in the role of president for several months.

The Session

What happened was that he would spend the first half hour updating me. Following up on tasks or elements from our previous coaching session, things he would like to do differently or change within the organization. And what came up repeatedly was that he was frustrated that his leadership team was not taking leadership responsibility, making decisions and being strategic. He felt that the leadership team was being more reactive and 'siloed' in their own areas of responsibility. The chief financial officer was focusing only on the finances, the vice president was focusing just on the core business, and the development officer was focusing only on fundraising and the capital campaign, but as a team they were not focusing on the future of the organization, and when he was away – without some intervention on his part – they failed to manage the issues that needed to be managed. Also, without his guidance, they did not really set the strategic direction of the firm. So there was one session where – and this was maybe the fourth or fifth time that he came in saying the same thing – I decided to intervene in a way that I hadn't intervened up until that point.

The Leap

What I did with him in that session was that I said to him, "If you would like, I would like to share with you my experience in working with you, because to some degree I am a direct report of yours, you hired me to be your coach, and I would like to compare what you have been like to me as a client compared to other senior executives other large organizations and just share with you some of my observations and then ask: how do you make sense of that …"

He said, looking at me with some hesitation: "Yes I would like you to tell me; what is it like, what has it been like to work with me?" And then I gave him very direct feedback, and what I said to him was, "Most clients who are presidents and chief executives at some level, senior vice presidents, whatever: I come into a coaching session and we have already agreed that there will be an agenda to the coaching session. The way that they use that coaching session is that they plan ahead, and they e-mail me what it is that they'd like to talk about, and then in the session they plan the time very carefully to make sure that they get at all the items that they want to get at. Some people don't do that, because they are more improvisational and more spontaneous. But most clients at the senior level think strategically and use the time with me as a coach very, very carefully. They want to make sure that the expectations for what I give them as a coach are very clear, and that I deliver on those. So other than my being there when you need me and to listen and to feed back what I hear, when it comes to the goals of the coaching that we have used, and a general guideline that we say that will cover those goals – most of the coaching sessions that we have, you don't really tell me what it is that you want, and you never give me any feedback as to whether or not I have done it. I really have no idea, as your coach, whether or not I am meeting your needs."

They Don't Know When You're Not Happy

He was a little bit angry ... he was a little bit angry and defensive at first and he said something like, "I think that I'm pretty direct with you, and I think a lot about our coaching sessions, and I think that I do make sure that we use our coaching session the way that I want to use them," and I acknowledged his perspective but reiterated the point that he did not come through with clear demands and constructive feedback as opposed to other executive clients I had experienced coaching. I said, "Whenever I ask you for feedback you hold back. You never told me anything constructive that you would like me to do differently and I can't believe that I'm a perfect coach!"

I said "Does this make you think of how you might be perceived and experienced by the people who report to you? Do you think some of them would want you to be more direct with your expectations and demanding? Because you never come across as demanding, and it strikes me that you want them to do much more than what they are doing. But I never get the sense that you really care about it. You don't show any emotion about it. And if you want me to be something different I would need to know that you care about it, and when you don't feel that I deliver. I interviewed your peers/reports, and none of them ever get that feeling from you. They don't know when you're not happy."

In the next coaching session he said "I did a lot of thinking about what you said, and I think there is something to it, and I need to be more demanding of my people, and I need to have a contract with each one of them that is written down as to what my expectations are with what things are most important and what I want them to do differently than what they are currently doing."

First we started with him and me, and I said, "What do you want me to do in our next coaching session? What do you want me to do differently than what I had been doing – is this perfect for you, are you getting everything you need?" And he said, "Well I don't particularly like this session," and I said, "Okay, so If I was going to give you feedback in a better way next time, what would I do?" He said, "Well, be a little softer," and I said, "Okay, tell me what I would do to be softer?" He said, "Well I don't know!" I said, "Well, let's talk about it, because that is what you need to do with your people, you need to talk with them about the best way that they receive feedback and the best way you can give it to them. You need to have that dialogue, but you never talk about it. It's always there in the background, but you need to bring it into the present, you need to talk about the way that you work, not just what you want from them but the way that you work. So let's talk about the way that we work." And then I rehearsed it with him, doing it with me, and me giving him feedback and him giving me feedback.

Then I said, "Alright; who is the first person you want to meet with in your executive team to do this with? What is the agenda, what do you want from him, what do you want him to do differently? What words would you use to describe that? And how will you talk about it with him before you have that meeting, and what will you say to him, so that he will be prepared for that meeting?"

And so he went back to his senior people, one at a time, and had a serious conversation with them about what he wanted them to accomplish within the next three months, and how he wanted them to act differently. We actually worked on those the next three months, following up on each one of those conversations and planning and rehearsing them.

We practiced with him being more demanding, and he was a bit frustrated at first: "I can't be a very emotional person. I'm not gonna pound my fist!" I said, "Leaders don't need to pound their fist. Obama doesn't pound his fist. Lots of leaders don't pound their fist, they use powerful words – words that stand out. Let's pick some words for you that would stand out, because you need to have words and timing and weighed deliberately without necessarily becoming an emotional person that you aren't. We need to stay true to the seed, but we need to also change some habits that are getting in the way of that seed growing. If there is no sun it doesn't help for you to be an apple tree, so what are those things, and we need to do some pruning."

So there are things we need him to stop doing, and then we need to add some nutrients to his dialogue with people. The nutrients are some new habits, and in his case, the nutrients would be different words and a pause – for example, he never pauses, after he has said something important. For a person who is not an emotionally expressive person, using a pregnant pause ... is a very powerful tool. So for him, we practiced this over and over again.

The Gardener: Reflecting on the Session
You could call this a very skill-based/instrumental type of coaching. In my mind, the fallacies, the thing that does not work well in coaching is when people have artificial divisions and separations of what happens in coaching.

Yesterday I went to a religious service, and the minister had a sermon about this seed, and how you can't change the core of who you are. Today is the first time I have had the opportunity to use that metaphor as part of my description of coaching and of growth and change, and it felt very comfortable for me. It really worked for me and gave me an opportunity to practice it. I will use it from now on, with the concept of gardening. Gardening really has within it the complexity of the coaching at work – the concept of the seed and the watering and the sun and the pruning and the seasons and the growth and all of that – it's just a wonderful metaphor.

Applying this to my approach to coaching, my many roles as a coach and my palette of tools, models and approaches, I am the gardener at times, and at other times I am another tree in the garden, and at other times I'm the water coming up around the roots, and at other times I'm the person planting with the person. They are the gardener, and I am a partner ... gardening with them. At other times I'm a mirror, and at other times I'm the reflector, and at other times I'm the teacher. There are so many different roles, and different roles are activated at different times. In any one session I might activate ten different roles, and they might take different roles with me.

Dividing coaching into separate approaches, like developmental versus skill-based or mindfulness coaching versus confrontational coaching or communications coaching versus cognitive behaviour coaching, is artificial, and in fact they are all needed. You won't succeed with skill-based coaching unless you have all the rest. And then let's say you have all the skills, and your habits have been pruned, and they have been added to, and you work on that – so you have brought the person to the place where they have their mind and their heart prepared to be as good as they can be. When I had done all of that with the client, I had the person confront himself and ask himself, "Is this working? And if it isn't working, what might I do differently?" Then in the follow-up sessions it goes into skills, it goes into habits and it actually rehearses and does successive approximations, it builds those micro skills, micro-habits, it shapes them, you help the person shape their own behaviour and then get feedback from the people. I always ask them to keep a log of every experience they have as part of the follow-up to the coaching and end every dialogue with a person they interact with by asking "What happened here? What worked for you? What would you like to be different next time?" and then jot that down for themselves together with their own reflections:

- *how did they feel about that, and what worked, and*
- *what didn't work, and*
- *what would they like to do differently themselves?*

And then we start the next coaching session by reviewing that first. It's a kind of homework. They exercise, they train new skills, and then they come back to me. If they are far away in a meeting they will have the follow-up meeting with me on the phone or by Skype or by e-mail. They will give me the incremental things that are going on in between our sessions, which are usually two to three weeks apart. In my approach, most of the work in coaching happens between the coaching sessions, so the interaction and the exchange that have to go on between me and my coachee often take place between the coaching sessions.

Ready for Coaching?
In my first meeting with someone that I might potentially coach, I have a checklist. It's a checklist on readiness for coaching, and ... whether or not the person is ready for coaching, and if the boss is ready for coaching, and the organization is ready for coaching, and that we are ready to work with each other in coaching, and that the family is ready for coaching, that everything is in the right place for coaching to work, and as part of that I ask them, "What other coaches have you ever worked with? In any role in your life, as an athlete, as a student, as a friend, who has ever helped you be as good as you can be, and what did they do to help you do that? And what works best for you?" And then I ask them, "So in this relationship, what

would you need from me, and what wouldn't you want from me?" I have a checklist of about 20 things to do with directness, worthiness, honesty, tactfulness, political savvy, mentoring and advocacy, and we go down the list, and I ask them, "What would be an ideal relationship at this moment for you, if I was to work with you? Let's decide whether or not, given what you are experiencing of me, and what I am experiencing of you, we would have a good match. And if so, let's write it down, and you'll have a copy, and I'll have a copy, and we'll adjust it as we go, based on what we learn works for us." I make it very explicit. Obviously, the first and most important ingredient in establishing a good coaching relationship is trust. So they need to believe that I am there for them, that I accept them for who they are, that whatever they want, I am there to help them achieve that, that I am not biased, that I won't betray our confidence, that I'll give them anything within my power, that I will respect them, and that I will be objective. The explicit and thorough preparation I do with a new client regarding history, readiness, contracts and goals is important for establishing this trust.

As a coach I empathize with my client; I take their point of view and look at the world through their eyes, and what I add to the interaction is, "Yes I am YOU, but I am now you with all my years of expertise and my objectivity. And what I am now going to do is to share with you what I see through your eyes with some new viewpoints and ask you, 'How do you view that?'" I am not sharing something as an equal, I am sharing something as an expert – and I am sharing something as a consultant. And I am sharing something as someone who can provide new perspective.

Models

I would like to share the models that I used with this person, models which I often use. There are two main models that I use in the session, one is metaphorical, and one is practical. The metaphorical model is about a tree and a seedling, and the idea that every person is like a seed when they are born. That seed has certain potentials, and it has certain characteristics; an apple seed can only become an apple tree, it can't be a cherry tree. Now, you could graft a cherry tree onto an apple tree, and you could look like a cherry tree, but you are still an apple tree at the root, and that doesn't mean that you are going to be an apple tree, as the seed could wither and die; nor does it mean that you are going to be a healthy or vibrant apple tree which will produce a great deal of apples or offer shade or whatever you want from the apple tree.

The other model is a practical model. I use what goes on in the coaching relationship and in the coaching session as an example of what the coachee does and hold up a mirror to the coachee – sort of as an analogue that you will simply reflect back what has been going on between you and the coachee as a coach and ask a question that will get them to look at themselves in a reflective way and in a new way by giving them a model of "What do leaders do?" or "What do planners do?" or "What does whoever do?" I call it the present processing model – where you process the present: the present relationship, the present communication, the present interaction, the present ... whatever is going on in the present meeting within the coaching relationship and the coaching dialogue. This specific method has grown out of my early practice, where I spent the first part of my professional life as a video-self-confrontation expert. I spent many years sitting with people and videotaping them and watching their video tapes with them and giving them models, observation guides to use to look at themselves in light of different criteria. This has developed into its own model, which I apply in my coaching, where I offer my client the opportunity or this idea/image of looking at themselves 'on video' – be it literally or metaphorically.

Other models that we use are the LPI model – the Leadership Practices Inventory Model – addressing the core competencies of a leader. The conflict and confrontation model, addressing how to deal with differences, where you look at yourself and you look at another person, and you look at how you view the world, and how they view the world. The coachee had also worked with the 'vintage' model in his mindverbals, inter-verbals, nonverbals, thoughts, actions, goals and emotions. And he had used the growth model – there is a cycle of growth, where you go from unconscious incompetence to conscious incompetence, to conscious competence to unconscious competence. So those were examples of models that he had already used, and then he had shared with me – but not fully – what he was looking for from his leadership team. That was the next step down into the matter, which we took in that particular session together.

Afterthoughts: Unconditional Regard for Someone

I will be very direct and honest with you. I have spent a lot of my life on this through running a graduate program in coaching and supervising coaches and getting supervision myself on coaching, going for counselling myself. I spend a lot of time trying to improve myself, so none of what you talked about is new for me. It's simply a matter of feeding back to you what I said.

I must say that one of the things that I have learned about myself – I've gotten feedback from my students over the years that I come across as a very direct and sometimes even harsh – and when I go back to what I actually do in coaching, its much softer. Somehow, when I talk about it, it comes across as much more macho. When I'm actually in a coaching session, I'm kinder and gentler, and for some reason, when I describe it to people it comes across as more direct and hard, and most of my clients perceive me as a caring, empathic and warm person. When necessary, I say things in a very direct fashion, but I do it in a descriptive way, not in an evaluative way. And I think that is what is most important – that unconditional regard for someone. If you give feedback you're not telling them that they're doing something wrong, you're simply telling them what they are doing and the impact of what they are doing and asking them, whether that is the impact that they want to have, and if it isn't "What are the other options?" and then providing a model to think about it. So, I think what happens is that I get excited about coaching and its potential, and then when I talk about it, it comes across stronger.

7.3 Kathrine

Kathrine has more than 20 years' experience in clinical psychology, psychotherapy and coaching. She is a trained psychologist and a certified coach, and she has a Ph.D. in clinical psychology. She works with coaching and coaching psychology as her professional driving force, in supervision and as a teacher, researcher and practitioner. Here is Kathrine's story:

> Some time ago, I had a client, a woman who was a high level partner at a multi-national firm. On the one hand, she was the most outstanding in terms ... of client relationship, the most outstanding in terms of problem-solving and basically in terms of her ability to manage and relate to other people ... she was like a standard deviation and a half below any of her peers. I was called in because nobody could stand working with her as a peer, as her direct reports. That was the situation.

The First Meeting

I was pushed towards her like she was a lion that was going to attack the people who were feeding her. That was sort of the feeling when I arrived. I got two hours of intro with her, and this called for general executive coaching skills. I liked her a lot. I experienced the woman as delightful, open, curious, brilliant, and interpersonally clueless. She had zero idea of her impact on others.

I talked to her for an hour and forty minutes, no intervention, no nothing, and time was running out – the meeting was set for two hours. And I was actually getting a little worried about it, because I thought, "It's business, we have to talk about her relationship with these people."

Backing Up to the Agenda

According to her there were no problems, she didn't see that there were any problems at all. So I tried to listen to my intuition. I just had to create some kind of relationship with her. And since she loved learning, she was just asking me lots of questions about coaching. So I just really tried to engage with her on whatever she wanted to engage with, with the fierce belief that I then needed to back my way towards what we needed to work on. I couldn't walk forward to it. I had to back up towards it.

You basically have to play the relationship like a musical instrument. And then you have to have faith in the process. There is a very famous psychoanalyst in Boston who described this ... beautifully. He said he could talk to really, really schizophrenic people that no one else could talk to, and they said, "How do you do it?" He said, "Oh, it's very easy, I just cross the bridge over to where they are, and then I back up step by step." So it's like you go to where they are, and you back up step by step to the agenda, and if you back up, and they come forward, that's great, you can keep going, and a little more ... you don't allow the distance to happen. And then you try to use, again, the emergent process. When they say anything that relates to what the agenda is, you just fish that baby right out of the water and start looking at it.

So, at the end, in the last twenty minutes is when she talked about. . . I was sort of lobbing questions her way, and it was like Teflon, I was not getting anything. The lack of self-awareness was so significant. Only at the end, when I kept trying to back up toward her social relationships and social skills and her relationships with people. And then eventually, I said something like, "What is it like running your teams? You have so many teams, what is it like?" And that's when she said, "Oh, my gosh, they are so boring." I'm like, "Really? I'm really interested in boredom. Tell me about what makes it boring?"

As soon as she just said anywhere near the scatter plot, I just exuded interest in it. And that is when we got to the first place, because in my mind, it's like, uh-oh, you find it boring; I can only imagine how much you must emanate how bored you are. What I did say to her was, "You know there is this huge agenda of what everyone wants from you, let us just figure out for ourselves what your own agenda may be, and what is interesting to you."

This conversation I am talking about is even before she's decided that she is going to accept coaching. But when we got to something that was very interesting to her and useful and for her, it was a nugget of something she hadn't thought of before.

Curiosity as Key
How to just let her know just how seriously horrible everyone experienced relating to her?

. . . I connected with her around her curiosity. So then, if I could pull on her curiosity, then I could say anything to her. It was just very remarkable. I took a host of responses to her that I knew about and started with somebody whom she said she really liked a lot. I told this person that she was the first I spoke to because she likes her more than everybody else, and she replied, "I didn't know that. I had no idea she liked me at all." This seemingly benign information was really important – and a great first step – because it basically showed a serious disconnect in my client's perception and reality. So we began there, just trying to be curious together about what the factors might be contributing to the fact that this woman had no idea my client liked her. That meant that I could do a powerful process confrontation with very benign content. And then I had to have us just step down and step down and step down to tougher and tougher content.

In order to work on from there, I framed a very serious issue as a branding problem. So I just say, "Listen; clearly, numbers of people love you, other groups of people really don't, so we just kind have a branding problem. We have to figure out how you can change your brand with these people because clearly you have the skill." So that goes immediately toward the sense of empowerment, not feeling like "I can't make that change."

What also came up my first intervention with her actually was based . . . a little bit on Ellen Langer's work about the creative mind list. Because the other thing was, her team couldn't stand her, and at this point she doesn't know she is going to lose all of her direct reports. When we talked about how she felt about running meetings, it turned out she would be running meetings and be extremely bored.

So one of the very novel ideas that intrigued her, and this is actually when I first met her, and this is the point where she picked up a pen and really started writing, which indicated to me that she was getting interested. I asked, "How about we think of ways that you could make them more interesting to you?"

I then gave her this assignment: "When you are talking with one of your subordinates, and you are about to get bored as usual, you look at them and think, 'How is this conversation with this individual different from any other conversation?'" I told her about research done with dolphins, where people were trained to think that way about their dolphins. Half the people were trained to think about how their dolphin is like all other dolphins, the other half were trained to think how their dolphin is different from any other dolphin. And they found that the people in that category had dolphins that bonded with them more quickly and swam to them faster. So I used that as an example of what you emanate is very powerful.

I then said, what if it was her job to make people interesting? That was just a novel idea to her, so she liked the novelty; it really hooked into her curiosity. What it was really was me (or us) trying to build up a sense of social awareness, because really she had everything else.

Bright Eyes

People would say, "You just do not want to argue with this woman, she will not only win any argument, she will just keep pummelling you after she has beaten you and killed you, she will just keep on, she just can't stop." When she would see that people weren't getting it, or people weren't interested, she would be more forceful, thinking that that would capture them. Unknowingly, she was creating a paradox: that by trying hard to capture these people and get them to believe in what she has to say, she was actually alienating them. People described her as the bulldog.

Benjamin Zander talks about how, when people are excited about what you are saying, their eyes light up; they have got these bright eyes. I asked her, "How can you tell when people are interested in what you have to say, and when they are not interested in what you have to say?"

I said, "Here is a piece of information for you," and I told her about the bright eye observations. I said, "So tell me, when you are talking to people, would it be helpful to sort of track how bright their eyes are?" And she loved that, she loved that idea. I remember the next time I saw her, she came in and said, "I was speaking with my boss, and we were talking, and I made a comment. Things were going very well, his eye brightness was quite adequate. And then I said something, and I could see he lost 50% of eye brightness, so what I attempted to do was to back off and regain eye brightness and end the conversation," and she continued "I was able to regain about 25% of the lost eye brightness before I left."

Afterthoughts: The Interview

In talking to you about my practice as a coach and what theories I used, I think a lot of things ... I think what was implicit to me became a little more explicit. For example, my using relational cultural theory ... I actually feel better about the first session now; in terms of acknowledging the fact that I really had to give up everything to really connect with this person. So this has become clearer to me, and makes me appreciate more clearly how you back up toward goals.

The other thing I hadn't thought of really before was Kegan's work. That this was really looking at the subject/object, the balance. In her case, her behaviours as becoming an object rather than a subject.

You did make me realize one other piece of information: warmth. To really try to match whatever the warmth level is of your client, to be a tiny bit warmer. You can't be hugely warmer than they are; otherwise you sort of scare them, but to emanate warmth and positivity, interest in them. Remember what I said about the branding? By subtle means emanating your faith in them – implicitly . . . I think that is also what helped in her case.

Building a Relationship

There was this deciding moment when they approached me initially, they were going to make some organizational changes which involved her position, and the number two and the number three person in the company wanted to talk to me, to ask me how they should approach her about this. I said no. I explained that I appreciated that they wanted input, but that they had also told me that this woman was very unlikely to accept coaching, and if it worked great for the first session or two, and if I then had conversations with them, and if they revealed in any way that I knew about these developments before she did, it would trash the relationship.

On top of this, what made it work was also that a) They picked me. They thought she would like me, that she might like me. They were trying to be intelligent about who they match. And b) I really tried to walk in and leave my judgments at the door. All the things that I had heard; that people couldn't stand to work with her; that she had her own agenda; that she just drove people into the ground, etcetera, etcetera. I sweep all of this information over to the side like a curtain. And just say, "Okay, I am just going to experience who this person is and find my own way of liking her." So it's not so much you try to work on getting them to like you, you work on getting yourself to like them. And find what's interesting about them and then also sort of follow the energy. In the beginning, I think if you are too agenda-focused, it can hurt you.

Let's have a look at some of the theories I use:

Strength

I would try to get her to use her own strengths in a new way. Her strength of curiosity could be used for her to figure out how to make other people interesting. This idea is taken from positive psychology and 'strength orientation'.

Eye-Brightness Barometer

This spoke to a relational perspective. The first thing with this woman is to bond with her and to help her feel connected, and to do that by meeting her where she was, exploring her strengths, and having the kind of conversation with her that increased her energy and was engaging to her. And sort of just being very much aware of building that relationship first, because if you don't have that, nothing else will happen.

Social Intelligence
I therefore also used [Kegan's] subject/object work, because what we (as in her and I) wanted to do was to get her to be curious about her behaviour and what it emanates. It was evident that she needed help with is social intelligence: She emanates wealth and class, but she lacks that whole idea of emotional intelligence, where you try to recognize your emotions and understand them and utilize them and manage them. In this particular case, she would have judgmental feelings about people, and we would figure out how to help her or confront her about that. So for example in the emotional intelligence category we have her on a warmth campaign. Where she has to be aware of emanating warmth where she is, whether she is on e-mail, on the telephone or in person.

Assessment and Evaluation
A lot of people have coaching preparation forms, where they give the client something before the session. For some reason, I hate that. I don't know why I hate that, it's just whimsical for me. But I love giving people coaching reflection forms after the session. So first of all, I will usually end the session with, "Okay, let's go through what we learned today, what was particularly intriguing for you, what was useful to you, what's something that you might want to try practicing?" So sort of lightly bring it to an agenda. And in this case, it was really matching up with her agenda, which is she wants to have a vibrant and exciting career, and this is one thing that could get in her way, so she is willing to work on it. And part of what she needs to do to make her work interesting is her relationships.

So how do you connect the agenda of your client with the organization agenda? Particularly, when in your own heart of hearts, you know it's the right thing for them. So this whole conversation would have been different if the company wanted something from her which was not really in her best interest. But in this case, how could it not be in her best interest to understand her impact on other people? You wonder whether some of the games would be felt by her family and kids; it couldn't be that she was just experiencing these things at work.

Backing up to the agenda is probably a good idea and worked here. It may help you when you feel guilty and pressured to 'perform' as the coach, which can then make you clumsy. ... But I do remember that first hour and forty minutes, I was really starting to think, "Oh my gosh, what am I going to do?" Then I just sort of had faith in the coaching process.

7.4   Martha

Martha has an M.Sc. in Human Resource Management from the Copenhagen Business School, is a trained business coach and holds a management position in a Danish coaching and consultancy firm. Martha works with executive coaching, team coaching, leadership development, leadership network groups, change management, negotiation and conflict management. She teaches in leadership education programmes and is the education coordinator of a comprehensive coaching education programme. Martha has also co-authored a book on coaching. Among the coaches presented here, she is the one who is closest to a form of third-generation coaching. Here is Martha's story:

Building a Relationship
In my work as a coach I view the relationship between coach and focus person as paramount. A concrete example from my practice, where the importance of that became clear to me is the following: It was a situation where I was going to coach a team embroiled in a conflict. It was a conflict where a majority in the group did not want a particular person in the group. The team was in a fixated and rather critical situation, which was difficult for the organization to resolve, and the organization contacted our consultancy firm for help. We managed to resolve the conflict for some reason, which did not become clear to me until a while later; what I think we managed to do was for me to connect with them on an emotional level – with the group that was angry with an individual – in a way where they felt that they were being met. My explanation of what happened in this group is that when many people are upset with one person, they become shameful, because they don't feel that it's okay to gang up on someone. It seems mean; it goes against their norms and self-concept of showing solidarity and building a community. They know that, in the sense that they can feel it, but the fact that they were actually met around the emotions that they did not have words for felt like a huge relief and was very helpful for them. In the process where they explained what had happened I developed a hypothesis that perhaps, as the conflict became increasingly tense it wasn't so much that they were angry with him. It was more what the situation activated in them. That they lived in a culture where the sense of community was the most important. So in fact, it was the feeling they were confronted with in themselves, and which they had no words for, that was hardest for them to bear. That was actually worse for them than his presence. So the fact that I asked them what was worst – this feeling inside themselves or his presence – totally deflated the conflict. It ended, and in a shared effort they developed an understanding for themselves and for what was happening to them, but they were also able to put their anger towards this one co-worker into perspective, so that they understood that maybe this was not about him but rather about them!

Earning Their Trust
Being able to connect emotionally with people who are suffering is crucial for a successful outcome of a project like that. And that is what I managed/was lucky enough to achieve in the example above.

How do I manage to build a good relationship with a focus person? By somehow earning the other's trust. Succeeding in deserving being shown their vulnerabilities and making them confident that I can manage these vulnerabilities. And that's a huge thing, I think, and I don't always succeed. Sometimes it takes more conversations, especially the higher up the managers are in the hierarchy in the organization, the more cautious they are. So there I have to proceed with caution, I think.

Something that's fundamental for me as a coach – something that's really, really important to me – is that every time I walk into a room I don't know if I'll be good enough; not knowing whether I'll be successful. And it's a matter of principle to me to maintain that I can't know that.

How Did We Get Here?
That brings me to how I find out what's important, and what it might be relevant to work with for the individual. I had a manager in a company recently where we do sales coaching. After I had been coaching her for an hour and a half, she said, "How did we get here?" When I asked her what she meant by that, she said, "Well, this wasn't exactly what I thought we were going to be talking about." I reflected on this, "Now, I don't know whether I'm right, but I think we got here because that's what was important to you. I hope so." To this she replied, "Yes, it was. It was really important." She told me in a later coaching session that just after her session she had said to her management colleagues, "We need to change our strategy completely." So I think my work involves – in the best protreptic tradition – searching for what is essential for whoever is sitting here right now ... and that most of the time I'll succeed in doing that if I manage to seize the other's heavy/weighty thought.

I was lucky enough to manage to meet her on something that she was actually all alone with, and which she didn't know how to handle, so it's a difficult case to generalize from, but here I draw on protreptics, and I use it by remaining insistent; asking follow-up questions about the things she actually says. Taking her word for it, as protreptics prescribes. I insist on sticking to what comes up. In this particular case we worked with a concept where I first had to observe a sales follow-up she did with one of her managers there. Subsequently, we were going to discuss how it went. And she began generally by speaking about her situation as a manager in the organization. And I sensed that she was frustrated. So I asked her whether my feeling was correct. And she replied, "Yes, I guess it is." So we continued along that track, and that's where I discovered that she was in fact frustrated by her conditions, and she invested a lot of energy into counteracting something that she couldn't actually do anything about, and that's what I see as one of the six protreptic eventuals, Heterotelos, which means orderliness, a basic feeling of wonder and creation,[4] which consists in being able to tell what is within my power, and what is not, and to discern the best and most productive use of one's energy.

70 % Presence, 30 % Readiness – or: 70 % Intuition and 30 % Theory
This kind of example is actually an image of how I work with my full register. I sense a mood and ask questions about it, and based on what I get in return, I continue asking based on my theoretical ballast. In the example, this involved elements of protreptics, where we were able to deconstruct the frustration and discover where

---

[4]See Kirkeby, 2009, p.132: "The goal of protreptic is Otherness. This could be named by the neologism 'heterotelos', ('the Other person as goal') ... to act as the non-servile servant of the other person."

it came from. And of course I constantly check whether I am correct. I would never say to her, "You're frustrated." I would never say that to anyone. Because I don't know anything about that. I just know that something strikes me as something or other, and I can then bring that into the conversation, and then she can say, "No, Martha, you're barking up the wrong tree!" It's a hypothesis, which they have the right to reject at any time. I don't return to it if they reject it. It's very important for me to maintain that I can never know … I don't know, after all, who they are, and what they want, and what sorts of problems they have, but maybe I can bring them closer to what it's important for them to talk about.

The intuitive is essential to develop as a coach and a protreptician – intuition as a form of readiness. In that connection, it's relevant to ask how my theoretical foundation is balanced with my immediate presence in the situation. Right now I am working with managers in the hospital sector. He is a chief physician – a gynaecologist – who told me they had had a delivery were the mother subsequently went into cardiac arrest. And what he was able to study as the team had to treat the patient for cardiac arrest; everything went completely by the book. And after six minutes of arrest, the mother's heart actually started beating again. He observed this and saw that everyone had instilled the procedures so that they were second nature to them! They knew exactly what to do, and when - technically speaking. So I would say that what they did was use their knowledge, a sort of theoretical foundation, but at the same time they acted intuitively. And I don't know if you see the parallel, but that is my ambition for the students [in our coaching training programme], and I do it myself. I practice new techniques/methods/models over and over again and keep at it until they're second nature! In coaching conversations, at one point I stopped working in a model framework, because I felt it was getting too automated. Then I decided to forget about models and to focus instead on being present. So for me today the effort is to manage to be present, first of all. And then draw on what I have but letting the distribution be about 70:30 – that is, 70% attentiveness and presence and 30% readiness.

Training New Coaches
I try to do the same when I teach, first of all to be present, to capture 'the mood in the room', seizing it and presenting it by saying, "How about we look at this together?" In my experience, that's a learning approach that gives the students a sense of attentive presence as well as new insights.

When I teach I am very focused on making sure they remember that the precondition of coaching in the first place is not to know anything and not to want anything on behalf of the other. Now, I'm fully aware that there are learning processes where they have to get to know some tools, and where in many ways that is a difficult and oddly external thing to deal with. In visual terms I believe that they have to go through a process where they try out the tools repeatedly, are supervised and reflect in groups on the conversations, and everything goes pear-shaped, because they can't maintain an attentive presence while practicing, asking questions in a non-judgmental and non-steering way. But once they're done learning about all those tools, well, we're never really done, but at least the ones in the curriculum, then they need to let go of them and practice just being there. Then it's my hope that the tools they have worked with, that they have become so second nature that they show up automatically when they're needed. We have established a practice in our coaching programme, Module 2, for the exam, which is a practical exam, where the students coach a focus person, and then they reflect on how it went, together with an internal and an external examiner and their fellow students. Here we try to really focus on those moments in the coaching conversation where there are breaches or breakthroughs, some might call them golden opportunities, in order to give the students an experiential base and prepare them to be able, as coaches, to capture these moments and thus add important/crucial new perspectives and insights to the conversation.

A Process That I Am Not Supposed to Take Over
So how do I evaluate what happened, and what should happen in the future? I mean, we don't just say goodbye, perhaps we'll meet again. Specifically, I always ask, when we complete a session, what they're taking home. And I ask whether there is something they would like to see more of.

In a way, then, I don't evaluate the coaching in a traditional sense. But I do ask them what they'll be taking home, and whether there's anything they would like to see more of. And sometimes they make suggestions, and sometimes I actually let the focus person summarize what he or she would now like to take home and might like to continue working with. I don't take notes. They bring back to the following session what thoughts they've had since the last time we met. So I see this as their process, which I'm not supposed to take over the responsibility for. A process that I have to avoid assuming too much responsibility for, because as I see my role or my purpose as a coach – and that applies both to individual coaching and to team coaching – it's to make myself superfluous, and in fact the goal is to work toward a situation where they can handle things themselves. So I don't see myself as someone they are or will be dependent on – on the contrary. That's also why it's important for me not to be the judge on whether they have done stuff since the previous session. I might even step in if I think they're going to be too hard on themselves in the process. But I should not make them dependent on me. My goal is to create as much freedom for them as possible to make their choices. Maybe for a period in their life I can help qualify the process where it gets tough.

Afterthoughts
I would like to be interviewed about my practice as a coach a little more often, because it offers a chance to think more about what my reasons are for doing what I do and being who I am. It's nice, actually, to be forced to answer what actually is my role in the coaching conversation, and what sort of people I represent when I do that.

And also, the whole thing about trust has become very clear to me during the interview. To have to earn their trust. When I said that, I was like, "Of course!

That's the way it is …" It really feels right, just at that moment. So I recall that as a key thing, which I haven't articulated exactly in those terms before. That that's the principle of my coaching.

7.5 Reflections on Practitioner Reflections

In my assessment, a cross-analysis of the four coaching narratives highlights three topics as especially prominent and essential for the involved coaching experts' reflections on their own practice.[5] I specify these topics under the following headings:

- Building and developing a relationship.
- The coach's way of being
- Relationship with theory and method

In the following I will look at these topics in depth, first by searching for similarities and differences in the four coaches' stories and secondly by including relevant theory and research in a further discussion of the topics.

7.5.1 Building and Developing a Relationship

This topic is addressed in manners both divergent and similar by the four coaches. There are differences among the specific coaching situations, which call for different responses, and in addition the individual coaches adopt different theoretical and methodological positions, just as they all have their own personal style and manner in the way they relate to their conversation partner. Two of the coaches, Peter and Kathrine, speak explicitly about experiencing sympathy, respectively fascination, in their relationship with the coachees in the stories. Martha and, especially, Steven seem to engage in a more rational and task-related collaborative relationship. But all four coaches, regardless of their more or less evident level of sympathy, seek to develop a productive collaborative relationship. Peter invites his coachees to tell stories where he begins to search for relevant issues, which might lie beyond the coachee's awareness. He defines his practice as being always relational. Steven expresses an interest in putting himself in the other person's place while still maintaining some form of objectivizing distance. Kathrine speaks about listening

---

[5]Of course, to some extent, these topics were highlighted as topics of interest. But at the same time, it is important to maintain that all four coaching practitioners were very interested in and focused on reflecting on these exact topics. Other topics that I was also interested in (for example the coach's view of human nature or his or her meta-theoretical reflections) did not resonate with the interviewees to the same degree.

to her intuition and following the coachee's lead in terms of what the coachee would like to focus on. Here, Steven seems much more goal-oriented by aiming for an agenda and a clear strategic perspective from his coachee – a perspective that he can then follow up on. Martha focuses on the coachee's sense of being met as well as on her own experience, where she searches for something meaningful for herself in what the coachee is focused on. She says in her story: "I just know that something strikes me as something or other, and I can then bring that into the conversation." In a sense, Steven does something similar. He brings himself into the process by saying to his coachee that he would like to receive some clear feedback on what was addressed in the previous sessions. Steven encourages his coachee to relate more clearly to him as a coach. In my assessment, bringing oneself in play, *being a fellow human being* by aiming for symmetry in the relationship, is an important dimension in third-generation coaching. Martha does it the same way that I prefer to do it: by engaging both parties in the shared coaching process, exploring meaningful aspects and the coach and coachee's similarities, differences and underlying values in relation to a particular situation or event. In his specific case, Steven had a strategic purpose with bringing himself into play, actively using himself in the ongoing coaching relationship as a model for the coachee's learning and developmental process.[6]

What does research have to say about creating and developing the relationship? Essentially, a collaborative relationship is considered paramount for the therapeutic alliance. Horvath and Bedi (2002) thus write, "There is support for therapists assuming a 'collaborative stance' as a useful relational position" (p. 61). Research has found an especially high degree of empirical evidence for the importance of collaboration in the introduction phase of the relationship. As emphasized in Chap. 6, in his *relational coaching* approach de Haan recommends a development from intervention to interaction, an important shift in perspective and attention focus in the coaching relationship, which underscores the collaborative nature of the relationship. In a study involving depressive patients, Webb et al. (2011) examined differences between relationships based on, respectively, collaboration and sympathy and the impact of the relationship on the outcome of psychological treatment; they reach the following conclusion: Just as Horvath and Bedi (2002), Webb et al. document the role of the collaborative relationship as an especially important factor for a successful therapeutic outcome, while sympathy between therapist and client appears to play a lesser role. However, the study did find that the client's sympathy for the therapist grows relative to the successful outcome of

---

[6]In therapy research, *self-disclosure* is a relatively controversial form of intervention where the therapist discloses something of a personal nature. Research shows that clients generally perceive self-disclosure as helpful (Hill & Knox, 2002). In the literature, it is further found that humanist and experiential therapists use this form of intervention more frequently than therapists with, e.g., a psychoanalytic outlook. In my understanding of third-generation coaching, self-disclosure takes a particularly self-reflective form in the coach and thus takes on crucial importance for the collaborative process. This essentially turns intervention into *interaction*.

the therapy. Thus, the sympathy relationship was seen to be more effect than cause in effective therapy. We might expect something similar to apply to the coaching relationship (see also Duncan et al. 2010).

7.5.2   The Coach's Way of Being

Fundamentally, the four coaches have fairly similar views on this issue – although there are many noteworthy nuances. In the early stages of the coaching process, Kathrine is particularly focused on *displaying interest*. She describes this very vividly: "I just exude interest." In this, she definitely displays a quality as a coach that stems especially from her background in positive psychology. She highlights curiosity as the key to building trust and a connection with the coachee. In relation to the coachee in her story who was considered so problematic by the managers and colleagues, it was especially crucial for Kathrine to *remain non-judging* ("leave judgments at the door"). Here Kathrine highlights qualities in a coach that are crucial for developing a trusting relationship. Peter highlights *authenticity* and *being genuine* as key qualities and underscores fundamental human and *empathic understanding* as essential ways of being in his coaching. Steven uses a variety of metaphors to describe himself in his role as a coach. He sees himself as a *gardener* but also as *another tree* in the garden next to the coachee or as the *water* that nourishes the growth process. He may also function as a reflecting *mirror* or as a *teacher*. He highlights the possibility of taking on multiple roles even within a single coaching session. Martha highlights the quality of being insistent by *asking follow-up questions about what the coachee actually says*. In this, she is clearly influenced by the protreptic approach, which focuses on what is important in the coachee's life (Kirkeby, 2009). At other times, she is very aware of the need to *avoid taking over too much of the responsibility*. In this balance between challenge, collaboration and responsibility for the process, she attempts to create as much freedom as possible for the coachee to make his or her own choice.

What does research have to say about how the coach should be? De Haan (2008) has presented research findings with relevance for coaching. He points to three main characteristics as the most helpful from the coachee's point of view: *Listening, understanding* and *encouragement* followed by *knowledge, empathy, authenticity* and *involvement*. Somewhat less relevant factors are *calmness, humour* and *warmth*. In psychotherapy research, empathy has been a particularly prominent factor and a hot research topic since the 1990s (see Bohart, Elliot, Greenberg, & Watson, 2002, in their overview article, which I will refer to further down). The lack of consensus on a definition has posed a problem in empathy research. Concepts such as *perspective-taking* or *connected knowing* highlight cognitive aspects. A concept such as *reflection of feeling* highlights emotional aspects. Rogers (1980) defines empathy as

... the therapist's sensitive ability and willingness to understand the client's thoughts, feelings and struggles from the client's point of view. [It is] this ability to see completely through the clients eyes, to adopt his frame of reference ... (p. 85).

It means entering the private perceptual world of the other ... being sensitive, moment by moment, to the changing felt meanings which flow in this other person (p. 145).

With this definition, empathy becomes an overarching concept with a number of subcategories that help capture what is essential for a therapist's and definitely also a coach's capacity to attune with his or her conversation partner[7]:

- *Personal empathy:* This is about the coach's capacity for grasping and understanding the coachee's experiential world, where the coach develops an experiential and sensuous understanding of the other's life world (Bohart & Greenberg, 1997) as a key condition for being able to meet the other.
- *Empathic understanding and support:* In the context of coaching one might speak about the coach's capacity for understanding what the coachee is attempting to describe. A compassionate display of interest and an ability to sympathize and to be able to put the coachee's statements into words is a precondition for this form of empathy, which can also be described as the *coach's responsiveness.*
- *Communicative attunement:* This category is a form of process empathy and describes the coach's capacity for attuning with the coachee – from moment to moment. It also requires the coach's bodily-sensory sense of the other. In Chap. 3 I discussed relational attunement, which I described as a *shared or co-created articulation*, where a sense, a sensory expression or a theme is addressed in a shared process, and where the parties manage to meet. In my understanding, both parties are involved in a process of coordinated meaning-making.

These three categories might be seen as a hierarchy of empathy with growing degrees of complexity. First, the focus is on the coach's capacity for opening up and taking the other in. The next level concerns the capacity for reflecting and articulating what one senses and hears. And finally, the concern is with developing the relationship together, creating something new, a new understanding or narrative in relation to a task, a situation, an event or a process – going on a journey and learning and developing together as coach and coachee.

7.5.3 Relationship with Theory and Method

This topic is clearly the one farthest removed in the coaching experts' awareness – it is almost like a sort of background knowledge that they draw on, and which has become 'second nature'. Peter discusses his *eclectic* or *integrated approach*, where he moves freely among the various theoretical approaches, depending on

---

[7]The importance of *acceptance, empathy and authenticity* were already addressed by Rogers (1961).

the case and the person at hand. However, his main focus is on building a good relationship with his coachee. Steven basically shares Peter's view in his assertion that the distinction between different and separate coaching approaches is contrived. Later in his story, however, he does mention a number of models that he always incorporates, and which serve to qualify his actual work as a coaching psychologist: (1) a metaphorical model, where the person is seen as a seed that grows into a tree, (2) a practical model where he might, for example, act as a reflecting mirror for the coachee, (3) a Leadership Practice Inventory Model, which addresses a manager's core competences, (4) a conflict and confrontation model aimed at highlighting experiential and perceptual differences between the coach and coachee and, finally, (5) a growth model where the goal is to outline the coachee's developmental process from unconscious incompetence to conscious incompetence, then conscious competence and finally unconscious competence. With his background of knowledge and experience within practice, theory and research, Steven is clearly capable of relating these models to specific theoretical approaches. But in his story, these models appear as practical models for action in specific contexts and as *reflection-on-practice*, as Steven works as the unconscious competent expert in the situation.

Both Kathrine and Martha clearly mention *intuition* as something that they are both aware of in their reflection on the coaching process. Their theoretical knowledge is visible in a few glimpses, but they both explicitly state that their focus is on the coaching process itself. Like Steven, Kathrine mentions a number of action-oriented models: (1) Using the coachee's strength in a new way – here she is clearly drawing on positive psychology, (2) an eye-brightness-barometer as an indicator for what catches the coachee's interest in the conversation and (3) social intelligence, where she includes Robert Kegan's works in the field of developmental psychology.[8] Martha describes how she questions the coachee based on her particular theoretical ballast, but she also states that she relies mostly on her sense of the situation and of what will help move the dialogue forward. She describes this *intuition as a form of skill* that she activates in the situation when it is appropriate. But she also works with *deliberate practice* (see Chap. 6, Sect. 6.4), where she repeatedly tests a particular technique, method or model in order to develop professionally. At other times she deliberately chooses to push a given model aside in favour of being *fully present*. In her assessment, she works with 70 % intuition and presence and with 30 % theory as the basis of her skills repertoire.

---

[8]Robert Kegan is a developmental psychologist and a professor of adult learning at the Harvard Graduate School of Education and one of Kathrine's collaborators. Among other titles, he co-authored *How the Way We Talk Can Change the Way We Work: Seven Languages for Transformation* (together with Lisa Lahey). 2001.

7.6 Afterthoughts

The four coaching experts clearly indicate where their focus lies in the process. Their main focus is on how the coach can create a good collaborative relationship with his or her conversation partner, and on *the best way of being* for the coach in order to frame the optimal learning and developmental process. Theory, method and technique form integrated elements of the collaboration process, but in the actual situation, during the conversation, theory and method take on relatively little prominence. The coach is in the action flow – fully present – drawing on his or her theoretical skills and acting on intuition. Expert-level coaching is a way of being that is intentionally oriented toward dialogue and collaboration with another person – and which is ethically anchored. Martha puts it in philosophical terms: One has to earn the other's trust – or, as Kirkeby (2004) put it: *prove worthy of the event.*

In this chapter I have attempted to capture and expand on the way that coaching experts work, from moment to moment, and how they articulate their reflection-on-practice. Their competence is partially unconscious and impossible to impart to a novice in a simple manner. This expertise requires sound training, many years of experience in combination with ongoing continuing/additional training and an ambition of being a reflective practitioner. And ultimately, practice develops in a permanent reflection during the process – as an underlying flow that constitutes the expert's invisible competence. In closing, I quote Johns (2004), who has worked with reflective practice. He describes the practitioner's capacity for *reflections- in-the-moment* as follows:

> Being aware of the way I am thinking, feeling and responding in the unfolding moment and dialoguing with self to ensure that I am interpreting and responding congruently to whatever is unfolding. It is having some space in your mind to change your ideas rather than being fixed to certain ideas (p. 2).

Chapter 8
In Conclusion

We are almost at journey's end. A process that has lasted several years, tough at times but also very rewarding, is drawing to a close. I am delighted to have come this far and to be able to present this book. I am hopeful that, like my first book on coaching, it will contribute to the ongoing qualification of coaching and other dialogue forms. In the time between the release of the first book and the present, I have moved from second to third-generation coaching – a journey that is definitely not over. As Martha puts it in her story earlier in the book (Chap. 7), we are sometimes more successful than we are at other times. That is the basic condition of coaching and of dialogues in general. All things being equal, it is also a matter of how good the match is between coach and coachee in the situation and in relation to the topic they are addressing.

Twelve years ago I was working on the closing chapter to my first book on coaching under the strong influence of the terrorist attack in the United States on September 11, 2001. My hope and my wish at the time were that a growing use of coaching would (1) help people experience their personal interactions with others and their working life as more meaningful and rewarding, (2) that conversations could develop in a more appreciative direction in relation to what we can and hope to accomplish, and (3) that we would get better at living with differences and diversity in our organizations and in society at large. Generally speaking, the world has probably not become a better place since then, but the hope is still there, and it confirms my belief that I may be able to offer my small contribution to a better world. I pin my hope on the bright points, large and small, that make life worth living. Conversations can help bring these bright points out in our own and others' minds. There is no time like the present to get started. It 'only' requires us to pluck up our courage and invite a new agenda for meetings, conversations and gatherings.

Not without reason are coaching advocates accused of being slightly naive with regard to the applications of coaching. Coaching contributes to individualizing certain issues, which are in fact systemic, say the critics; for example, stress coaching for individual employees does not solve the problems that are situated in the organizational structure, internal communication and excessive workloads.

R. Stelter, *A Guide to Third Generation Coaching: Narrative-Collaborative Theory and Practice*, DOI 10.1007/978-94-007-7186-4_8,
© Springer Science+Business Media Dordrecht 2014

All I can say is that I am not naive. I know that there are growing pressures in
the labour market, and that our lives in general are not a walk in the park. But
working with group coaching has made me optimistic. I sincerely hope that the
form of third-generation coaching as a dialogue between fellow human beings that I
promote in this book will help humanist considerations and community thinking
grow. As documented in my research, group coaching can help develop social
capital, a dimension that clearly helps promote social coherence and contributes
to the development of social communities, as people engage in social relationships
based on networks, shared values and trust. These communities can be developed in
the workplace and in civil society, for example by developing coaching or coaching-
oriented dialogues that match working methods, developmental projects or goals in
the given context.

With this book my aim is not only to promote coaching in its pure form. I want
to invite people to engage in dialogue. *Dialogue* is in stark contrast to *discussion*.
A discussion is about fielding the 'best' arguments and superior rhetoric – and
unfortunately, the parties rarely arrive at a shared conclusion, or they are forced
to accept compromises they really do not feel like living with. Dialogue is about
something else entirely: presenting one's reflections, sharing with the other(s) and
reason over what was said – using the others' thoughts and reflections as impulses
for putting their stories into perspective in one's own life universe. Witnessing procedures and other forms for community-building rituals from narrative collaborative
practice offer new ways of sharing sensations, emotions and thoughts; conversation
forms that contain a special community-developing dimension. We reflect on what
we heard, *without* judging and evaluating. Listening to the other while suspending
one's own assessment can unleash a collective intelligence that we use far too
rarely. When we listen to each other, ideally, all the participants in the conversation
can move forward to a new place, a new perspective. In dialogues, *synergy* can
become more than just an empty buzzword. The narrative collaborative practice
initiates a shared movement, where everybody assumes a position of appreciative
interest in each other and is willing to listen in order to learn. This lets the dialogue
become a process of shared meaning-making toward a new understanding for all the
participants. The American consultant and lecturer at MIT School of Management
William Issacs (1999) expresses the potential of the dialogue as follows:

> Dialogue fulfills deeper, more widespread needs than simply 'getting to yes'. The aim of a
> negotiation is to reach agreement among parties who differ. The intention of dialogue is to
> reach new understanding and, in doing so, to form a totally new basis from which to think
> and act. In dialogue, one not only solves problems, one dissolves them. We do not merely
> try to reach agreement, we try to create a context from which many new agreements might
> come. And we seek to uncover a base of shared meaning that greatly help coordinate and
> align our actions with our values. (p. 19; italics in original)

That also describes the ambition that I pursue with the third-generation coaching
approach that is presented here: to reach agreement between one's actions and the
values one wishes to apply as a guideline for one's actions. Having an intentional
orientation, a purpose behind one's actions, matters more than having an objective.
Our actions are imbued with a *purpose* and above all a *meaning* that rests on

fundamental values that should be articulated and thus be brought out into the light (see Fig. 3.3). *Searching for meaning and embodying one's values* – also in the communities one engages in – provide a fundamental direction for one's actions or plans. Here, third-generation coaching and similar forms of dialogue can help unleash, emancipate and develop social capital.

As a lecturer in the Master of Public Governance programme, I am in contact with several hundred managers in government organizations, and here I sense a high degree of commitment and many ambitions of improving working life, despite growing pressures from the political decision-makers. I am hugely impressed with how much the managers reflect and think about their employees, and how high the management ideals and values are that guide their leadership. Although the managers rarely act as coaches for their staff, through the courses that Ole Fogh Kirkeby and I teach, they do become aware of the possibility of applying basic principles from third-generation coaching in everyday dialogues with their employees or in the management teams or collegial forums that they are part of. Dialogues resembling coaching can contribute to the ongoing development of personal leadership. Personal leadership is based on relational qualities, on taking a dialogue-based approach. Managers earn their leadership position by engaging in dialogue and developing authority from the bottom up, by being inclusive and reflective – but also by offering direction. Here it can be helpful for managers to receive coaching in order to achieve clarity about their goals and aspirations – based on the general values that underpin their leadership.

Today, coaching and coaching psychology are largely associated with a work and business context. There are many indications that this focus is going to prove too narrow in the future. Already now, there are countless projects and initiatives that seek to incorporate coaching in other contexts, for example in relation to career guidance, studying,[1] reducing student drop-out rates and addressing cross-cultural issues. I am also very pleased to see that this form of coaching psychology is increasingly being used in the world of sport, where the emphasis is on talent development, and where there is a need to develop good elite environments to ensure successes while maintaining a socially responsible perspective.

Perhaps the greatest future growth area in coaching will be healthcare, rehabilitation and healthy living. I too plan to initiate research projects in this field in the future. Based on my previous research findings, I see very promising perspectives in replacing the often individual expert counselling with coaching, where individuals or groups of patients/clients can share their life experiences and develop knowledge that is based on their specific challenges. Healthcare staff or other professionals appear less in the role of experts offering advice and more like partners in a process where their patients/clients can share experiences and help each other find a way

---

[1] In the Department of Nutrition, Exercise and Sports, since autumn 2010 we have had a project on coaching and studying with the goal of promoting the student community, improving motivation and preventing drop-outs by enhancing their focus on what they consider essential in the programme with regard to their job perspectives.

to (re-) establish a life characterized by a high level of well-being. There has been great interest in my lectures on health coaching. Here I see a considerable need to develop coaching strategies that do not individualize health and lifestyle challenges but instead promote empowerment and sharing among the people who know best how they feel, and where they want to go in their lives.

Regardless of how the reader uses this book, I hope that my contributions can help stimulate reflections on coaching, coaching psychology, leadership, dialogues, learning and development. I also hope to contribute to strengthening the development of the practice field. Coaching is in many ways a grey market, and it will take many years before it will come to constitute an actual and generally recognized profession. Meanwhile, coaching and coaching-like dialogues will continue to be an integrated element in other professions. Thus, individuals are encouraged to develop in their personal and professional lives by becoming reflective practitioners who take charge of their own ongoing development on a personal basis, in collegial forums, via supervision and in continuing education.

References

Allen, J. G., Fonagy, P., & Bateman, A. (2008). *Mentalizing in clinical practice*. Washington, DC: American Psychiatric Publishing.

Alrø, H. K., Nørgård Dahl, P., & Frimann, S. (Eds.). (2011). *Coaching – Fokus på samtalen*. Copenhagen: Gyldendal.

American Psychological Association. (2006). Evidence-based practice in psychology. *American Psychologist, 61*(4), 271–285. doi:10.1037/0003-066X.61.4.271.

Anderson, H. (1995). Collaborative language systems: Toward a postmodern therapy. In R. Mikesell, D. D. Lusterman, & S. McDaniel (Eds.), *Integrating family therapy: Family psychology and systems theory* (pp. 27–44). Washington, DC: American Psychological Association.

Anderson, H. (1997). *Conversation, language, and possibilities: A postmodern approach to therapy*. New York: Basic Books.

Anderson, H. (2007a). The heart and spirit of collaborative therapy: The philosophical stance – "A way of being" in relationship and conversation. In H. Anderson & D. Gerhart (Eds.), *Collaborative therapy – Relationships and conversations that make a difference* (pp. 43–59). New York: Routledge.

Anderson, H. (2007b). People creating meaning with each other and finding ways to go on. In H. Anderson & D. Gerhart (Eds.), *Collaborative therapy – Relationships and conversations that make a difference* (pp. 33–41). New York: Routledge.

Anderson, H., & Gehart, D. (2007). *Collaborative therapy. Relationships and conversations that make a difference*. New York/ London: Routledge.

Argyris, C. (1992). *On organizational learning*. Cambridge, MA: Blackwell.

Argyris, C., & Schön, D. (1978). *Organizational learning: A theory of action perspective*. Reading: Addison Wesley.

Asen, E., & Fonagy, P. (2011). Mentalization-based therapeutic intervention for families. *Journal of Family Therapy*. (Online 9.6.2011; doi:10.1111/j.1467-6427. 2011.00552.x).

Backhausen, W., & Thommen, J. P. (2006). *Coaching: Durch systemisches Denken zu innovativer Personalentwicklung* (3rd ed.). Wiesbaden: Gabler.

Bale, L. S. (1995). Gregory Bateson, cybernetics, and the social/behavioral sciences. *Cybernetics & Human Knowing, 3*(1), 27–45.

Barkham, M., & Margison, F. (2007). Practice-based evidence as a complement to evidence-based practice: From dichotomy to chiasmus. In C. Freeman & M. Power (Eds.), *Handbook of evidence-based psychotherapy: A guide for research and practice* (pp. 443–476). Chichester: Wiley.

Barkham, M., Hardy, G. E., & Mellor-Clark, J. (2010). *Developing and delivering practice-based evidence: A guide for the psychological therapies*. Chichester: Wiley- Blackwell.

Bateson, G. (1972). *Steps to an ecology of mind*. New York: Ballantine.

Bateson, G. (1979). *Mind and nature: A necessary unity*. New York: Dutton.

Beck, U. (2000). *What is globalization?* Oxford: Policy.

Berg, I. K., & De Jong, P. (1996). Solution-building conversations: Co-constructing a sense of competence with clients. *Families in Society, 77*(6), 376–391.

Berg, I. K., & Szabó, P. (2005). *Brief coaching for lasting solutions*. New York: W.W. Norton.

Berger, P. L., & Luckmann, T. (1966). *The social construction of reality: A treatise in the sociology of knowledge*. Garden City: Anchor Books.

Biswas-Diener, R. (2010). *Practicing positive psychology coaching*. Hoboken: Wiley.

Biswas-Diener, R., & Dean, B. (2007). *Positive psychology coaching – Putting the science of happiness to work for your clients*. Hoboken: Wiley.

Bochner, A. P. (2001). Narrative's virtue. *Qualitative Inquiry, 7*(2), 131–157.

Bohart, A. C., Elliot, R., Greenberg, L. S., & Watson, J. C. (2002). Empathy. In J. C. Norcross (Ed.), *Psychotherapy relationships that work. Therapist contribution and responsiveness to patients* (pp. 89–108). Oxford: Oxford University Press.

Bohart, A. C., & Greenberg, L. S. (1997). Empathy: Where are we and where do we go from here? In A. C. Bohart & L. S. Greenberg (Eds.), *Empathy reconsidered: New directions in psychotherapy* (pp. 419–450). Washington, DC: American Psychological Association.

Bohart, A. C., & Tallman, K. (2010). Clients: The neglected common factor in psychotherapy. In B. L. Duncan, S. D. Miller, B. E. Wampold, & M. A. Hubble (Eds.), *The heart & soul of change* (2nd ed., pp. 83–111). Washington, DC: American Psychological Association.

Bohm, D. (1996). *On dialogue*. London: Routledge.

Boscolo, L., & Bertrando, P. (1996). *Systemic therapy with individuals*. London: Karnac Books.

Boscolo, L., Cecchin, G., Hoffman, L., & Penn, P. (1987). *Milan systemic family therapy: Conversations in theory and practice*. New York: Basic Books.

Bottrup, P. (2007). *Medarbejderforankret værdiarbejde – Refleksioner over arbejdet med værdier i arbejdslivet*. Report prepared for the Danish Confederation of Trade Unions by Kubix ApS (www.nye-vaerdier-i-arbejdslivet.socialfonden.net/files/upload/refleksionsrapp.pdf)

Bourdieu, P. (1983). Forms of capital. In J. C. Richards (Ed.), *Handbook of theory and research for the sociology of education*. New York: Greenwood Press.

Bourdieu, P. (1988). *Homo academicus*. Stanford: Stanford University Press.

Bourdieu, P. (1993). *The field of cultural production*. Cambridge: Polity Press.

Brandi, S., & Hildebrandt, S. (2008). *Leadership*. Copenhagen: Børsens Forlag.

Brinkmann, S., & Tanggaard, L. (2012). An epistemology of the hand: putting pragmatism to work. In P. Gibbs (Ed.), *Learning, work and practice: New understandings* (pp. 147–163). Dordrecht: Springer Science + Business Media.

Bruner, J. (1986). *Actual minds, possible worlds*. Cambridge, MA: Harvard University Press.

Bruner, J. (1990a). *Acts of meaning*. Cambridge, MA: Harvard University Press.

Bruner, J. (1990b). Culture and human development: A new look. *Human Development, 33*, 344–355.

Bruner, J. (1991). The narrative construction of reality. *Critical Inquiry, 18*(1), 1–21.

Bruner, J. (1996). *The culture of education*. Cambridge, MA: Harvard University Press.

Bruner, J. (2002). *Making stories – Law, literature, life*. Cambridge, MA: Harvard University Press.

Bruner, J. (2006). Culture, mind and narrative. In J. Bruner, C. F. Feldman, M. Hermansen, & J. Mollin (Eds.), *Narrative learning and culture* (New social science monographs, pp. 13–24). Copenhagen: Copenhagen Business School.

Bryant, F. B., & Veroff, J. (2007). *Savoring: A new model of positive experiences*. Mahwah: Lawrence Erlbaum.

Buber, M. (1999). The genuine dialogue. In J. Buber Agassi (Ed.), *Martin Buber on psychology and psychotherapy: Essays, letters, and dialogue* (The Estate of Martin Buber). New York: Syracuse University Press.

Buber, M. (2004). *I and Thou*. London: Continuum (German original from 1923).

Buytendijk, F. J. J. (1933). *Wesen und Sinn des Spiels*. Berlin: Kurt Wolf Verlag.

Carr, D. (1986). *Time, narrative and history*. Bloomington: Indiana University Press.

Cavanagh, M. J. (2006). Coaching from a systemic perspective: A complex adaptive conversation. In D. R. Stober & A. M. Grant (Eds.), *Evidence based coaching handbook* (pp. 313–354). Hoboken: John Wiley.

Cavanagh, M. J., & Grant, A. M. (2010). The solution-focused approach to coaching. In E. Cox, T. Bachkirova, & D. Clutterbuck (Eds.), *The complete handbook of coaching* (pp. 54–67). London: Sage.

Cecchin, G. (1987). Hypothesizing, circularity, and neutrality revisited: An invitation to curiosity. *Family Process, 26*(4), 405–413.

Cecchin, G. (1992). Constructing therapeutic possibilities. In K. J. Gergen & S. McNamee (Eds.), *Therapy as social construction* (pp. 86–95). London: Sage.

Cecchin, G., Lane, G., & Ray, W. A. (Eds.). (1993). *Irreverence: A strategy for therapists' survival.* London: Karnac.

Charon, R. (2006). The self-telling body. *Narrative Inquiry, 16*(1), 191–200.

Charon, R. (2011). The novelization of the body, or how medicine and stories need one another. *Narrative, 19*, 33–50.

Clandinin, D. J., & Connelly, F. M. (2000). *Narrative inquiry: Experience and story in qualitative research.* San Francisco: Jossey-Bass.

Cochrane, A. (1972). *Effectiveness and efficiency – Random reflections on health services.* London: The Nuffield Provincial Hospitals Trust.

Cohn, P. J. (1990). An exploratory study on sources of stress and athlete burnout in youth golf. *The Sport Psychologist, 4*(2), 95–106.

Coleman, J. C. (1990). *Foundations of social theory.* Cambridge, MA: Harvard University Press.

Cooperrider, D. L., & Srivastvas, S. (1987). Appreciative inquiry. In W. Pasmore & R. Woodman (Eds.), *Research in organizational change and development* (pp. 129–169). Greenwich, CT: JAI Press.

Cooperrider, D. L., & Whitney, D. (2005). *Appreciative inquiry – A positive revolution in change.* San Francisco: Berrett-Koehler.

Cooperrider, D. L., Whitney, D., & Stavros, J. M. (2008). *Appreciative inquiry handbook. For leaders of change.* San Francisco: Crown Custom Publishing/Berrett-Keohler Publishers.

Cooren, F. (2004). Textural agency: How texts do things in organizational settings. *Organization, 11*(3), 373–393.

Corrie, S., & Callahan, M. M. (2000). A review of the scientist-practitioner model: Reflections on its potential contribution to counselling psychology within the context of current health care trends. *British Journal of Medical Psychology, 73*, 413–427.

Cox, E., Bachkirova, T., & Clutterbuck, D. (Eds.). (2010). *The complete handbook of coaching.* London: Sage.

Cox, M., & Theilgaard, A. (1987). *Mutative metaphors in psychotherapy.* London/New York: Tavistock.

Cronen, V., & Lange, P. (1994). Language and action: Wittgenstein and Dewey in the practice of therapy and consultation. *Human Systems: The Journal of Systemic Consultation & Management, 5*, 5–43.

Crossley, M. (2000). *Introducing narrative psychology.* Buckingham: Open University Press.

Crossley, M. L. (2003). Formulating narrative psychology: The limitations of contemporary social constructionism. *Narrative Inquiry, 13*, 287–300.

Cunliffe, A. L. (2002). Social poetics: A dialogical approach to management inquiry. *Journal of Management Inquiry, 11*, 128–146.

Czarniawska-Joerges, B. (2004). *Narratives in social science research.* Thousand Oaks: Sage.

de Haan, E. (2008). *Relational coaching – Journey towards mastering one-to-one learning.* Chichester: Wiley.

De Jong, P., & Berg, I. K. (2002). *Interviewing for solutions.* Belmont: Thomson.

De Shazer, S., & Berg, I. K. (1997). What works? Remarks on research aspects of solution-focused brief therapy. *Journal of Family Therapy, 19*(4), 121–124.

Depraz, N., & Varela, F. J. (2000). The gesture of awareness. In M. Velmans (Ed.), *Investigating phenomenological consciousness* (pp. 121–136). Amsterdam: John Benjamins.

Depraz, N., Varela, F. J., & Vermersch, P. (2003). *On becoming aware*. Amsterdam: John Benjamins.

Derrida, J. (1978). *Writing and difference* (p. 1978). Chicago: University of Chicago.

Drake, D. B. (2007). The art of thinking narratively: Implications for coaching psychology and practice. *Australian Psychologist, 42*(4), 283–294.

Drake, D. B. (2009a). Evidence is a verb: A relational approach to knowledge and mastery in coaching. *International Journal of Evidence Based Coaching and Mentoring, 7*(1), 1–12.

Drake, D. B. (2009b). Narrative coaching. In E. Cox, T. Bachkirova, & D. Clutterbuck (Eds.), *The Sage handbook of coaching* (pp. 120–131). London: Sage.

Dreier, O. (2008). *Psychotherapy in everyday life*. Cambridge: Cambridge University Press.

Dreier, O. (2009). Persons in structures of social practice. *Theory & Psychology, 19*(2), 193–212.

Dreyfus, H. L. (1992). *What computers still can't do: A critique of artificial reason*. Cambridge, MA: MIT Press.

Duncan, B. L., Miller, S. D., Wampold, B. E., & Hubble, M. A. (Eds.). (2010). *The heart & soul of change* (2nd ed.). Washington, DC: American Psychological Association.

Edwards, D., & Potter, J. (1992). *Discursive psychology*. London: Sage.

Ehrenreich, B. (2009). *Smile or die: How positive thinking fooled America and the world*. London: Granta.

Elbe, A. M. (2008). *The Danish version of the recovery-stress questionnaire for athletes*. Ref. Type: Unpublished Work.

Elliott, R., & Greenberg, L. S. (2007). The essence of process-experiential/emotion-focused therapy. *American Journal of Psychotherapy, 61*, 241–254.

Ericsson, K. A. (2006). The influence of experience and deliberate practice on the development of superior expert performance. In K. A. Ericsson, N. Charness, P. Feltovich, & R. R. Hoffman (Eds.), *Cambridge handbook of expertise and expert performance* (pp. 685–706). Cambridge: Cambridge University Press.

Espedal, G., Svendsen, T., & Andersen, T. (2006). *Løsningsfokusert coaching*. Oslo: Gyldendal.

Etherington, K., & Bridges, N. (2011). Narrative case study research: On endings and six session reviews. *Counselling and Psychotherapy Research, 11*(1), 11–22.

Ferdig, M. A. (2007). Sustainability leadership: Co-creating a sustainable future. *Journal of Change Management, 7*(1), 25–35.

Fillery-Travis, A., & Passmore, J. (2011). A critical review of executive coaching research: A decade of progress and what's to come. *Coaching: An International Journal of Theory, Research and Practice, 4*(2), 70–88.

Fink-Jensen, K. (1998). *Stemthed – En basis for æstetisk læring*. Copenhagen: Danmarks Lærerhøjskole.

Fitzgerald, S. P., Murrell, K. L., & Newman, H. L. (2002). Appreciative inquiry – The new frontier. In J. Waclawski & A. H. Church (Eds.), *Organization development: Data driven methods for change* (pp. 203–221). San Francisco: Jossey-Bass Publishers.

Ford, J. D. (1999). Organizational change as shifting conversations. *Journal of Organizational Change Management, 12*(6), 480–500.

Foucault, M. (1972). *The archaeology of knowledge and the discourse on language*. New York: Pantheon Books.

Foucault, M. (1991). Nietzsche, genealogy, history. In P. Rabinow (Ed.), *The foucault reader* (pp. 76–100). London: Penguin.

Frederickson, B. L., & Losada, M. F. (2005). Positive affect and the complex dynamics of human flourishing. *American Psychologist, 60*(7), 678–686.

Fredrickson, B. L. (2004). Gratitude, like other positive emotions, broadens and builds. In R. A. Emmons & M. E. McCullough (Eds.), *The psychology of gratitude* (pp. 145–166). New York: Oxford University Press.

Fredrickson, B. L. (2009). *Positivity: Groundbreaking research reveals how to embrace the hidden strength of positive emotions, overcome negativity, and thrive*. New York: Crown.

Freemann, A. (1994). Operative intentionality: Notes on Merleau-Ponty's approach to mental activities that are not the exclusive product of the conscious mind. *Journal of Phenomenological Research, 24*(1), 78–89.

Frølund, L., & Ziethen, M. (2011). Relationel eksistentialisme – Om konsulentens komplementar-blik og translogiske dømmekraft. *Erhvervspsykologi, 9*(1), 38–57.

Gallwey, W. T. (1974). *The inner game of tennis* (1st ed.). New York: Random House.

Gazzaniga, M. S. (2005). *The ethical brain*. New York: Dana Press.

Geertz, C. (1973). Thick description: Toward an interpretive theory of culture. In C. Geertz (Ed.), *The interpretation of cultures: Selected essays* (pp. 3–30). New York: Basic Books.

Gendlin, E. T. (1978). *Focusing*. New York: Everest House.

Gendlin, E. T. (1996). *Focusing-oriented psychotherapy*. New York/London: The Guildford Press.

Gendlin, E. T. (1997). *Experiencing and the creation of meaning*. Evanston: Northwestern University Press (original from 1962).

Gergen, K. J. (1973). Social psychology as history. *Journal of Personality and Social Psychology, 26*(2), 309–320.

Gergen, K. J. (1990). Die Konstruktion des Selbst im Zeitalter der Postmoderne. *Psychologische Rundschau, 41*, 191–199.

Gergen, K. J. (1991). *The saturated self – Dilemmas of identity in contemporary life*. New York: Basic.

Gergen, K. J. (1994). *Realities and relationship – Soundings in social constructionism*. Cambridge, MA: Harvard University Press.

Gergen, K. J. (1997). *Realities and relationships, soundings in social construction*. Cambridge MA: Harvard University Press.

Gergen, K. J. (2009a). *An invitation to social construction*. London: Sage.

Gergen, K. J. (2009b). *Relational being: Beyond self and community*. Oxford: Oxford University Press.

Gergen, K. J., & Gergen, M. M. (2003). *Social construction: A reader*. London: Sage.

Gergen, M. M., & Gergen, K. J. (2006). Narratives in action. *Narrative Inquiry, 16*(1), 112–121.

Germer, C. K. (2005). What is mindfulness? In C. K. Germer, R. D. Siegel, & P. R. Fulton (Eds.), *Mindfulness and psychotherapy* (pp. 3–27). New York/London: The Guilford Press.

Gibson, J. J. (1966). *The senses considered as perceptual systems*. Boston: Houghton Mifflin.

Gibson, J. J. (1979). *The ecological approach to visual perception*. Boston: Houghton Mifflin.

Giddens, A. (1991). *Modernity and self-identity: Self and society in the late modern age*. Stanford: Stanford University Press.

Gingerich, W. J., & Eisengart, S. (2000). Solution- focused brief therapy: A review of the outcome research. *Family Process, 39*(4), 477–498.

Goffman, E. (1959). *The presentation of self in everyday life*. Garden City: Doubleday.

Grant, A. M. (2007). Past, present and future. The evolution of professional coaching and coaching psychology. In S. Palmer & A. Whybrow (Eds.), *Handbook of coaching psychology*. London: Routledge.

Grant, A. M., & Cavanagh, M. (2004). Toward a profession of coaching: Sixty five years of progress and challenges for the future. *International Journal of Evidence Based Coaching and Mentoring, 2*, 8–21.

Grant, A. M., & Stober, D. R. (2006). Introduction. In D. R. Stober & A. M. Grant (Eds.), *Evidence based coaching handbook* (pp. 1–14). Hoboken: John Wiley.

Grawe, K., Regli, D., & Schmalbach, S. (1994). *Psychotherapie im Wandel: Von der Konfession zur Profession*. Gottingen: Hogrefe.

Green, L. W. (2006). Public health asks of systems science: To advance our evidence-based practice, can you help us get more practice-based evidence? *American Journal of Public Health, 96*(3), 406–409.

Greenberg, L. (2002). *Emotion-focused therapy: Coaching clients to work through feelings*. Washington, DC: American Psychological Association Press.

Greenhalgh, T., & Hurwitz, B. (1999). Narrative based medicine: Why study narrative? *BMJ, 318*(7175), 248–250.

Greenwald, A. G. (1980). The totalitarian ego – Fabrication and revision of personal history. *American Psychologist, 35*(7), 603–618.

Greif, S. (2007). Advances in research on coaching outcomes. *International Coaching Psychology Review, 2*(3), 222–249.

Greif, S. (2008). *Coaching und ergebnisorientierte Selbstreflexion*. Göttingen: Hogrefe.

Greismas, A. J., & Courtes, J. (1976). The cognitive dimension of narrative discourse. *New Literary History, 7*(3), 433–447.

Grencavage, L. M., & Norcross, J. C. (1990). Where are commonalities among the therapeutic common factors? *Professional Psychology: Research and Practice, 21*, 372–378.

Groeben, N., & Scheele, B. (2000). Dialogue- hermeneutic method and the "Research program subjective theorie" [9 paragraphs]. *Forum Qualitative Sozialforschung/Forum: Qualitative Social Research, 1*(2), Art. 10. http://nbn-resolving.de/urn:nbn:de:0114-fqs0002105

Groeben, N., Wahl, D., Schlee, J., & Scheele, B. (1988). *Das Forschungsprogramm Subjektive Theorien. Eine Einführung in die Psychologie des reflexiven Subjekts*. Tübingen: Francke.

Hansen, F. T. (2002). The use of philosophical practice in lifelong and self-directed learning. In H. Herrestad, A. Holt, & H. Svare (Eds.), *Philosophy in society: Proceedings from the 6th International Conference on Philosophy in Practice*. Oslo: Oslo Academic Press.

Hansen, M. T. (2009). *Collaboration: How leaders avoid the traps, create unity, and reap big results*. Boston: Harvard Business School Publishing.

Hansen, K. V. (2010). Terapi er koncentreret liv. *Psykolog Nyt, 64*(12), 16–17.

Hansen, J., & Henriksen, K. (2009). *Træneren som coach – En praktisk guide til coaching i sport*. Virum: Dansk Psykologisk Forlag.

Hansen-Skovmoes, P., & Rosenkvist, G. (2002). Coaching som udviklingsværktoj. In R. Stelter (Ed.), *Coaching – læring og udvikling* (pp. 107–128). Copenhagen: Dansk Psykologisk Forlag.

Hardman, A. J. (2011). *The ethics of sports coaching*. London/New York: Routledge.

Haslebo, G., & Haslebo, M. L. (2012). *Practicing relational ethics in organizations*. Ohio: TAOS Institute Publications.

Hay, J. (2007). *Reflective practice and supervision for coaches*. Maidenhead: Open University Press.

Hede, T. (2010). *Coaching – Samtalekunst og ledelsesdisciplin*. Frederiksberg: Samfundslitteratur.

Helth, P. (Ed.). (2009a). *Lederskabelse: Det personlige lederskab* (2nd ed.). Copenhagen: Samfundslitteratur.

Helth, P. (2009b). Ledelse i den relationsskabte organisation. In P. Helth (Ed.), *Lederskabelse: Det personlige lederskab* (2nd ed., pp. 39–60). Copenhagen: Samfundslitteratur.

Hieker, C., & Huffington, C. (2006). Reflexive questions in a coaching psychology context. *International Coaching Psychology Review, 1*(2), 46–55.

Hildebrandt, S. (2003). Dårlig ledelse skaber stress. Interview. In L. Lyngbjerg Steffensen (Ed.), *Effektiv uden stress*. Børsens Forlag: Copenhagen.

Hill, C. E., & Knox, S. (2002). Self-disclosure. In J. C. Norcross (Ed.), *Psychotherapy relationship that works. The rapist contribution and responsiveness to patients* (pp. 255–265). Oxford: Oxford University Press.

Holmgren, A. (2006). Poststrukturalistisk coaching – Om coaching og ledelse. *Erhvervspsykologi, 4*(3), 36–76.

Hornstrup, C., Loehr-Petersen, J., Madsen, J. G., Johansen, T., & Vinther, A. J. (2012). *Developing relational leadership: Resources for developing reflexive organizational practices*. Chagrin Falls: The Taos Institute Publications.

Horvath, A. O., & Bedi, R. P. (2002). The alliance. In J. C. Norcross (Ed.), *Psychotherapy relationship that works. The rapist contribution and responsiveness to patients* (pp. 37–69). Oxford: Oxford University Press.

Hougaard, E. (2006). *Psykoterapi – Teori og forskning* (2nd ed.). Copenhagen: Dansk Psykologisk Forlag.

Hougaard, E. (2007). Evidens: Noget for psykologer. *Psykolog Nyt, 20*, 14–21.

Huizinga, J. (1950). *Homo ludens: A study of the play element in culture*. New York: Roy Publishers.

Husserl, E. (1931). *Ideas: General introduction to pure phenomenology*. London: George Allen & Unwin.

Husserl, E. (1950). Konstitution der Intersubjektivität. In E. Husserl (Ed.), *Gesammelte Werke. Bd. 1: Cartesianische Meditationen und Pariser Vorträge* (pp. 121–163). Den Haag: Martinus Nijhoff.

Husserl, E. (1985). Encyclopaedia Britannica. In E. Husserl (Ed.), *Die phänomenologische Methode I* (pp. 196–206). Stuttgart: Reclam (English version at http://www.stanford.edu/dept/relstud/faculty/sheehan.bak/EHtrans/5-eb.pdf; retrieved on 31 Dec. 2012).

Ihde, D. (1977). *Experimental phenomenology: An introduction.* New York: Putnam's Sons.

Illeris, K. (2004). Transformative learning in the perspective of a comprehensive learning theory. *Journal of Transformative Education, 2,* 79–89.

Illeris, K. (2007). *How we learn: Learning and non-learning in school and beyond.* London: Routledge.

Isaacs, W. (1999). *Dialogue: The art of thinking together.* Strawberry Hills: Currency.

Jackson, P. Z., & McKergow, M. (2007). *The solutions focus: Making coaching and change simple* (2nd ed.). London/Boston: Nicholas Brealey.

Jarvis, P. (1999). *The practitioner-reseacher – Developing theory from practice.* San Francisco: Jossey-Bass.

Johns, C. (2004). *Becoming a reflective practitioner* (2nd ed.). Oxford: Blackwell.

Kabat-Zinn, J. (1994). *Wherever you go, there you are: Mindfulness meditation in everyday life.* New York: Hyperion.

Katz, A., & Shotter, J. (2004). On the way to "presence": Methods of a "social poetics". In D. A. Pare & G. Larner (Eds.), *Collaborative practice in psychology and therapy* (pp. 69–82). New York: The Haworth Clinical Practice Press.

Kegan, R., & Lahey, L. (2001). *How the way we talk can change the way we work: Seven languages for transformation.* San Francisco: Jossey-Bass/Wiley.

Keupp, H., Ahbe, T., Gmür, W., Höfer, R., Mitzscherlich, B., Kraus, W., et al. (1999). *Identitätskonstruktionen. Das Patchwork der Identitäten in der Spätmoderne.* Reinbek: Rowohlt.

Kierkegaard, S. A. (2010). *Kierkegaards skrifter, SKS*.* Copenhagen: Søren Kierkegaard Forskningscenter (online edition: www.sks.dk).

King, P., & Eaton, J. (1999). Coaching for results. *Industrial and Commercial Training, 31*(4), 145–151.

Kirkeby, O. F. (2000). *Management philosophy. A radical-normative perspective.* Heidelberg/New York: Springer.

Kirkeby, O. F. (2004). The eventum tantum. To make the world worthy of what could happen to it. *Ephemera, 4*(3), 290–308.

Kirkeby, O. F. (2006a). Coaching: For madonnaer eller ludere? *LPF-nyt om ledelse, 9*(2), 10–11.

Kirkeby, O. F. (2006b). *Begivenhedsledelse og handlekraft.* Copenhagen: Børsens Forlag.

Kirkeby, O. F. (2007). *The virtue of leadership.* Copenhagen: CBS Press.

Kirkeby, O. F. (2008). *Selvet sker – Bevidsthedens begivenhed.* Frederiksberg: Samfundslitteratur.

Kirkeby, O. F. (2009). *The new protreptic – The concept and the art.* Copenhagen: Copenhagen Business School Press.

Kjerulf, S. (2008). *Personlig handlekraft.* Copenhagen: Gyldendal Business.

Klafki, W. (1983). *Kategorial dannelse og kritisk- konstruktiv pædagogik* (Udvalgte artikler og indledning ved Sven Erik Nordenbo). Copenhagen: Nyt Nordisk Forlag Arnold Busck.

Klafki, W. (2000). The significance of classical theories of Bildung for a contemporary concept of Allgemeinbildung. In I. Westbury, S. Hopmann, & K. Riquarts (Eds.), *Teaching as a reflective practice. The German Didaktik tradition* (pp. 85–107). Mahwah: Erlbaum.

Kling-Jensen, H. (2008). *Kierkegaard og refleksion: Fra enkelt-refleksion til dobbeltrefleksion* (Skriftserie: Refleksion i praksis). Aarhus: Institut for Filosofi og Idehistorie.

Knudsen, H., & Thygsen, N. T. (2009). Ledelse og værdier. In P. Helth (Ed.), *Lederskabelse: Det personlige lederskab* (2nd ed., pp. 77–93). Copenhagen: Samfundslitteratur.

Kolb, D. A. (1984). *Experiential learning. Experience as the source of learning and development.* Englewood Cliffs: Prentice Hall.

Kolb, D. A. (2000). Den erfaringsbaserede læreproces. In K. Illeris (Ed.), *Tekster om læring* (pp. 47–66). Frederiksberg: Roskilde Universitetsforlag.

Kraus, W. (2006). The narrative negotiation of identity and belonging. *Narrative Inquiry, 16*(1), 103–111.

Kure, N. (2010). http://www.asb.dk/en/aboutus/newsfromasb/newsarchive/article/artikel/feature_
the_hr_departments_sicilian_offer-1/

Kvale, S. (Ed.). (1992). *Psychology and postmodernism*. London: Sage.

Kvale, S. (2007). Professionspraksis som erkendelse – Om dilemmaer i terapeutisk forskning.
In S. Brinkmann & L. Tanggaard (Eds.), *Psykologi: Forskning og profession* (pp. 69–95).
Copenhagen: Hans Reitzels Forlag.

Ladkin, D. M. (2010). *Rethinking leadership: A new look at old leadership questions*. Cheltenham:
Edward Elgar Publishing.

Lakoff, G. (1987). *Women, fire, and dangerous things*. Chicago/London: University of Chicago
Press.

Lakoff, G., & Johnson, M. (1980). *Metaphors we live by*. Chicago: University of Chicago Press.

Lambert, M. J., & Barley, D. E. (2002). Research summary on therapeutic relationship and psychotherapy outcome. In J. Norcross (Ed.), *Psychotherapy relationship that works* (pp. 17–32).
Oxford: Oxford University Press.

Lane, D. A., & Corrie, S. (2006). *The modern scientist-practitioner – A guide to practice in
psychology*. London: Routlege.

Lane, D. A., Stelter, R., & Stout-Royston, S. (2010). The future of coaching as a profession.
In E. Cox, T. Bachkirova, & D. Clutterbuck (Eds.), *Sage handbook of coaching and mentoring*
(pp. 337–348). London: Sage.

Lang, W. P., Little, M., & Cronen, V. (1990). The systemic professional: Domains of action
and the question of neutrality. *Human Systems: The Journal of Systemic Consultation and
Management, 1*, 39–56.

Langdridge, D. (2007). *Phenomenological psychology: Theory, research and method*. Harlow:
Pearson Education.

Langer, E. J. (1993). A mindful education. *Educational Psychologist, 28*(1), 43–50.

Langer, E. (1997). *The power of mindful learning*. Cambridge, MA: Perseues Books.

Lave, J., & Wenger, E. (1991). *Situated learning: Legitimate peripheral participation*. Cambridge
England: Cambridge University Press.

Lavendt, E. (2010). Køb af coaching – Råd og vejledning om effekt, forbrugersikkerhed og
værdi for pengene. Retrieved October 19, 2011 from http://www.sebc.dk/uploads/artikler/
Køb_af_coaching.pdf

Law, H. C., Ireland, S., & Hussain, Z. (2007). *Psychology of coaching, mentoring & learning*.
Chichester: John Wiley & Sons.

Lowe, R. (2005). Structured methods and striking moments. *Family Process, 44*(1), 65–75.

Luhmann, N. (1980). *Gesellschaftsstruktur und Semantik: Studien zur Wissenssoziologie der
modernen Gesellschaft I*. Frankfurt: Suhrkamp.

Luhmann, N. (1995). *Social systems*. Stanford: Stanford University Press.

Luhmann, N. (1998). *Die Gesellschaft der Gesellschaft*. Suhrkamp: Frankfurt/M.

Luhmann, N. (2006). System as difference. *Organization, 13*(1), 37–57.

Lyotard, J. (1984). *The postmodern condition: A report on knowledge*. Manchester: Manchester
University Press.

Manning, P. K. (1987). *Semiotics and fieldwork*. Newbury Park/London: Sage.

Markus, H., & Wurf, E. (1987). The dynamic self-concept: A social psychological perspective.
Annual Review of Psychology, 38, 299–337.

Maturana, H. R. (1978). Biology of language: The epistemology of reality. In G. A. Miller &
E. Lenneberg (Eds.), *Psychology and biology of language and thought* (pp. 27–63). New
York/London: Academic Press.

Maturana, H. R., & Varela, F. J. (1980). *Autopoiesis and cognition. The realization of human living*.
Boston: Reidel.

Maturana, H. R., & Varela, F. J. (1992). *The tree of knowledge: The biological roots of human
understanding*. Boston: Shambhala.

McAdams, D. P. (1993). *The stories we live by: Personal myths and the making of the self*.
New York: The Guilford Press.

McDonald, P. W., & Viehbeck, S. (2007). From evidence-based practice making to practice-based evidence making: Creating communities of (research) and practice. *Health Promotion Practice,* *8*(2), 140–144.

McNamee, S. (2004). Social construction as practical theory: Lessons for practice and reflection in psychotherapy. In D. A. Pare & G. Larner (Eds.), *Collaborative practice in psychology and therapy* (pp. 9–21). New York: The Haworth Clinical Practice Press.

Mead, G. H. (1934). *Mind, self and society.* Chicago: University of Chicago Press.

Merleau-Ponty, M. (1993). Douche. In G. A. Johnson (Ed.), *The Merleau-Ponty aesthetics reader: Philosophy and painting.* Evanston: Northwestern University Press.

Merleau-Ponty, M. (2012). *Phenomenology of perception.* London: Routledge.

Mezirow, J., & Associates. (1990). *Fostering critical reflection in adulthood. A guide to transformative and emancipatory learning.* San Francisco, CA: Jossey Bass.

Mezirow, J., & Associates. (2000). *Learning as transformation: Critical perspectives on a theory in progress.* San Francisco, CA: Jossey-Bass.

Miller, S. D., Duncan, B. L., Brown, J., Sparks, J. A., & Claud, D. A. (2003). The outcome rating scale: A preliminary study of the reliability, validity, and feasibility of a brief visual analog measure. *Journal of Brief Therapy, 2*(2), 91–100.

Miller, S. D., Duncan, B. L., Sorrell, R., Brown, G. S., & Chalk, M. B. (2006). Using outcome to inform therapy practice. *Journal of Brief Therapy, 5*(1), 5–22.

Moltke, H. V., & Molly, A. (Eds.). (2010). *Systemisk coaching – En grundbog.* Virum: Dansk Psykologisk Forlag.

Myerhoff, B. (1982). Life history among the elderly: Performance, visibility and remembering. In J. Ruby (Ed.), *A crack in the mirror: Reflexive perspectives in anthropology.* Philadelphia: University of Pennsylvania Press.

Nay, R., & Fetherstonhaugh, D. (2007). Evidence-based practice: Limitations and successful implementation. *Annual of the New York Academy of Science, 1114,* 456–463.

Nechansky, H. (2008). Elements of a cybernetic epistemology: Decisions, control and principles of societal organization. *Kybernetes, 37*(1), 83–93.

New Oxford Dictionary of English. (1999). Oxford: Oxford University Press.

Nielsen, K. (2006, June 17). Apprenticeship at the Academy of Music. *International Journal of Education & the Arts, 7*(4). Retrieved December 31, 2012 from http://ijea.asu.edu/v7n4/

Nielsen, K. (2008). Scaffold instruction at the workplace from a situated perspective. *Studies in Continuing Education, 30*(3), 247–261.

Nielsen, K.S. (i samarbejde med M. Klinke & J. Gegersen). (2010). *Narrativ coaching – en ny fortælling.* Virum: Dansk Psykologisk Forlag.

Nielsen, K., & Kvale, S. (1997). Current issues of apprenticeship. *Nordisk Pedagogik, 17,* 130–139.

Nitsch, J. R. (1986). Zur handlungstheoretischen Grundlegung der Sportpsychologie. In H. Gabler, R. Singer, & J. R. Nitsch (Eds.), *Einführung in die Sportpsychologie, Teil 1: Grundthemen* (pp. 188–270). Schorndorf: Hofmann.

Norcross, J. C. (Ed.). (2002). *Psychotherapy relationships that work. Therapist contribution and responsiveness to patients.* Oxford: Oxford University Press.

Nørlem, J., Alrø, H. K., & Dahl, P. N. (Eds.). (2009). *Coachingens landskaber – Nye veje – Andre samtaler.* Copenhagen: Hans Reitzels Forlag.

O'Broin, A., & Palmer, S. (2010). Introducing an interpersonal perspective on the coaching relationship. In S. Palmer & A. McDowall (Eds.), *The coaching relationship – Putting people first* (pp. 9–33). London: Routledge.

O'Connell, B., & Palmer, S. (Eds.). (2003). *Handbook of solution-focused therapy.* London: Sage.

O'Connor, J., & Lages, A. (2004). *Coaching with NLP: How to be a master coach.* London: Element.

Olsen, T., & Lund-Jakobsen, D. (2006). Værdier – Snuble- eller ledetråde? *Erhvervspsykologi,* *4*(2), 50–68.

Orem, S. L., Binkert, J., & Clancy, A. L. (2007). *Appreciative coaching – A positive process for change.* San Francisco: Jossey-Bass.

Orford, J. (2008). *Community psychology: Challenges, controversies and emerging consensus.* Hoboken: John Wiley and Sons.

Palmer, S., & McDowall, A. (Eds.). (2010). *The coaching relationship – Putting people first.* London: Routledge.

Palmer, S., & Szymanska, K. (2007). Cognitive behavioural coaching: An integrative approach. In S. Palmer & A. Whybrow (Eds.), *Handbook of coaching psychology – A guide for practitioners* (pp. 86–117). London: Routledge.

Palmer, S., & Whybrow, A. (Eds.). (2007). *Handbook of coaching psychology – A guide for practitioners.* London: Routledge.

Pare, D. A., & Larner, G. (2004). *Collaborative practice in psychology and therapy.* New York: The Haworth Clinical Practice Press.

Park, N., & Peterson, C. (2006). Character strengths and happiness among young children: Content analysis of parental descriptions. *Journal of Happiness Studies, 7*, 323–341.

Parker, I. (1992). *Discourse dynamics: Critical analysis for social and individual psychology.* London: Routledge.

Passmore, J., & Marianetti, O. (2007). The role of mindfulness in coaching. *The Coaching Psychologist, 3*(3), 131–137.

Passmore, J., Peterson, D., & Freire, T. (Eds.). (2012). *Wiley-Blackwell handbook of the psychology of coaching and mentoring.* Chichester: Wiley-Blackwell.

Pearce, W. B. (1994). *Interpersonal communication. Making social worlds.* New York: Harper Collins College Publishers.

Pearce, W. B., & Cronen, V. (1980). *Communication, action and meaning.* New York: Praeger.

Pedersen, D. (2001). *Offentlig ledelse år 2010: Fremtiden som udfordring.* BUPL: Copenhagen.

Pemberton, C. (2006). *Coaching to solutions: A manager's toolkit for performance delivery.* Oxford: Butterworth-Heinemann.

Perls, F. S., Goodman, P., & Hefferline, R. F. (1951). *Gestalt therapy: Excitement and growth in the human personality.* New York: Julian Press.

Peterson, C., Park, N., & Seligman, M. E. P. (2006). Greater strengths of character and recovery from illness. *The Journal of Positive Psychology, 1*, 17–26.

Peterson, C., Ruch, W., Beermann, U., Park, N., & Seligman, M. E. P. (2007). Strengths of character, orientations to happiness, and life satisfaction. *The Journal of Positive Psychology, 2*(3), 149–156.

Peterson, C., & Seligman, M. (2004). *Character strengths and virtues: A handbook and classification.* New York: Oxford University Press.

Phillips, L. (2011). *The promise of dialogue: The dialogic turn in the production and communication of knowledge.* Amsterdam: John Benjamins.

Philosophia (1993). Tidsskrift for filosofi. Volume 22, 3–4: Den levede krop.

Piaget, J. (1962). *Play, dreams and imitation in childhood.* New York: W. W. Norton & Company.

Piaget, J. (1999). *The construction of reality in the child* (International library of psychology, developmental psychology, Vol. XX). London: Routledge.

Plutchik, R. (2002). *Emotions and life: Perspectives from psychology, biology, and evolution.* Washington, DC: American Psychological Association.

Polkinghorne, D. (1988). *Narrative knowing and the human sciences.* Albany: SUNY Press.

Putnam, R. D. (1995). Bowling alone: America's declining social capital. *Journal of Democracy, 6*(1), 65–78.

Putnam, R. D. (2000). *Bowling alone: The collapse and revival of American community.* New York: Simon & Schuster.

Ramian, K. (2007). *Casestudiet i praksis.* Copenhagen: Academica Gyldendal.

Ramian, K. (2009). Evidens på egen praksis. *Psykolog Nyt, 2*, 18–25.

Rauen, C. von (2005). *Handbuch coaching* (3rd Rev. ed.). Gottingen: Hogrefe.

Ravn, I., & Soderqvist, T. (1987). Dette er en kosmologi, og som sådan er den fuldstændig. In H. Maturana & F. Varela (Eds.), *Kundskabens træ* (pp. 9–28). Århus: Forlaget ASK.

Reivich, K., & Shatte, A. (2002). *The resilience factor: 7 keys to finding your inner strength and overcoming life's hurtles.* New York: Broadway Books.

Rennison, B. (2009). Refleksiv ledelse. In P. Helth (Ed.), *Lederskabelse: Det personlige lederskab* (2nd ed., pp. 121–132). Copenhagen: Samfundslitteratur.

Richardson, L., & Pierre, E. A. St. (2005). Writing. A method of inquiry. In N. K. Denzin & Y. S. Lincoln (Eds.), *The Sage handbook of qualitative research* (pp. 959–978). Thousand Oaks: Sage.

Riessman, C. K. (2008). *Narrative methods for the human sciences.* Thousand Oaks: Sage Publications.

Robinson, P. E. (2010). *Foundations of sports coaching.* London: Routledge.

Rock, D., & Page, L. J. (2009). *Coaching with the brain in mind: Foundations for practice.* Hoboken: Wiley.

Rogers, C. R. (1942). *Counseling and psychotherapy: Newer concepts in practice.* Boston: Houghton Mifflin Company.

Rogers, C. R. (1951). *Client-centered therapy: Its current practice, implications, and theory.* Boston: Houghton Mifflin.

Rogers, C. R. (1959). A theory of therapy, personality and interpersonal relationships as developed in the client-centered framework. In S. Koch (Ed.), *Psychology: A study of a science. Vol. 3: Formulations of the person and the social context.* New York: McGraw Hill.

Rogers, C. R. (1961). *On becoming a person. A therapist's view of psychotherapy.* Boston: Houghton Mifflin.

Rogers, C. R. (1980). *A way of being.* Boston: Houghton Mifflin.

Rosenthal, R., & Jacobson, L. (1992). *Pygmalion in the classroom* (Expanded ed.). New York: Irvington.

Ryle, G. (1949). *The concept of mind.* London: Hutchinghouse.

Sackett, D. L., Rosenberg, W. M. C., Gray, J. A. M., Haynes, R. B., & Richardson, W. S. (1996). Evidence-based medicine: What it is and what it isn't. *British Medical Journal, 312,* 71–72.

Sampson, E. E. (1985). The decentralization of identity. Towards a revised concept of personal and social order. *American Psychologist, 40*(11), 1203–1211.

Sampson, E. E. (1996). Establishing embodiment in psychology. *Theory & Psychology, 6,* 601–624.

Sandler, C. (2011). *Executive coaching: A psychodynamic approach.* Berkshire: Open University Press.

Sarbin, T. R. (Ed.). (1986). *Narrative psychology: The storied nature of human conduct.* New York: Praeger.

Schein, E. (1992). *Organizational culture and leadership.* San Francisco: Jossey-Bass Publishers.

Schmidt, L.-H. (1999). *Diagnosis I – Filosoferende eksperimenter.* Copenhagen: Danmarks Pædagogiske Institut.

Schön, D. A. (1983). *The reflective practitioner: How professionals think in action.* New York: Basic Books.

Segal, Z., Williams, M., & Teasdale, J. (2002). *Mindfulness-based cognitive therapy for depression. A new approach to preventing relapse.* London: Guildford.

Seligman, M. E. P. (2002). *Authentic happiness: Using the new positive psychology to realize your potential for lasting fulfillment.* New York: Free Press.

Seligman, M. E. P., & Czikszentmihalyi, M. (2000). Positive psychology: An introduction. *American Psychologist, 55*(1), 5–14.

Seligman, M. E. P., Steen, T., Park, N., & Peterson, C. (2005). Positive psychology progress: Empirical validation of interventions. *American Psychologist, 60*(5), 410–421.

Selvini-Palazzoli, M., Boscolo, L., Cecchin, G. M. S., & Prata, G. (1980). Hypothesizing – Circularity – Neutrality: Three guidelines for the conductor of the session. *Family Process, 19*(1), 3–12.

Sennet, R. (1992). *The fall of public man.* New York: Knopf.

Shotter, J. (1993). *Conversational realities: The construction of life through language.* London: Sage. New edition from 2008 published by The Taos Institute Publications.

Shotter, J. (2003). 'Real presences': Meaning as living movement in a participatory world. *Theory & Psychology, 13*(4), 435–468.

Shotter, J. (2006). Understanding process from within: An argument for 'witness'-thinking. *Organization Studies, 27*, 585–604.

Shotter, J., & Katz, A. M. (1996). Articulating a practice from within the practice itself: Establishing formative dialogues by the use of a 'social poetics'. *Concepts and Transformation, 1*, 213–237.

Shotter, J., & Lannamann, J. W. (2002). The situation of social constructionism: Its 'imprisonment' within the ritual of theory – criticism – and-debate. *Theory & Psychology, 12*(5), 577–609.

Siegel, D. J. (2007). *The mindful brain: Reflection and attunement in the cultivation of well-being.* New York: Norton.

Sieler, A. (2010). Ontological coaching. In E. Cox, T. Bachkirova, & D. Clutterbuck (Eds.), *The complete handbook of coaching* (pp. 107–119). London: Sage.

Singer, R. N., Hausenblas, H. A., & Janelle, C. (Eds.). (2001). *Handbook of sport psychology.* New York: Wiley.

Skårderud, F. (2000). *Uro – En rejse i det moderne selv.* Copenhagen: Tiderne Skifter.

Skårderud, F. (2001). The global body. In M. Nasser, M. Katzman, & R. Gordon (Eds.), *Eating disorders and cultures in transition.* Chichester: Routledge.

Sloan, T. (Ed.). (2000). *Critical psychology: Voices for change.* New York: St. Martin's Press.

Søholm, T. M., Storch, J., Juhl, A., Dahl, K., & Molly, A. (2006). *Ledelsesbaseret coaching.* Copenhagen: Børsens Forlag.

Søltoft, P. (2008). Kierkegaard som coach. *Erhvervspsykologi, 6*(1), 2–17.

Sommerbeck, L., & Larsen, A. B. (2011). *Accept, empati og ægthed i psykoterapeutisk praksis.* Copenhagen: Dansk Psykologisk Forlag.

Spaten, O. M. (2010). *Coaching forskning – På evidensbaseret grundlag (e-book, PDF).* Alborg: Aalborg Universitetsforlag.

Spence, G. (2008). *New directions in evidence- based coaching: Investigations into the impact of mindfulness training on goal attainment and well-being.* Saarbrücken: VDM Verlag Dr. Mueller.

Spinelli, E. (2010). Existential coaching. In E. Cox, T. Bachkirova, & D. Clutterbuck (Eds.), *The complete handbook of coaching* (pp. 94–106). London: Sage.

Stacy, R. D. (2007). *Strategic management and organisational dynamics: The challenge of complexity* (5th ed.). Harlow: Pearson Education.

Stam, H. J. (Ed.). (1998). *The body and psychology.* London: Sage Publications.

Stam, H. (Ed.) (2001). Social constructionism and its critics. *Theory & Psychology, 11*(3), 291–296.

Stam, H. (Ed.). (2002). Varieties of social constructionism. *Theory & Psychology, 12*(5), 571–576.

Stelter, R. (1996). *Du bist wie dein Sport – Studien zur Selbstkonzept- und Identitätsentwicklung.* Schorndorf: Hofmann.

Stelter, R. (1998). The body, self and identity. Personal and social constructions of the self through sport and movement (review article). *European Yearbook of Sport Psychology, 2*, 1–32.

Stelter, R. (1999). *Med kroppen i centrum – Idrætspsykologi i teori og praksis.* Copenhagen: Dansk Psykologisk Forlag.

Stelter, R. (2000). The transformation of body experience into language. *Journal of Phenomenological Psychology, 31*(1), 63–77.

Stelter, R. (Ed.). (2002a). *Coaching – Læring og udvikling.* Copenhagen: Dansk Psykologisk Forlag.

Stelter, R. (2002b). Hvad er coaching? In R. Stelter (Ed.), *Coaching – Læring og udvikling* (pp. 21–44). Copenhagen: Dansk Psykologisk Forlag.

Stelter, R. (2002c). Bevægelsens betydning i børns identitetsudvikling. Teoretiske refleksioner og analyse af en case. *Nordisk Psykologi, 54*(2), 129–144.

Stelter, R. (2006). Sich-Bewegen – Auf den Spuren von Selbst und Identität (Invited review article). *Motorik, 29*(2), 65–74.

Stelter, R. (2007). Coaching: A process of personal and social meaning making. *International Coaching Psychology Review, 2*(2), 191–201.

Stelter, R. (2008a). Learning in the light of the first-person approach. In T. S. S. Schilhab, M. Juelskjær, & T. Moser (Eds.), *The learning body* (pp. 45–65). Copenhagen: Danish University School of Education Press.

Stelter, R. (2008b). Exploring body-anchored and experience-based learning in a community of practice. In T. S. S. Schilhab, M. Juelskjær, & T. Moser (Eds.), *The learning body* (pp. 111–129). Copenhagen: Danish University School of Education Press.

Stelter, R. (2009a). Coaching as a reflective space in a society of growing diversity – Towards a narrative, postmodern paradigm. *International Coaching Psychology Review, 4*(2), 207–217.

Stelter, R. (2009b). Experiencing mindfulness meditation – A client narrative perspective. *International Journal of Qualitative Studies on Health and Well-Being, 4*(3), 145–158.

Stelter, R. (2010a). Narrative coaching: A community psychological perspective. In T. Ryba, R. Schinke, & G. Tennenbaum (Eds.), *The cultural turn in sport psychology* (pp. 335–361). Morgantown: Fitness Information Technology.

Stelter, R. (2010b). Experience-based and body-anchored qualitative interviewing. *Qualitative Health Research, 20*(6), 859–867.

Stelter, R. (2012). Narrative approaches. In J. Passmore, D. Peterson, & T. Freire (Eds.), *Wiley-Blackwell handbook of the psychology of coaching and mentoring* (pp. 407–425). Chichester: Wiley-Blackwell.

Stelter, R., & Law, H. (2010). Coaching – Narrative-collaborative practice. *International Coaching Psychology Review, 5*(2), 152–164.

Stelter, R., Nielsen, G., & Wikmann, J. (2011). Narrative-collaborative group coaching develops social capital – A randomized control trial and further implications of the social impact of the intervention. *Coaching: Theory, Research and Practice, 4*(2), 123–137.

Stern, D. N. (2004). *The present moment in psychotherapy and everyday life.* New York: W.W. Norton.

Stevens, R. (2000). Phenomenological approaches to the study of conscious awareness. In M. Velmans (Ed.), *Investigating phenomenal consciousness* (pp. 99–120). Amsterdam/Philadelphia: John Benjamins.

Stevens, M. J., & Morris, S. J. (1995). A format for case conceptualization. *Counselor Education and Supervision, 35*(1), 82–94.

Stober, D. R., Wildflower, L., & Drake, D. (2006). Evidence-based practice: A potential approach for effective coaching. *International Journal of Evidence Based Coaching and Mentoring, 4*(1).

Storch, J., & Søholm, T. M. (Eds.). (2005). *Teambaserede organisationer i praksis. Ledelse og udvikling af team.* Virum: Dansk Psykologisk Forlag.

Storch, J., Soholm, T. M., & Molly, A. (2005). Gensyn med domæneteorien. *Erhvervspsykologi, 3*(2), 54–80.

Strauss, D. (2002). *How to make collaboration work.* San Francisco: Berrett Koehler.

Svendsen, G. L. H. (2001). Hvad er social kapital. *Dansk Sociologi, 12*(1), 49–61.

Swann, W. B., Jr. (1987). Identity negotiation: Where two roads meet. *Journal of Personality and Social Psychology, 53*, 1038–1051.

Tanenbaum, S. J. (2005). Evidence-based practice as mental health policy: Three controversies and a caveat. *Health Affairs, 24*(1), 163–173.

Thorgard, K., & Jensen, U. J. (2011). Evidence and the end of medicine. *Medicine, Healthcare and Philosophy, 14*, 273–280.

Thybring, A., Søholm, T. M., Juhl, A., & Storch, J. (2005). Teamudviklingssamtale. In J. Storch & T. M. Søholm (Eds.), *Teambaserede organisationer i praksis* (pp. 95–128). Virum: Dansk Psykologisk Forlag.

Thyssen, O. (2004). Dannelse i moderniteten. In E. L. Dahle & K. Krogh-Jespersen (Eds.), *Uddannelse og dannelse – Læsestykker til pædagogisk filosofi* (pp. 331–353). Århus: Klim.

Thyssen, O. (2009). *Business ethics and organizational values – A systems theoretical analysis.* Basingstoke: Palgrave Macmillan.

Tomaschek, N. (2006). *Systemic coaching. A target-oriented approach to consulting.* Heidelberg: Carl Auer International.

Tomm, K. (1984). One perspective on the Milan systemic approach (part 1): Overview of development, theory and practice. *Journal of Marital and Family Therapy, 10*, 113–125.

Tomm, K. (1988). Interventive interviewing: Part III. Intending to ask lineal, circular, strategic, or reflexive questions? *Family Process, 27*(1), 1–15.

Tomm, K. (1989). Externalizing the problem and internalizing personal agency. *Journal of Strategic and Systemic Therapy, 8*(1), 16–22.

Tomm, K. (1998). A question of perspective. *Journal of Marital and Family Therapy, 24*(4), 409–413.

Trinder, L., & Reynolds, S. (Eds.). (2000). *Evidence-based practice: A critical appraisal.* Oxford: Blackwell Science.

Turner, V. (1967). *The forest of symbols: Aspects of Ndembu ritual.* Ithaca: Cornel Paperbacks.

Væksthuset for Ledelse. (2005). *Ledere der lykkes – En undersøgelse af kernekompetencer hos succesfulde ledere på kommunale arbejdspladser.* http://www.vaeksthusforledelse.dk/ ImageVault/Images/id_41322/ImageVaultHandler.aspx. Retrieved 2 January, 2013.

Varela, F. J., & Shear, J. (1999). First-person methodologies: What, why, how? In F. J. Varela & J. Shear (Eds.), *The view from within first-person approaches to the study of consciousness* (pp. 1–14). Imprint Acadamic: Thorverton (Concurrent: *Journal of Consciousness Studies, 6*, 2–3).

Varela, F. J., Thompson, E., & Rosch, E. (1993). *The embodied mind.* Cambridge, MA: MIT Press (Concurrent: *Journal of Consciousness Studies, 6*, 2–3).

von Bertalanffy, L. (1981). In P. A. LaViolette (Ed.), *A systems view of man: Collected essays.* Boulder: Westview Press.

von Glasersfeld, E. (1995). *Radical constructivism – A way of knowing and learning.* London: Routledge Falmer.

Vygotsky, L. (1962). *Thought and language.* Cambridge, MA: M.I.T. Press, Massachusetts Institute of Technology.

Walji, N. (2009). Leadership: An action research approach. *AI & Society, 23*, 69–84.

Wampold, B. E. (2001). *The great psychotherapy debate: models, methods and findings.* Mahwah: Lawrence Erlbaum.

Wampold, B. E. (2010a). *The basics of psychotherapy. An introduction to theory and practice.* Washington, DC: American Psychological Association.

Wampold, B. E. (2010b). The research evidence for the common factors models: A historically situated perspective. In B. L. Duncan, S. D. Miller, B. E. Wampold, & M. A. Hubble (Eds.), *The heart & soul of change* (2nd ed., pp. 49–81). Washington, DC: American Psychological Association.

Watkins, J. M., & Mohr, B. J. (2001). *Appreciative inquiry: Change at the speed of imagination.* San Francisco: Jossey-Bass/Pfeiffer.

Watzlawick, P. (1978). *The language of change: Elements of therapeutic communication.* New York: Basic Books.

Watzlawick, P., Jackson, D. D., & Beavin, J. (1967). *The pragmatics of human communication.* New York: W. W. Norton.

Webb, C. A., DeRubeis, R. J., Amsterdam, J. D., Shelton, R. C., Hollon, S. D., & Dimidjian, S. (2011). Two aspects of the therapeutic alliance: Differential relations with depressive symptom change. *Journal of Consulting and Clinical Psychology, 79*(3), 279–283.

Wenger, E. (1998). *Communities of practice. Learning, meaning and identity.* Cambridge: Cambridge University Press.

Wenger, E. (2011). *Communities of practice.* Retrieved from http://www.ewenger.com/theory/. Accessed 9 March 2011.

White, M. (2004). Narrative practice and the unpacking of identity conclusions. In M. White (Ed.), *Narrative practice and exotic lives: Resurrecting diversity in everyday life (Chapter 4)* (pp. 119–148). Adelaide: Dulwich Centre Publications.

White, M. (2007). *Maps of narrative practice.* New York: Norton.

Whitmore, J. (2002). *Coaching for performance – GROWing people, performance and purpose.* London: Nicholas Brealey.

Winslade, J., & Monk, G. (2001). *Narrative mediation.* San Francisco: Jossey-Bass.

Wittgenstein, L. (1953). *Philosophical investigations*. Oxford: Blackwell.

Wittrock, C., Didriksen, V., & Stelter, R. (2009). Coaching Barometer 2009: En foreløbig oversigt over coachingens udbredelse og anvendelse i Danmark. Special insert with *Personale Chefen*, *6*, December 2009 (16 pages), (see also: www.ifi.ku.dk/coaching)

Yin, R. K. (1994). *Case study research. Design and methods*. Thousand Oaks: Sage.

Zachariae, B. (2007). Evidensbaseret psykologisk praksis. *Psykolog Nyt, 12*, 16–25.

Zahavi, D. (2003). *Husserl's phenomenology*. Stanford: Stanford University Press.

Index

R. Stelter, *A Guide to Third Generation Coaching: Narrative-Collaborative*
Theory and Practice, DOI 10.1007/978-94-007-7186-4,
© Springer Science+Business Media Dordrecht 2014

CPSIA information can be obtained at www.ICGtesting.com
Printed in the USA
LVOW10*1601240314

378692LV00015B/913/P